MANAGEMENT OF RESEARCH AND DEVELOPMENT ORGANIZATIONS

ETM WILEY SERIES IN ENGINEERING & TECHNOLOGY MANAGEMENT

SERIES EDITOR: Dundar F. Kocaoglu, Portland State University

PROJECT MANAGEMENT IN MANUFACTURING AND HIGH TECHNOLOGY OPERATIONS
Adedeji B. Badiru, University of Oklahoma

MANAGERIAL DECISIONS UNDER UNCERTAINTY: AN INTRODUCTION TO THE ANALYSIS OF DECISION MAKING
Bruce F. Baird, University of Utah

INTEGRATING INNOVATION AND TECHNOLOGY MANAGEMENT
Johnson A. Edosomwan, IBM Corporation

CASES IN ENGINEERING ECONOMY
Ted Eschenbach, University of Missouri-Rolla

ENGINEERING ECONOMY FOR ENGINEERING MANAGERS: WITH COMPUTER APPLICATIONS
Turan Gonen, California State University-Sacramento

MANAGEMENT OF RESEARCH AND DEVELOPMENT ORGANIZATIONS
Ravinder K. Jain, U.S. Army Corps of Engineers
Harry C. Triandis, University of Illinois

STATISTICAL QUALITY CONTROL FOR MANUFACTURING MANAGERS
William S. Messina, IBM Corporation

KNOWLEDGE BASED RISK MANAGEMENT IN ENGINEERING: A CASE STUDY IN HUMAN-COMPUTER COOPERATIVE SYSTEMS
Kiyoshi Niwa, Hitachi, Ltd. and Portland State University

MANAGING TECHNOLOGY IN THE DECENTRALIZED FIRM
Albert H. Rubenstein, Northwestern University

MANAGEMENT OF TECHNOLOGICAL CHANGE
Yassin Sankar, Dalhousie University

PROFESSIONAL LIABILITY OF ARCHITECTS AND ENGINEERS
Harrison Streeter, University of Illinois at Urbana-Champaign

MANAGEMENT OF RESEARCH AND DEVELOPMENT ORGANIZATIONS

MANAGING THE UNMANAGEABLE

R. K. JAIN
U.S. Army Corps of Engineers
Champaign, Illinois
Adjunct Professor
University of Illinois, Champaign
Research Affiliate
Massachusetts Institute of Technology
Cambridge, Massachusetts

H. C. TRIANDIS
Professor
University of Illinois
Urbana, Illinois

WILEY

A WILEY–INTERSCIENCE PUBLICATION
JOHN WILEY & SONS
NEW YORK   CHICHESTER   BRISBANE   TORONTO   SINGAPORE

Library of Congress Cataloging in Publication Data:

Jain, R. K. (Ravinder Kumar), 1935–
    Management of research and development organizations:
Managing the unmanageable/R. K. Jain, H. C. Triandis.
        p. cm.—(Wiley series in engineering and technology
management).
    "Wiley Interscience publications."
    Bibliography: p.
    Includes index.
    1. Research, Industrial—Management. I. Triandis, Harry
Charalambos, 1926– . II. Title. III. Series.
T175.5.J35 1989
658.5'7—dc20   89–14687
ISBN 0–471–50791–1   CIP

To Anna and Avra, Pola and Louisa

CONTENTS

PREFACE

When asked, "How do you manage research conducted by the many faculty members and staff in your school," a Dean at Harvard replied, "We don't." He asked, "Have you ever tried to manage prima donnas?"

Managing R&D organizations and focusing on their *productivity* and *excellence* presents unique problems and unusual challenges. This uniqueness stems from two basic reasons: (1) the character of the enterprise and (2) the type of people involved in R&D.

John Naisbitt and Daniel Bell have suggested that one of the major trends in the 1980s and 1990s will be the transformation of an industrial society (i.e., manufacturing) into an informational society. Nobel Laureate Ken Arrow has stated "the central economic fact about the processes of invention and research is that they are devoted to the production of information" [Arrow, 1974, p. 152]. The generation of information requires research; therefore, research is going to be one of the most important jobs in the society of the 1990s. Just as farmers in preindustrial society were central players, particularly in periods of famine, so the researchers will be the central players in the future, especially in the advanced industrialized economies.

In addition to the R&D organizations' focus on information, the work itself involves considerable uncertainty since the output can never be predicted perfectly from the various inputs used. Ken Arrow stated "even human consciousness itself would disappear in the absence of uncertainty" [Arrow, 1974, p. 1]. Uncertainty, therefore, gives R&D enterprises a unique quality, and people involved in research and development have some unique characteristics. The obvious ones are postgraduate training and high aptitude. Perhaps, more importantly, people working in R&D have been social-ized differently from others. This process occurred during their graduate training, since in order to do well, they had to work autonomously and show some initiative and curiosity. To some degree, it was a self-selection process.

Commenting on managing R&D organizations, an eminent R&D man-ager (Keith Williams, Industrial Fellow, Churchill College) stated, "It is more difficult to manage R&D organizations because of the nature of their activities and people involved—mostly the people. People are more inde-pendent and articulate...so they need to be handled differently."

How differently? Well as an example, a progressive manager would be well advised to use few sticks and every available carrot. Also, accepting "odd" behavior and granting considerable autonomy to the researcher are highly desirable. In Chapter 3 we discuss "the Amadeus complex," which reminds us that genius is associated with behaviors that some people would call immature. The manager has to learn to tolerate a broad range of behavior from subordinates.

In managing an R&D organization, one also has to understand the ethos of a scientific community with its focus on universalism and sharing of scientific knowledge.

Managing an R&D organization, then, is essentially the art of integrating the efforts of diverse, creative, and rather intelligent and autonomous indi-viduals. Paraphrasing John D. Rockefeller Jr., good management consists of showing superior people how to do the work of near geniuses.

Why Such a Book?

This book, as the reader will see from the background of the authors, is a collaboration between an engineer/scientist and a social and organizational psychologist.

Besides the interest and experience of the authors in R&D, which en-compasses managing and directing significant R&D programs, teaching, and writing about many technical, social, and behavioral issues related to orga-nizations, we feel R&D is a very important activity of a modern technologi-cal society. For R&D, the United States alone will spend about $132 billion in 1988 [Mosbacher, 1988]. The important role R&D plays in the effective-ness of a technology-based organization, the profitability of a business enter-prise, and in the economic well-being of a nation, can hardly be overstated. These and other related science policy issues are explored more fully in the book.

Much has been written recently about this country's loss of competitive-ness to the Japanese and others. Much of this loss can be traced to the spen-ding pattern of R&D funds. While the Japanese have researched the U.S. market and developed products that can sell here, we have spent the over-whelming portion of our R&D budget on military hardware that becomes obsolete every few years. No one questions the importance of national defense. The question is: Is the United States carrying a disproportionate share of this burden? Thus a word about our science policy in a book discussing the management of R&D is in order. The managers of R&D must influence science policy and redirect it in the 1990s.

There is evidence [Nadiri, 1980] that return on R&D investment in industry is higher than on other activities. Some studies showed that the *average* return on this investment is 30 to 1. Furthermore, there is evidence that technology stimulates science [Bondi, 1967], science stimulates technology [Gibbons and Johnston, 1974], and both stimulate the economy [Freeman, 1982].

A few conclusions about R&D funding and researcher productivity are worth stating at the outset:

1. Basic research is more likely to be supported by government or foundations than by private enterprises.
2. Some of the cost of basic research is covered by the researcher, because researchers are people of great talent and dedication who put in considerable extra time for which they are rarely reimbursed.
3. The most productive researchers do some basic as well as applied research (Chapter 1).
4. R&D investment in the United States has slipped in recent years, relative to Japan and Germany, particularly when we examine the non-defense-related R&D funding.

Looking ahead, in the next 10 years U.S. industry will have to learn to develop products for the global industrial society [Brown and Kay, 1987]. The reality of the 1990s is going to be that with Europe becoming a unified market (after 1992), and Japan converging with the industrial countries in taste, there will be a market of about one billion people interested in products that current R&D might develop. Corporations that sell only in the United States will be at a disadvantage, because they will be dividing their R&D costs by 250 million instead of by one billion potential customers. But to design products for the global industrial society one will need to be quite familiar with that society; in fact, as familiar with it as with U.S. society. This will require a much broader cross-cultural education for the R&D manager.

This book has resulted from the experiences of the authors in actually managing R&D organizations, teaching courses in R&D management, and conducting research in theories of management and organization psychology. Many of the topics are evolving, as new research brings in new theoretical perspectives. Knowing the needs of physical scientists and engineers for practical suggestions, rather than for a review of the pros and cons of various theories, we used our best judgment of what constitutes the most appropriate answer to a theoretical controversy, rather than burden the reader with such controversies. This means that some managers and scholars in the field would disagree with some of our positions, but that is inevitable in a fast-changing field where precise answers are rarely available.

For Whom Is This Book?

This book focuses on ways one can improve R&D organization productivity and foster excellence in such organizations. Thus, it is written for principal investigators and their colleagues and supervisors in research and development organizations. While the profile of such individuals frequently includes a Ph.D. in a physical or biological science or engineering, whatever they learned in behavioral science courses they took as undergraduates has long since been forgotten. Basically, they have been given the job of managing people without much training in how to do this. We assume that individuals in such a role will want to have a short, easily accessible guide to the literature on the best way to manage a major research enterprise or a small research group.

Much of the inspiration concerning what topics to cover in the book came from a needs assessment that David Day and Harry Triandis, of the University of Illinois, Urbana–Champaign, carried out in R. K. Jain's laboratory. Over a period of several months, we spoke to groups of principal investigators (P.I.s) about their management problems in order to assess what they needed to know. Although these P.I.s did not want to become social psychologists or organizational theorists, they expressed a need to learn something about the behavioral sciences. The needs assessment determined that topics such as how to resolve conflicts, how to change attitudes, how to motivate subordinates, how to design the best work environment, how to make decisions about priorities, and leadership theory were of the greatest concern and probable utility to the principal investigators.

In addition, R. K. Jain, as supervisor of many principal investigators, noted that they would do their job better and get more funds to support their research if they had a broader perspective about science policy. So, in addition to the "micro" topics identified in the needs assessment, we have included some "macro" topics that will help the principal investigators in their search for research funding.

In writing this book we have kept this kind of person in mind. However, there are others—for example, university department heads, consulting engineers, managers responsible for sponsoring research, and policymakers concerned with science and technology—who should find the information presented here of interest. Some reviewers suggested that the book provides information that is quite relevant and useful to all managers of creative and rather autonomous personnel.

We will cover some topics that will already be familiar to some of the readers. To help the reader go through the book most efficiently, and skip sections in the book of insufficient interest, we will provide, at the beginning and end of each chapter, an introduction and summary.

In writing this book we thought of it as opening doors for further study and discussion. Consequently, at the end of each chapter, we have provided a list of Questions for Class Discussion and Suggested Further Readings. The list of questions can be used for paper topics, group projects, homework assignments, or for developing case studies related to R&D organizations.

What the Book Is All About

Managing a research and development (R&D) organization is to a great degree the art of coordinating and integrating the efforts of highly trained and rather autonomous participants. The manager has to provide order, purpose, and foresight and do this while dealing intelligently with the uncertainty inherent in an R&D enterprise. It is hoped that discussions and ideas presented in this book focus on ways one can improve the productivity of R&D organizations and foster excellence in such organizations. Based on needs assessment and the experience of the authors, topics that we thought to be most helpful to R&D managers and their colleagues have been covered. As the book outline shows, the topics range from motivation of individuals to science policy.

Chapter 1 develops a typology of R&D activities and the people who engage in them. What is research and development and what is unique about managing R&D organizations are discussed. A section examines the question: What to research? To some extent this is a key question for an R&D manager and for the organization.

Chapter 2 covers basic elements needed for an R&D organization: people, ideas, and funds. It examines communication networks and the innovation process. The discussion of the R&D organizational culture includes avoiding the not-invented-here syndrome, fit of the person and the job, and managing antithesis and ambiguity. The discussion has implications for the selection of people in R&D organizations and the shaping of the culture of such organizations.

The key role for a manager is to create a productive and effective R&D organization, which is the topic of Chapter 3. We ask questions such as What is organizational effectiveness? Who are the inventors and innovators? How are new ideas generated? Formation of the teams and the ethos of a scientific community that are likely to result in effective organization are discussed.

Chapter 4 focuses on the design of jobs, careers, and organizational hierarchies, and on keeping researchers as innovative as possible throughout their careers. Chapter 5 covers influencing people, peoples' attitude, and how attitudes can be changed. A behavioral science case and its analysis are also presented. Chapter 6 examines what is relevant about human motivation, with special emphasis on rewards, communication, and social and organizational structures that are likely to motivate R&D personnel. It also examines how to develop a sense of control and community for a research organization.

Leadership is the topic of Chapter 7. We examine a number of theories of leadership and the leadership styles that are likely to be effective in R&D organizations.

Chapter 8 provides a discussion of conflict in organizations. Three kinds of conflict (within a person, between individuals, and between groups) are discussed. Conflict is not always undesirable. There is productive as well as destructive conflict. We explore how to take advantage of productive conflict, how to reduce destructive conflict, and the ethics that are likely to achieve such ends in R&D organizations.

Chapter 9 is on performance appraisal. We make suggestions concerning how to successfully structure a performance appraisal system in R&D organizations. To do that, the discussion takes into account the different goals and activities of scientists and engineers. Monetary rewards, status, and other rewards can be associated with the results of the appraisal, but some of the dangers of too close a connection between appraisal and monetary rewards are also explored. A performance appraisal implementation strategy and example performance appraisal systems at research organizations are presented.

To be effective, an R&D organization must also be successful in technology transfer, which is the subject of Chapter 10. We ask: What are the stages of such transfer? What factors affect technology transfer? What is the optimal strategy for such transfer?

Chapter 11 provides the manager with an overview of organizational change, what goes on in organizational change, and how to evaluate it.

Finally, a discussion of research and development and society as well as issues important for developing science policy is provided in the Appendix. It examines R&D expenditures and their effect on economic development. A discussion of the need and the level of resource allocation for basic research is included. Some European perspectives on innovation and a discussion of mutual benefits from university–industry linkage are also provided.

Confessions and Acknowledgments

When all is said and done, one reflects on one's completed work and finds many shortcomings. In other words, reality sets in. One could argue that there is not much here that has not already occurred to or been postulated by others. We hope our attempt to integrate and formalize some of the concepts will be of value to our readers.

First, R. K. Jain is indebted to the Construction Engineering Research Laboratory, U.S. Army Corps of Engineers, for providing a rich experience in managing and directing a significant research program for over 18 years.

Many of the concepts discussed here were developed during Jain's stay as a Fellow at Churchill College, Cambridge University, a distinct honor and a memorable experience.

The cases that appear in this book were developed by Harry Triandis and David Day, both of the University of Illinois, Urbana–Champaign, in the course of a training needs assessment at Jain's laboratory, organized and directed by David Day. The cases have been distorted, exaggerated, and changed sufficiently so that no one can recognize the players, least of all Jain!

We benefited immensely from the review of the manuscript and interaction with the following colleagues and eminent managers of R&D organizations: Sir Hermann Bondi, Master, Churchill College, Cambridge University; Mr. Keith Williams, Industrial Fellow Commoner, Churchill College (formerly of Shell International Petroleum); The Rt. Hon. Aubrey Jones, Industrial Fellow Commoner, Churchill College (former Minister in the British government and author of many books); Sir William Hawthorne, former Master, Churchill College, Cambridge University and former Hunsaker Professor of Aeronautical Engineering at MIT; Professor David Day, Industrial and Labor Relations, University of Illinois, Urbana–Champaign; Professor David Marks, Professor and Department Head, Civil Engineering, Massachusetts Institute of Technology (MIT); Professor Andrew Schofield, Engineering Department, Cambridge University.

We are grateful to Pola Triandis, who improved the writing style of the book by meticulously editing the entire manuscript, and to Debbie Curtin, who carefully typed and checked the manuscript provided to the publisher. Many individuals at John Wiley were most generous with their assistance in finalizing the manuscript and producing the text. Working with Frank J. Cerra, Editor, Wiley–Interscience Division, was a pleasure; he tactfully provided many critical comments to improve the manuscript. Personal attention provided to this project by Mr. Cerra made the crucial difference in effectively completing this long, demanding, and exciting journey and finally producing a published volume.

Although the assistance and support provided by our organizations and colleagues are gratefully acknowledged, the responsibility for what is presented in the book is solely that of the authors.

R. K. JAIN,
H. C. TRIANDIS

Champaign, Illinois
Urbana, Illinois
September 1989

____1

R&D ORGANIZATIONS AND RESEARCH CATEGORIES

Clockmakers were the first consciously to apply the theories of mechanics and physics to the making of machines. Progress came from the collaboration of scientists—Galileo, Huygens, Hooke, and others—with craftsmen and mechanics.

DANIEL J. BOORSTIN
The Discoverers

The historic collaboration between scientists and craftsmen to create the clock, which Boorstin calls "the mother of machines," represents a rudimentary R&D organization.

Today the complexity of the technology has created correspondingly complex organizations, with sometimes hundreds of employees. Many disciplines have to be coordinated and it is the manager who brings the many components together so they can function smoothly, each making an optimal contribution to the R&D organization. Thus, today, as in the past, progress requires collaboration.

Managing a research and development (R&D) organization is, to a great degree, the art of integrating the efforts of its many participants. Beyond this, the manager has to provide order, purpose, and foresight and do this while dealing intelligently with the uncertainty inherent in an R&D enterprise. Considering the important role R&D plays in the economic well-being of a nation, the profitability of a business enterprise, the effectiveness of a technology-based governmental agency (for example, the Department of Defense), and the enormous investment nations make in R&D activities ($132 billion in 1988 in the United States), effective R&D management can have profound and far-reaching consequences. Effective management, coupled with a vigorous research and science policy, is necessary for a nation to sustain economic growth, provide a strong national defense at an affordable cost, and maintain a position of leadership in the international community. It is, therefore, important to understand R&D organizations and their relationship to society. For this reason, the first chapter provides some basic definitions of research categories and research organizations and the Appen-

1

dix covers macro issues related to R&D and science policy. This information should be useful to those who conduct and manage research, and especially to those who seek funding support for research and who want to develop allies in influencing science policy.

Chapter 1 first provides a perspective on R&D management and then discusses research and development definitions and categories. Sections that follow examine the question: What to research? This is in some respects a key question for an R&D manager. To what extent, for instance, should the manager allow basic research to be done in addition to the applied research needed by the organization? What is the best way to establish priorities among competing research projects? There are numerous suggestions in the literature on how to do that, and we provide a guide to that literature in the form of an annotated bibliography at the end of each chapter. Since a question is often raised as to what is so unique about an R&D organization management, a discussion of this issue is included in this introductory chapter.

1.1 HOW INFORMATION CAN BE USED

Some readers may want to take a cursory look at the information presented in this chapter and keep in mind how some of it may help them. In addition to having important implications for R&D management, this information has other possible uses as well. Some examples follow.

As a principal investigator (PI), if you are interested in being involved primarily in basic research, in what kind of an organization should you be seeking employment? If you are working in industry you should not be too surprised if you are required to focus your efforts on "products and profits." As shown in Figure 1.1, on the average 76% of industrial R&D is focused on product development and only 4% of the total industrial R&D is devoted to basic research.

In this chapter, indeed in this book, we argue that, in a productive and effective research organization, a researcher should have a mix of activities including basic, applied, and product development research. Examples of successful organizations and results of studies conducted are provided to support this assertion. For a manager of an R&D organization interested in productivity and effectiveness, understanding this issue is crucial and has important managerial implications. If we are successful in persuading you to include basic research in your mix of activities, even if your organization focuses on product development, would you not use the information in this chapter to persuade corporate decision-makers to allow this flexibility?

Is there any R&D manager who has not been accused of being unresponsive to customer needs and of focusing on esoteric, nonproductive research activities? Throughout this book a strong case has been made for customer participation in needs assessment and in the innovation process. The issue is much broader. Let us consider an R&D organization that works only on

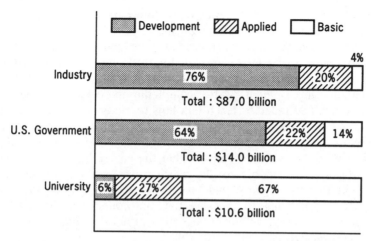

Figure 1.1. U.S. R&D spending by category for 1986. (Source: National Science Foundation.)

those research needs identified by the customer. Would such an organization not be working on yesterday's, or, at best, today's problems in a very narrow framework? Using this approach, during World War II, would researchers have been working on bigger and better binoculars to detect incoming airplanes rather than on developing radar? We propose a two-tier model, which includes an economic index model and a portfolio model, that should overcome some of these difficulties. Further, a systematic and a conceptual approach for prioritizing potential projects is presented. Depending on the organizational setting and the decision-makers involved, this approach provides a crucial mechanism for research project selection and effective decision-making. By being systematic, it also gives psychological comfort to the decision-makers.

Oh yes, how about these mundane definitions! Anyone involved in research knows them, or should know them. Maybe so. Careful reading would show that there are some key points brought out that are not commonly appreciated. For example, what really differentiates basic research from applied research? Basic research is not inevitably unapplied. Differences lie elsewhere. If nothing else, these definitions may facilitate communication among the various actors involved in conducting and sponsoring research.

1.2 A PERSPECTIVE ON R&D MANAGEMENT

The ideas presented in this book focus on ways to improve the productivity of R&D organizations and foster excellence in such organizations. The book is primarily aimed at principal investigators, their colleagues, and supervisors. As indicated, others may also find the information presented here interesting.

In mathematics or physics most concepts can be readily judged as useful or worthless. Management concepts, on the other hand, are more difficult to evaluate. The following example might illustrate the case.

One well-known scientist was recruited to be vice-president of a biotechnology company. In trying to prepare for this important new position he took a course at the California Institute of Technology on "Managing Research and Development." After completing the course the scientist felt that the course had failed to teach him how to motivate employees, how to say no, and how to focus or how to organize highly trained scientists. Furthermore, the course failed to teach him how to prioritize research projects. On his evaluation he stated that the course had been "expensive and worthless." In response to this criticism, the course program director pointed out that the scientist had "completely misunderstood the goals of the course." According to the director, the course was geared toward planning research and development activities rather than managing scientists [*Wall Street Journal*, November 10, 1986].

Managing researchers is one of the most daunting tasks a manager can undertake. It is not clear how one plans or anticipates a "scientific breakthrough." If this is the case, is there any point in undertaking extensive efforts in stretegic planning or doing any planning at all? Scientists are thought to be dedicated to ideas and research. However, as shown in Figure 1.1, except at universities, a great majority of the research is devoted to product development and very little to basic research. The challenge then is to provide a mix of activities to achieve organizational goals and sustain the researcher's motivation and curiosity, which are essential to scientific breakthroughs and product development.

The effect public policy and management decisions have on the resources available for R&D is well understood; one needs to consider and understand, also, the important role engineers and scientists can and should play in developing science policy. Of the approximately 1.94 million engineers in the United States as of 1983, approximately 78,800 work in research and 585,800 work in development [*Science Indicators*, 1985, p. 242]. The remaining engineers are involved in many forms of professional practice, such as consulting engineers. Consulting engineers undertake creative activities that are, in many ways, responsible for closing the loop between research and development and application. Figure 1.2 shows primary work activities of doctoral engineers and all engineers.

A doctorate is a research degree and the majority of scientists and engineers with PhDs work in research, development, and teaching. It is significant that relatively few engineers, as compared to scientists, hold doctoral degrees. In 1983, 61,500 engineers held doctorates, which represented only about 3% of all employed engineers. The percentage of employed engineers in different disciplines holding a doctorate is shown in Figure 1.3. This percentage has not changed much. For example, the same proportion held doctorates in 1976. Among scientists, however, about 20% hold doctorates [*Science Indicators*, 1985, p. 61].

We favor managers of R&D organizations with high-level technical skills,

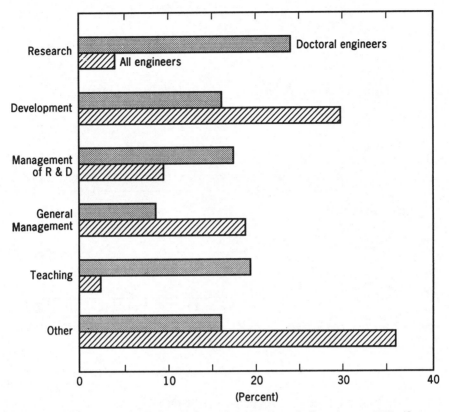

Figure 1.2. Primary work activities of doctoral engineers and all engineers: 1983. (Source: *Science Indicators*, 1985, p. 62.)

because studies have clearly shown that where supervisors were rated highest in technical skills the research groups were most innovative. And where supervisors did not possess excellent technical skills (but had high-level administrative skills), the research groups were least innovative [Farris, 1982, p. 340]. These findings in no way minimize the importance of administrative skills, but rather point to a fundamental need for a supervisor in an R&D organization who possesses excellent technical skills. Ideally, both kinds of skills should be available to a manager. Consequently, the role of a scientist* in managing R&D organizations has and will continue to be an important one.

To make sure we communicate effectively, we must first define some basic terms. We will do this in the next section.

* Whenever we are considering engineering, technology, or pure science for the purpose of this book, this word *scientist* is used to apply to a person (engineer or scientist) who possesses the technical knowledge and skills that are essential to the work of an R&D organization

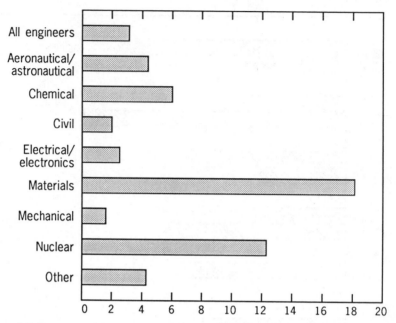

Figure 1.3. Percentage of employed engineers holding a doctorate: 1983. (Source: *Science Indicators*, 1985, p. 61.)

1.3 WHAT IS RESEARCH AND DEVELOPMENT

The National Science Foundation (NSF) classifies and defines research as follows [*Science Indicators*, 1985, p. 221]:

Basic Research. Basic research has as its objective "a fuller knowledge or understanding of the subject under study, rather than a practical application thereof." To take into account industrial goals, NSF modifies this definition for the industry sector to indicate that basic research advances scientific knowledge "not having specific commercial objectives, although such investigations may be in fields of present or potential interest to the reporting company."

Applied Research. Applied research is directed toward gaining "knowledge or understanding necessary for determining the means by which a recognized and specific need may be met." In industry, applied research includes investigations directed "to the discovery of new scientific knowledge having specific commercial objectives with respect to products or processes."

Development. Development is the "systematic use of the knowledge or understanding gained from research, directed toward the production of useful materials, devices, systems or methods, including design and development of prototypes and processes."

The Organization of Economic Co-operation and Development (OECD) in its publication, *The Measurement of Scientific and Technical Activities* [1970], defines some research activities as follows:

Basic research is original investigation undertaken in order to gain new scientific knowledge or understanding. It is not primarily directed towards any specific practical aim or application. Basic research focuses on the generality of the solution or the concept. *Pure basic research* is performed at the will of the individual scientist, while oriented basic research is steered in a general way by the individual's organization towards some field of particular interest. This further distinction between two types of basic research is interesting and can be useful in distinguishing between publicly and privately sponsored basic research. *Applied research* is also an original investigation undertaken in order to gain new scientific or technical knowledge. It is, however, directed primarily towards a specific practical aim or objective. Applied research develops ideas into operational forms. *Technological or experimental development* is the use of scientific knowledge in order to produce new or substantially improved materials, devices, products, processes, systems, or services.

Research and development covers many of these activities. The OECD defines R&D as "creative work undertaken on a systematic basis to increase the stock of scientific and technical knowledge and to use this stock of knowledge to devise new applications."

In order to provide functional and understandable definitions for various research activities, *Science Indicators* categorizes R&D activities as efforts in science and engineering as follows:

- Producing significant advances across the broad front of understanding of natural and social phenomena—*basic research*
- Fostering inventive activity to produce technological advances—*applied research and development*
- Combining understanding and invention in the form of socially useful and affordable products and processes—*innovation.*

Many United States governmental agencies have categorized research and development activities to provide a better focus on these activities and, ostensibly, to facilitate technology transfer. One such categorization for the U.S. Department of Defense (DOD) is depicted in Table 1.1. Since DOD accounts for 70% of the Federal Government's R&D expenditures, some understanding of its research program categorization would be helpful to those seeking research support from the DOD.

TABLE 1.1   U.S. Department of Defense Research Program Categorization

6.1   Research: Directed to the Development of Fundamental Knowledge. Includes scientific study and experimentation directed toward increasing knowledge and understanding in those fields of the physical, engineering, environmental, biological–medical, and behavioral–social sciences related to long-term national security needs. It provides fundamental knowledge for the solution of identified military problems. It also provides part of the base for subsequent exploratory and advanced developments in defense-related technologies and of new or improved military functional capabilities in areas such as communications, detection, tracking, surveillance, propulsion, mobility, guidance and control, navigation, energy conversion, materials and structures, and personnel support.

6.2   Exploratory Development: Directed to the Development of New Techniques, Methodologies, and Criteria. Includes all effort directed toward the solution of specific military problems, short of major development projects. This type of effort may vary from fairly fundamental applied research to quite sophisticated breadboard hardware, study, programming, and planning efforts. It would thus include studies, investigations, and minor development effort. The dominant characteristic of this category of effort is that it be pointed toward specific military problem areas with a view to developing and evaluating the feasibility and practicability of proposed solutions and determining their parameters.

6.3   Advanced Development: Concerned with Design and Development and Hardware (Material) Items for Experimentation. Includes all projects that have moved into the development of hardware for experimental or operational test. It is characterized by line item projects and program control is exercised on a project basis. A further descriptive characteristic lies in the design of such items being directed toward hardware for test or experimentation as opposed to items designed and engineered for eventual service use.

6.4   Engineering Development: Directed to Testing and Demonstration of New Techniques or Methodologies, and to Technical Systems Equipment. Includes those development programs being engineered for service use but that have not yet been approved for procurement or operation. This area is characterized by major line item projects and program control will be exercised by review of individual projects.

6.5   Management and Support: Directed to the Support of Installations for Their Operations and Maintenance and for the Procurement of Special Purpose Equipment. Includes research and development effort directed toward support of installations or operations required for general research and development use. Included would be test ranges, military construction, maintenance support of laboratories, operation and maintenance of test aircraft and ships, and studies and analyses in support of the R&D program. Costs of laboratory personnel, either in-house or contract operated, would be assigned to appropriate projects or as a line item in the research, exploratory development, or advanced development program areas, as appropriate. Military construction costs directly related to a major development program will be included in the appropriate element.

Source: AR70–9 Army Research Information Systems and Reports, May, 1981, NTIS, Springfield, VA.

For the purpose of this book, R&D, in a general sense, would include those activities that focus on innovation, product improvement, operation improvement, formulation of new theories, and provision of a better understanding of basic sciences and the fundamental mechanism of natural and human processes that are based on science and technology.

1.4 RESEARCH CATEGORIES

Harvey Brooks [1968, p. 46] has suggested a general set of dimensions and categories of research:

- The degree to which the research is fundamental or applied, for example, basic research versus applied research and development. The term "fundamental" refers to an intellectual structure, a hierarchy of generality, while the term "applied" refers to a practical objective. It is true that fundamental research is generally less closely related to practical application, but not inevitably so.
- The scientific discipline, for example, physics, chemistry, biology.
- The function of the research, or its primary focus, for example, defense, health, environment.
- The institutional character of research, for example, academic (university), governmental laboratory, industrial.
- The scale of research or style of research, for example, big science versus little science.
- The extent to which the research is multidisciplinary focusing on a single class of objects, for example, environment, space science, oceanography, or requiring multiple disciplines.

For planning purposes, Brooks [1968, p. 57] has suggested three broad categories of research organizations: mission-oriented research, scientific institutional research, and academic research.

Mission-Oriented Research Organizations

The term "mission" refers to an objective defined in terms of the long-range goals of the organization rather than a specific technical objective. Examples of such organizations include Department of Defense research laboratories and industrial research laboratories. Such research laboratories are vertically integrated organizations that conduct both basic and applied research and may provide technical support for operation or manufacturing. While their research may be of the most sophisticated and fundamental type, it is directed to fulfilling the objectives and the mission of the organization rather than to the development of science per se.

Scientific Institutional Research Organizations

This covers organizations whose mission is defined primarily in scientific terms; for example, advancement of high energy physics or molecular biology. Such research organizations follow some sort of a coherent program adapted to changing frontiers in their area of interest.

Academic Research Organizations

Academic research is usually small-scale basic research carried out in academic departments of universities by students or research associates under the direction of university professors who also teach.

1.5   WHAT TO RESEARCH

There are few discussions of research funding, research program planning, and execution that do not include comments about what really ought to be researched. Governmental agency and industry management hierarchies constantly talk about the need for a better focus on research programs so that research will meet agency and organization needs. Users in production departments, operational personnel in agencies, and consumers often complain about the lack of relevance of the research program and about the lack of timeliness of research results.

Let us take the case of a research laboratory where sponsors, though quite satisfied with the research output of the laboratory, nonetheless, provided these kinds of comments about the research program:

> Research takes too long.

> Our need to solve the groundwater contamination problem is now, not three years from now. We just can't wait for years for researchers to study the problem.

> We need answers quicker than researchers provide them.

> The research program is too esoteric. We need solutions that are practical.

> Researchers study the problem to death to find a one hundred percent solution. What is wrong with a quicker solution which is not quite one hundred percent?

> This problem seems to go on forever. Five years ago I worked at the Department of the Interior. We thoroughly studied the problem of land disposal of hazardous toxic waste. I thought we solved the problem or at least put the issues to bed. When asked whose bed and what were the results, the sponsor did not know.

> We always hear about your previous accomplishments. How about the future? What can we expect from you next year and the year after? Be specific.

First and foremost, R&D managers need to understand the sponsor's perspective and then develop a strategy for effective communication. Recall (Figure 1.1) that 96% of industry R&D expenditure is for applied research and development and 86% of U.S. government R&D expenditure also is for applied research and development. Consequently, the focus of such research is rather "specific," "commercial" and "product-oriented." For the sponsors to raise questions, as exemplified in the preceding quotes, is to some degree understandable. Consequently, the response of the R&D manager or the PI need not be defensive. For basic research, however, issues are likely to be of a different nature.

How, then, should one respond? One could take each question and provide extensive documentation to refute the sponsor's assertion. For example, one could prove that studying and solving the groundwater contamination problem, which was created through decades of neglect, would take some time. Solutions, especially cost-effective and environmentally safe solutions, may well take 3 years, or even longer, to find. One could also ignore sponsor assertions and go on with the research activity since the sponsor is not likely to find any other researcher who could do the work any faster anyway.

Another approach that an R&D manager could utilize would be a two-part strategy:

- First empathize with the sponsor's needs and be responsive in a genuine manner. This would translate to providing interim solutions, to the degree possible, for critical problems. Explain to the sponsor the limitations and uncertainties involved.
- Second, educate the sponsor regarding the nature of the research enterprise. Focus on why it is in his/her best interest to follow a systematic though time-consuming process of research and development so that solutions developed are scientifically valid, appropriate to the problem at hand, and truly provide a more advantageous solution to the problem than the existing technology does.

What to research is also affected by what our adversaries or competitors are doing. Some governmental agencies (for example, the Department of Defense) and some industries (for example, high technology) often are concerned about being surprised by a technological development by an adversary or competitor. This is simply because the payoff or effectiveness of the defense establishment of a nation, or profitability of an industry, depends on its own capabilities, and also on the capabilities of its adversaries or competitors. New technological developments of an adversary or a competitor can have a profound effect on the security of a nation and on the competitive success of an enterprise.

Other questions and issues related to the issue of what to research often include the following:

- How should user needs be considered?
- Who are the real users?
- How should a comprehensive and responsive research program be formulated?
- How should the tradeoffs between long-range research needs and short-range or immediate requirements be made?

Many approaches to formulating research programs have been proposed. For example, Merten and Ryu [1983, pp. 24–25] have proposed dividing an industrial laboratory's research activities into five categories:

- Background research
- Exploratory research
- Development of new commercial activities
- Development of existing commercial activities
- Technical services.

Schmitt [1985] has discussed generic versus targeted research and market-driven versus technology-driven research. Shanklin and Ryans [1984] contend that high technology companies can make a successful transition from being innovation-driven to being market-driven by linking R&D and marketing efforts.

A considerable literature is available related to R&D project selection. The proper approach applicable to an organization would clearly vary depending on the needs of an organization. Publications relevant to this are included under Further Readings at the end of the chapter.

Two criteria seem most important in deciding what to research: (1) What will advance the science? and (2) What do the customers of our research need? Once we have answered those questions, we need to ask: What are the prospects for a solution?

There are other considerations that may override them. Other criteria may apply in the solution of very specific problems. For example, in oil exploration, safety considerations may be a top research priority. Such problems may have to be solved regardless of cost because the organization would be wrong to ignore them. Research needed to protect human health and the environment from improper disposal of hazardous waste falls in the same category.

One of the most difficult problems is deciding when to abandon a problem that does not seem to be solvable. There is always the hope that with a few more months of work the problem will be solved. Yet, one usually has some sense of what is likely to happen. If one researcher is sure that the problem can be solved and no one else is so convinced, it is necessary to determine whether the one researcher is a "genius" or a "neurotic." People do get attached to hopeless causes and when that happens they exhibit a variety of other symptoms—extreme tension and inability to be self-critical. Managers must be sensitive to clues that indicate that the optimism about a project is unjustified. Since stopping such a project without destroying the motivation of the scientist is important, some suggested approaches to achieve this follow.

A manager may agree to give the scientist short deadlines and establish mutually agreed on milestones to ascertain whether tangible progress toward the goal is being made. If the project indeed is hopeless, lack of project progress during the milestone review would reveal the problem. In most cases, the scientist would, on his own initiative, agree to drop the project.

Should the scientist still request to continue the project, the manager should consider allowing the scientist to spend some time (say 20%) on the project and again establish agreed on milestones to review progress. If results again are not very promising and the scientist still perseveres and wants to continue, two options are possible. One, the manager may direct that the project be stopped. The other possibility is to still allow the scientist to spend some time on the project but strip away all support, such as for laboratory equipment, computer expenses, and technicians. In time the project will fade away.

The manager, however, should not be too surprised when some researchers supposedly pursuing unpromising theories or projects thought to be nonproductive in their early stages end up producing promising results. It is good for all concerned, especially for the manager, to keep in mind that predictions about the success or failure of research projects are most unreliable. Two examples come to mind, one dealing with fundamental research and the other with applied research.

Astrophysicist S. Chandrasekhar was working on the theory of black holes and white dwarfs. He sought to calculate what would happen in the collapse of larger stars when they burn out. He theorized that if the mass of a star was more than 1.4 times that of the Sun, the dense matter resulting from the collapse could not withstand the pressure and thus would keep on shrinking. He wrote that such a star "cannot pass into the white dwarf stage." His paper on this theory was rejected by the *Astrophysical Journal*, of which he was later to become a well-respected editor.

As reported in the *New York Times* (20 October, 1983), Sir Arthur, rejecting Dr. Chandrasekhar's theory, stated that "there should be a law of nature to prevent the star from behaving in this absurd way." Chandrasekhar was urged by other scientists to drop his research project because it did not seem very promising. Dr. Chandrasekhar persisted and in 1983 won the Nobel Prize for his discovery. His research led to the recognition of a state even more dense than that of a white dwarf: the neutron star. The so-called Chandrasekhar limit has now become one of the foundations of modern astrophysics.

As another example, a group of researchers developing a complex environmental impact analysis system and associated relational databases chose to pursue this research project by using a higher order computer language instead of the traditional Fortran. They also wanted to experiment using an operating system developed by the Bell Laboratories. Management attitudes ranged from enthusiastic support to tepid support, opposition, and down right hostility. The less technically knowledgeable managers were opposed and the further removed they were from the research group the more opposed they were to the continuation of this research project. Because of the creativity of the researchers and with some degree of support and acquiescence of the management, the project was allowed to continue in parallel with other activities. On completion the project was one of the most successful and one of the most widely used systems in the agency. It received the agency's highest R&D achievement award and became an archetype for future systems development research activities.

No one approach for categorizing or organizing research and for identifying the research needs of an agency or an industrial enterprise may satisfy the complex and, at times, unique needs of an organization. We propose a two-tier model for identifying "what to research" that is an effort to develop an approach that provides a flexible, systematic framework for integrating various requirements, that at times seem in conflict with each other. The model includes an economic index model and a portfolio model. This two-tier model may apply more readily to mission-oriented research than to scientific institutional or academic research. Further discussions of this model follow.

Economic Index Model

Under this model, research needs are defined as those needs designed to improve the operation or manufacturing efficiency of the organization or the enterprise. The emphasis is on building a "better mousetrap" to reduce the cost of doing things. Inputs for such needs come from the users, operation units, and scientists, and from looking at competitive products and operations.

Portfolio Model

Under this model, normative, comparative, and forecasted research needs are considered. *Normative needs* are those of the user (a user being the primary or follow-on beneficiary of the research product). *Comparative needs* relate to research needs derived from reviewing comparable organizations, competitive product lines, and related enterprises. *Forecasted research needs* focus on trend analysis in terms of consumer or organization needs derived from new requirements, changed consumer behavior, new technological developments, new regulations (for example, environmental, health, and safety regulations), and new operational requirements. Often the effectiveness of a commercial enterprise or of a national defense effort depends not only on how well the organization itself does but also on how well the organization does in comparison with its competitor or adversary. Consequently, it is necessary to have effective intelligence concerning the portfolio of a competitor in order to focus properly on comparative and forecasted research needs.

After defining research needs using these two models, some research projects would be essentially modifying, adapting, or adopting existing scientific knowledge and would correspond to applied research and development; other research projects would fill technology gaps and would correspond to basic or fundamental research.

Inevitably, there are more projects to be researched than there are funds available. This is a normal and a healthy situation. A model derived from the work of Keeney and Raiffa [1976], which takes into account multiple objectives, preferences, and value tradeoffs, is suggested for deciding which projects to select among competing requirements. The main problem in using such an approach is the tendency on the part of many technical users to quantify items that do not lend themselves to quantification.

In developing a policy (at higher levels) or in making specific project choices among competing demands (at lower levels), the decision-maker can assign utility values to consequences associated with each path instead of using explicit quantification. The payoffs are captured conceptually by associating to each path of the tree a consequence that completely describes the implications of the path. It must be emphasized that not all payoffs are in common units and many are incommensurate. This can be mathematically described as follows [Keeney and Raiffa 1976, p. 6]:

$$a' \text{ is preferred to } a'' \Leftrightarrow \sum_{i=1} P'_i U'_i > \sum_{j=1} P''_j U''_j$$

where a' and a'' represent choices, P probabilities, and U utilities; the symbol $<=>$ reads "such that."

Utility numbers are assigned to consequences, even though some aspects of a choice are either not in common units or are subjective in nature. This, then, becomes a multiattribute value problem. This can be done informally or explicitly by mathematically formalizing the preference structure. This can be stated mathematically [Keeney and Raiffa, 1976, p. 68] as:

$$v (x_1, x_2, \ldots, x_n) \geq v (x'_1, x'_2, \ldots, x'_n)$$
$$\Leftrightarrow (x_1, x_2, \ldots, x_n) \geq (x'_1, x'_2, \ldots, x'_n)$$

where v is the value function that may be the objective of the decision-maker, x_i is a point in the consequence space, and the symbol $\geq$ reads preferred or indifferent to.

After the decision-maker structures the problem and assigns probabilities and utilities, an optimal strategy that maximizes expected utility can be determined. When a comparison involves unquantifiable elements, or elements in different units, a value tradeoff approach can be used either informally, that is, based on the decision-maker's judgment, or explicitly, using mathematical formulation.

After the decision-maker has completed the individual analysis and has ranked various policy alternatives or projects, then a group analysis can further prioritize the policy alternatives or specific projects. A modified Delphi technique [Jain, 1981] is suggested as an approach for accomplishing this.

After research project selection and prioritization, an overall analysis of the research portfolio should be made. The research project portfolio should contain both basic and applied research. The mix would depend on the following:

- Technology of the organization
- Size of the organization
- Research staff capabilities
- Research facilities
- Access to different funding sources.

It should be noted that the distinction between basic and applied research can become rather blurred. What is *basic* research to one organization can be *applied* to another, and what is *basic* one year can be *applied* the next. Also, given the same general research project title, different emphases during project execution can affect the nature of research. As will be discussed below, to maximize R&D organizational effectiveness, scientists and work groups should be involved in a mix of basic and applied research.

1.6 EMPHASIS ON BASIC VERSUS APPLIED RESEARCH

We have discussed some research organization categorization and ways of developing an R&D portfolio. For planning purposes, three types of research organization categorization were presented. The emphasis on basic research versus applied research within each organization varies; consequently, there is a certain amount of conflict. The conflict is due to the fact that basic research is often dictated by the questions that science is asking. Such research may require activities that are not compatible with the mission-oriented research that a commercial or government organization is supposed to do. For example, a scientist while reading a scientific journal may have an insight that requires further experimentation. However, his supervisor may have already asked him to develop a particular product that meets particular specifications. Obviously the two activities are incompatible and some of the conflict that occurs within the scientist is due to the conflict between the need to discover and the requirements of the organization.

Some quite successful organizations, for example, 3M in Minnesota, have developed procedures that allow their scientists a certain amount of time to work on topics that are of interest to them. What percent of the scientist's time will be spent on such topics, and when such activities should take place, are matters of negotiation between the scientist and his or her supervisor. A successful scientist, who has had a better track record, may be given more time to discover other things by pursuing his or her own interest than one who does not have a good track record.

Pelz and Andrews [1966] did a study of 1300 scientists in 11 laboratories. They studied scientists in both industrial and government laboratories and they used five criteria to identify successful scientists: (1) the judgments of their peers, (2) the judgments of their boss, (3) the number of papers they published, (4) the number of patents they were awarded, and (5) the number of reports they issued. They then conducted intensive interviews to identify what discriminated the effective from the less effective scientists. One of the findings was that the more effective scientists did both basic and applied research. We will return to the study of Pelz and Andrews through-out this book, but for the time being one basic point that we should keep in mind when thinking about how to structure research and development organizations is that both kinds of research are done by the more effective scientists. It is obvious that if a scientist has an insight while reading a journal that requires an experiment, the inability to do the experiment will be quite frustrating. It is exactly this point that indicates that some sort of freedom to experiment should be allowed by the organization. If reading scientific journals results in frequent frustration, it is very likely that the scientist will become obsolete by giving up such reading. Similarly, the organization should encourage its scientists to publish, since this provides an opportunity for the organization to acquire prestige in the eyes of the scientific community and also tests the capabilities of the individual scientist to become effective in relating to the wider scientific community.

It should be remembered that there are about 7000 journal articles published every day in the sciences. Thus the output of any particular individual is a minute contribution to a very large pool of activity. However, the fact that a person has made a contribution essentially "buys" the ticket that allows him or her to interact with other scientists, to learn from them, and to discover what they are currently doing.

1.7 WHAT IS UNIQUE ABOUT MANAGING R&D ORGANIZATIONS

R&D organizations are different from other organizations because of the people working in such organization; the ideas that are generated; the funds or research support that are obtained; the culture of the organization. These four elements—people, ideas, funds, and culture—are the basic elements of an R&D organization and are discussed in detail in the next chapter. A brief review of each element as related to an R&D organization's uniqueness follows.

People. People in R&D organizations normally would have graduate training and relatively high aptitude. They are socialized during their graduate training to work autonomously and show considerable initiative.

An anecdote will help convey more clearly what is special about R&D personnel. The famous German scientist Hermann Helmholtz put a sign up on his lab: "Do not disturb." This was all that his students and collaborators were able to see for a month. After some 30 days Helmholtz emerged with an important new theory which eventually led to the development of radio and television (related in Boring, 1950).

Ideas. Ideas in an R&D organization are generated through a unique communication network (discussed in the next chapter) and facilitated by the ethos of a scientific community (discussed in Chapter 3).

Funds. In general, funding sources for R&D organizations are different from those for any similar large enterprise. For example, in the United States about 50% of funds for R&D are provided by the federal government. The federal government spends approximately four times as much on basic research as does industry. Even for academic institutions, the majority of research funding support (over 60%) is derived from the federal government. This funding support, coupled with research productivity benefits that accrue to society at large rather than the individual or the sponsoring organization, gives R&D organizations a unique characteristic.

Culture. The culture of an organization relates to both objective and subjective elements. For an R&D organization, objective elements such as research laboratory facilities and equipment and office buildings are different from those of other organizations. Subjective elements such as rules, laws, values, and norms for an R&D organization are also different. For example, scientific discoveries, whatever their source, are subjected to impersonal judgments and scientists often participate in organized skepticism and critically evaluate scientific ideas and discoveries. This permeates all aspects of an organization's function. Management decisions affecting individuals are thus critically evaluated and questioned by the researchers. After attending a senior management conference, a newly assigned deputy administrator of a federal research organization stated that he had never worked in an organization where people were so vocal and where management decisions were reviewed and discussed as openly and fully.

While the culture and indeed other elements vary from one R&D organization to another, as a group R&D organizations generally possess unique characteristics.

1.8 SUMMARY

We first pointed out that the essence of R&D management is the coordination of the activities of many individuals. An effective R&D organization should have a mix of research activities that are both basic and applied. The chapter provided definitions of terms such as basic and applied research and development, and reviewed proposals for a system of categories of research. One key issue is "What to research?" A model that deals with this question was presented. Finally, we examined what is unique about managing R&D organizations. One unique aspect is the need for the intricate coordination of people, ideas, funds, and culture. In the next chapter we discuss these elements and their coordination further, and the rest of the book is concerned with how a manager can be most effective and lead an organization that will be most productive.

1.9 QUESTIONS FOR CLASS DISCUSSION

1 How much R&D is too much for a corporation? When is it not enough?

2 How much R&D is too much for a country? When is it not enough?

3 Define and compare basic and applied research.

4 How much basic research is desirable in what kind of an R&D lab?

5 Take the actual case of a government or industry research laboratory. Develop a systematic procedure and a short-term and long-term research plan.

1.10 FURTHER READINGS

Allio, R. J. and D. Sheehan (1984). Allocating R&D resources effectively. *Research Management*, **27**(3), 14. The model proposed was used for R&D programs at the Allied Corporation. It suggests that R&D expenditures should support the business strategy and be sufficiently intensive and yield marketplace results that can be sustained in the face of vigorous competition. Technological innovations that do not improve competitive position are not cost-effective. R&D results should be converted into a product that is marketable in the face of vigorous competitive research response. Also, the business must have in place an appropriate marketing and distribution system and have adequate financial resources to withstand competitive situations.

Ellis, L. W. (1984). Viewing R&D projects financially. *Research Management*, March–April, **27**(2), 29. For project selection purposes, the paper focuses on R&D projects as investments for prospective return. Internal rate of return is offered as a tool for project selection and evaluation.

Fusfeld, A. R. (1981). Guidelines for project selection. MIT R&D 1981, Summer Session Notes. Other guidelines for R&D project selection suggested by Fusfeld include (1) using intuitive techniques where subjective assessment based on group or individual decision making is utilized and (2) using rational techniques where quantitative techniques are utilized for combining diverse data to objectively determine benefit ranking, or where financial ranking and optimization techniques are utilized.

Gibson. J. E. (1981). Rational selection of R&D projects. In *Managing Research and Development*. New York: Wiley, 289. This chapter discusses issues relating to ranking, scoring, or rating methods, economic rating methods, formal optimization methods, risk analysis, and decision analysis metods. Some examples of scoring methods for R&D projects are also presented. A staged approach to R&D project selection and some interactive decision analysis methods are also discussed.

Jackson, B. (1983). Decision methods for selecting a portfolio of R&D projects. *Research Management*, September–October, 210. This approach for selecting a portfolio of research projects is based on using analytical techniques such as linear programming, dynamic programming, and chance constraint programming techniques.

Krawiec, F. (1984). Evaluating and selecting research projects by scoring. *Research Management*, March–April, **27**(2), 21. In this paper, scoring, augmented by subjective probabilistic risk assessment, is seen as the most suitable ranking technique for developing a balanced R&D portfolio. Solar thermal R&D is used as an example.

Walters, J. E. (1965). Projects and programs formulation in R&D. In *The Management of R&D*. Washington: Sparten Books, 77. Examples of how research project selection is done by organizations such as General Electric Company, S.R.I. International, and Dow Chemical are provided. Basically, it is suggested that the selection of each project should be evaluated in terms of the objective of the project and the degree to which it services the objectives of the organization.

Winkofsky, E. P., R. M. Mason, and W. E. Sauder (1980). R&D budgeting and project selection: A review of practices and models. *TIMS Studies in the Management Sciences*, **15**, 183. This paper describes major aspects of R&D budgeting and project selection practices. This descriptive work is then used to evaluate the state of the art in quantitative models of R&D project selection.

___2
ELEMENTS NEEDED FOR AN R&D ORGANIZATION

The basic elements required for an R&D organization are (1) people, (2) ideas, (3) funds, and (4) cultural elements. These four basic ingredients have to be coordinated with skill by the management of R&D organizations in order to achieve high productivity and excellence. In this chapter we will cover some of the introductory topics concerning these basic elements. In later chapters we will focus more specifically on the task of coordinating and managing.

It is obvious that the most important element is creative people. Such people have the bright ideas and skills to do research and then translate research results into useful products. However, these people must be organized into structures that permit effective cooperation. In doing so it is important to keep in mind that certain mixes of people work better than others. To ensure a smoothly functioning organization one needs unstated assumptions, beliefs, norms, and values, in other words, an organizational culture that will favor creativity and innovation. Last, but not least, one needs funds.

2.1 PEOPLE

The kinds of people who are most likely to succeed in a R&D organization are those who are analytical, curious, independent, intellectual, introverted, and who enjoy scientific and mathematical activities. Such people tend to be complex, flexible, self-sufficient, task-oriented, and tolerant of ambiguity, and have high needs for autonomy and change and a low need for deference

[Winchell, 1984]. However, success in an R&D organization requires joint action; people should not be loners. So, the extreme introvert may simply not fit.

A person with a graduate degree probably already has many of these attributes. Other important attributes, however, may be lacking. For example, it is necessary to scrutinize very carefully a person's tolerance for ambiguity and need for autonomy and change.

People with internal standards and self-confidence are highly desirable, because in many cases research can be very discouraging. The person who is not easily discouraged and is sure of his goals and how to reach them is more likely to persist. Interaction with peers is also essential, since most new ideas are generated not by reading the literature but by talking with others who are working on similar problems. Finally, and this is admittedly cynical, a successful scientist needs to be able to tolerate what he might consider "bad management." The kind of person who gets upset too easily if the manager is insensitive to his needs may not be able to deal with a research environment. Most managers are technical people, interested in research rather than in managing others, so they are likely to do a less than optimal job. But there is a saving grace: research has shown that people who enjoy their job can tolerate poor supervisors!

Another desirable attribute is internal locus of control. This is the tendency to think that the causes of events are internal (e.g, ability, hard work) rather than external (e.g., help from others, luck). Research has shown that internals are better at collecting information, and deciding for themselves about the correct course of action [see Spector, 1982 for a review].

Creativity is, of course, highly desirable. Unfortunately there are few reliable and valid tests for this attribute. However, previous creativity is a good predictor of future inventiveness.

In summary, an effective scientist needs to be an individualist [Allen, 1977] with internal standards, self-confidence [Pelz and Andrews, 1966c], and persistence, who works in the right organizational environment. It is important to stress that even the most creative person will be a failure if the environment is not right. One can think of the analogy of a rectangle. The area of the rectangle depends on the size of both its sides. Similarly, creativity depends on both the attributes of the person and the environment. If either one is missing creativity can be zero.

2.2 SPECIALIZATION

The question of specialization is also related to both person and environment. Some people enjoy specialization while others prefer to be generalists. Some environments encourage and some discourage specialization. The literature suggests that successful R&D personnel are not overspecialized. They are interested in several topics, and are able to talk with others about *their* problems with ease. Specialization can be tolerated in the early stages of a career, but later one looks for broader interests and the ability to talk constructively with a wide range of colleagues.

In selecting people who have such attributes, the manager can look for specific behaviors. For example, the kind of person who tolerates answers such as "probably," "approximately," and "perhaps" is likely to be tolerant of ambiguity.

Finally, when selecting members of an R&D team, it is desirable to look for managerial talent. Since such talent is generally rare among highly technical people, when it occurs it should receive some special attention. While technical competence is of the utmost importance in managers of R&D organizations, their ability to deal with people makes them especially desirable. They should therefore be selected over their peers who are equally technically competent but lack interpersonal skills.

One more criterion should be kept in mind in putting together the R&D team: it is desirable to choose a diverse workforce. An R&D organization needs more than just idea generators. It needs entrepreneurs, project leaders, gatekeepers, coaches, public relations people, and others [Roberts and Fusfeld, 1981]. One should consider the mix of people, and the fact that conditions do change and what is popular today may not be popular or fundable in 10 years. With a sufficient mix one may be able to survive during periods of radical change in the environment of R&D organizations.

2.3   STAFFING

Often one hears managers say "people are our most important resource." Indeed, in an R&D organization highly trained, able, and motivated researchers, provided with well-equipped laboratories, are essential. Excellent and productive R&D organizations are all characterized by such assets.

In staff selection and staff development, some social issues, such as equal employment opportunity and biases against certain ethnic groups and women, are beyond the scope of this text. To be sure, these are important issues and there is clear and ample historical evidence of such biases. These biases first manifest themselves in the way people raise their children or in the initial counseling received in high school. They continue during interviews for the first job, and when decisions are made concerning pay, staff development, and promotion to higher administrative and executive level positions. Other staffing issues such as need identification, interviewing, selection, placement, staff development, promotion, and pay, are quite important but occur in R&D organizations just as in manufacturing organizations and are therefore already covered in the standard personnel literature. For this reason they will not be discussed here.

The selection of new employees should be done in collaboration with the people who are going to work with them. They are the ones who are most critical and the most involved. Furthermore, once they have participated, they will have some commitment to making that person a success in the organization. A work team interview is a good way to accomplish this.

The discussion here will focus primarily on the types of skills an R&D organization needs to facilitate the innovation process. These skills are categorized into three major areas:

- Support staff
- Technicians
- Research staff.

Support staff includes such functions as financial management, contracting, technical editing, reference library work, typing, and other clerical duties.

Technicians include laboratory technicians, fabricators of experimental models, computer technicians, and laboratory and field experimental support staff.

Making support staff and technicians true members of the team, along with the research staff, is crucial for the success of the innovation process. They make a significant contribution to the innovation process and their contribution needs to be recognized. Clockmakers were the first to apply scientific theories to the making of machines. Innovations came as a result of the collaboration among scientists, craftsmen, and mechanics. This collaboration, which was necessary for innovation centuries ago, is still required today. It is not uncommon for a clever technician to think of ways to set up an experiment or collect field data more efficiently, or for other support staff to facilitate administrative activities associated with the innovation process, thus saving time and effort. Often, the project sponsor's first contact is with the support staff (e.g., the receptionist or the secretary), and many technical assistance activities are handled by the technicians working closely with the user or the customer. Because of the crucial role support staff and technicians play in the innovation process, recruiting, training, and motivating them are quite important.

All the staff needs to become integrated, as the following true story suggests. Not long ago, a professor of psychology at the University of Illinois used fruitflies as part of an experiment in behavioral genetics. Several generations of fruitflies had been developed to obtain the particular type needed for the experiment. Then one evening a janitor opened the laboratory windows and the draft killed the fruitflies. Several years of the professor's work had been inadvertently destroyed! Obviously, had the janitor understood the significance of the work he would not have opened the windows.

A similar disaster to an experiment occurred on an oceanographic ship. The crew and the scientists did not get along. One of their disagreements concerned what should be placed in the refrigerator—the scientists' specimens or beer. After 6 months of collecting specimens in the Pacific, the scientists discovered, to their horror, that the crew had thrown the specimens overboard and put the beer into the refrigerator!

For the *research staff*, more than idea-generating personnel are needed. Other critical functions involve entrepreneuring (marketing), communicating, gatekeeping, coaching, and project leading or supervising [Roberts and Fusfeld, 1981, p. 25]. There is some overlap among these functions and an individual can perform more than one of them.

2.4 IDEAS

For idea-generating, the personnel needs to be technically competent in one or more fields and have the ability to conceptualize. They must be comfortable with abstract thinking and have a real interest in R&D.

In an R&D organization one finds that some people are particularly good at projecting beyond the obvious and thus generating ideas. To foster an idea-generating environment it is important to allow new ideas to be presented without immediately making judgments about their soundness. A group of researchers was once asked to present its ideas regarding some new research initiatives. After listening to the ideas, the managers quickly gave their comments and told the participants why the ideas were not particularly sound and thus could not be considered further. Participation in presenting new research decreased rapidly and after the initial two or three research presentations no one had anything more to offer. The research team finally disbanded because of low morale. Managers should not be too hasty to relegate ideas to the wastebasket.

Successful *entrepreneuring* or marketing requires individuals with the ability to sell or market new ideas to others and obtain resources for R&D projects. These individuals should be technically competent, possess a wide range of interests, and be energetic and willing to take risks. Entrepreneuring has some other important implications for organizational control and for organizational change. An organization that obtains much of its funding through the entrepreneuring activities of its research staff has to allow for more autonomy than others. Initiating new directions in research requires considerable participation by the affected research staff. A case in point is the type of research conducted at universities where much of the research funding is generated by individual faculty members. Consequently there is a strong tradition of faculty autonomy and dominance in academic institutions.

An important function in a laboratory is that of *key communicator* [Chakrabarti and O'Keefe, 1977]. A key communicator reads the literature in the field, particularly the "hard" papers, and talks frequently with outsiders and insiders in the laboratory. Chakrabarti and O'Keefe studied three government laboratories and found that about one-seventh of the professional staff could be described as doing that. Key communicators helped in a number of ways by providing desired information to others, locating written sources, participating in the generation of ideas, putting people in contact with each other, ending the search for nonexisting research in a particular area, evaluating ideas, offering support, selling a new idea, briefing key decision-makers about recent developments in the field, and making contacts both outside and inside the laboratory to promote an idea. Key communicators were in supervisory positions only half the time. Such people, when identified, deserve an increased personal budget to facilitate travel, release time, formal recognition, and special training and encouragement, since they are invaluable for a laboratory.

Related to the idea of key communicator is the idea of a gatekeeper, or of a person in a "boundary-spanning role" [Keller and Holland, 1975]. Keller and Holland tested the hypothesis that such people might suffer from role conflict and role ambiguity, and might be dissatisfied with their positions. Their data suggested that boundary-spanning activity did not produce much conflict, and even was positively correlated with job satisfaction with co-workers, pay, and promotions. However, it was negatively correlated with satisfaction with supervision. Thus, on the whole, this is a useful role that does not adversely affect those in it.

Also related to the role of key communicator is the role of "champion in product innovation" [Chakrabarti, 1974]. Such individuals are technically competent, know both the company and the market, are aggressive, and politically astute.

For gatekeeping,* individuals should posses a high level of technical competence, be personable and approachable, and enjoy contact with people and helping others. These individuals should keep themselves informed of related developments outside the organization via journals, professional conferences, and personal contacts. Gatekeeping is an informal role. Formalizing this role by assigning it to an individual or group would undermine the very purpose it is supposed to serve. In an R&D organization an individual with a high level of technical competence who has contacts with the wider scientific community and the appropriate personality frequently assumes this informal responsibility. Many times one hears the statement "If you have a question about acoustics check with Dr. X, he can tell you what is the latest." Often the supervisor acts as a gatekeeper, especially for locally oriented projects, which will be discussed later in this section.

It is clear from what was stated above that there is a controversy about the extent to which gatekeepers or key communicators should be identified

---

* The gatekeeping concept is further discussed in the Communication Network section of this chapter (2.5) and in Chapter 10 on Technology Transfer. A gatekeeper essentially links the organization to external information sources.

and rewarded. One view is that formalizing the role will undermine it; the other view is that by encouraging and rewarding the role these key functions could be done even better. We are inclined toward the latter view, but without too much emphasis on the singling out of the individual. Rather, top management might provide some extra travel allowances, some extra encouragement, and some more rewards without formally identifying the position of a key communicator or gatekeeper. It is the offering of support for the activity that is needed rather than a formalization of the role.

One can also make the case that it is not so much *how well* the role is carried out but how the *environment* in which the role is carried out is structured that determines the effectiveness of gatekeepers [Davis and Wilkof, 1988]. In a bureaucratic organization the best gatekeeper will fail; in an organic organization a moderately good gatekeeper will be effective. As Davis and Wilkof put it: "Most R&D groups long ago discovered that they cannot effectively operate with such a bureaucratic arrangement. They found that the restrictions and loss of autonomy inherent in the mechanistic structure stifled individual creativity and led to a sense of indifference and alienation, especially among those on the lower rungs of the organizational ladder" (p. 51).

In an organic organization professionals are recognized for their expertise, and not for their position in the organizational hierarchy. That means that an expert at the lowest level of the organization may be heard as much as a nonexpert at the top of the organization. The corporation is viewed as an individual/team initiative system within which ideas are bought and sold, packaged, organized, and implemented. Status is based on technical competence. Top honors go to those who generate, package, and sell ideas. Management screens ideas to ensure their compatibility with overall corporate objectives.

The organic form of organization encourages every team member to be a gatekeeper. Instead of identifying gatekeepers, the organization supports the function of gatekeeping for all team members. Thus, gatekeeping is the rule, not the exception. With more gatekeepers there is a higher probability of tapping broader sources of information. Information is transferred across project lines. There is a relative egalitarian structure, highly participatory project management, and the emphasis is on the group's "collective intelligence." It is the group that might assign the role of gatekeeper to a particular member, for a particular topic. Group meetings are important vehicles for information transfer.

The organic form of organization, desirable as it is, is not without its problems [see Davis and Wilkof, 1988, pp. 56–57], such as the neglect of routine functions and the danger of spending too much time in meetings. Managers will do well to move in the direction of organic organizations with prudence and caution so that routine functions and other essential organization needs are not ignored.

For *coaching*, individuals should be in a more senior position in the organization, be good listeners and helpers, and be technically competent enough to develop new ideas. They should provide encouragement, guidance, and act as sounding boards for others in the research group. Those coaching should have access to higher level management within and outside the organization and be able to buffer the projects from unnecessary organizational constraints. These individuals should have the ability to coach the members of the research team in a way that will enable them to develop their talents.

Project leading or *supervising* and coaching have some overlap and can often be accomplished by the same person. Project leading calls for individuals who are able to plan and organize the various project activities and can ensure that administrative and coordination requirements are met. They should have the ability to provide leadership and motivation and be sensitive to the needs of others. They must be able to understand the organizational structure, both formal and informal, so that they can get things done and balance the project goals with organizational needs. They should be interested in a broad range of disciplines and be able to handle multidisciplinary issues.

Clearly, as a manager in an R&D organization moves up in the organization, technical skills play a less direct role, while other skills such as human relations and administrative and conceptual skills become increasingly important.

As stated earlier, studies have clearly shown that research groups whose supervisors had high technical skills were the most innovative. On the other hand, those groups that had supervisors who did not possess high technical skills, but were in turn rated highest in administrative skills, were least innovative [Farris, 1982, p. 340]. Thus, the importance of an R&D supervisor's technical skills cannot be overemphasized. This is especially pertinent for organizations interested in productivity and excellence. Experience shows that an individual who does not have the training, the appreciation, and, indeed, the aptitude for science and technology is not likely to provide the necessary visionary leadership in an organization based on science and technology.

Creative people are likely to have good research ideas, but good ideas also come from communication with others. There is considerable research suggesting that communication patterns should be structured so that people can be stimulated by others who do similar work.

In R&D laboratories only a small percentage (11–18.5%) of all idea-generating information comes from the scientific literature [Allen, 1977, p. 63]. However, the scientific literature can be used for purposes other than generating ideas, such as problem definition at different stages associated with the total research process. But even in the problem definition stage, personal contacts provide more than five times the number of messages supplied by written sources [Allen, 1977, p. 65]. Therefore, communication through personal contacts is a crucial aspect of the innovation process.

In the next two sections, two related items—communication networks and the innovation process—will be discussed.

2.5 COMMUNICATION NETWORKS

There is considerable knowledge relevant to R&D activities that is not in books. Many ongoing R&D activities are not documented in the literature for some time. In addition, the written material is static and a limiting medium for communication, while personal contacts allow one to exchange ideas, analyze data more quickly, and obtain information that is more relevant to the research project concerned.

Because of the complexity of technological problems and the importance of analyzing and synthesizing relevant technical information, verbal communication plays an important role in modern-day R&D activities. Research has consistently demonstrated a linkage between high-performing individuals and projects and an extensive pattern of verbal communication [Tushman, 1982, p. 350]. Many new ideas are obtained while talking with people who do similar work. Sometimes talking with one person on Monday and another on Tuesday allows two apparently unrelated fields of research to merge in one's mind and leads to a new insight. Personal contacts and verbal communication therefore provide an efficient and effective communication medium within and between research and development communities.

The pattern of communication, however, depends on the nature of research activities. These research activities can be divided into three main areas: research projects, development projects, and technical service projects [Tushman, 1982, p. 351].

Research Projects: These involve work oriented toward developing new knowledge and concepts.

Development Projects: These are directed toward using existing scientific knowledge to address specific product problems. Generally, these types of projects correspond to technological or experimental development.

Technical Service Projects: These involve solving a specific technical problem using well-known stable technologies.

Based on a study [Tushman, 1982, p. 349] that compared and contrasted the communication networks of high- and low-performing research, development, and technical service projects, some patterns of communication activities were identified that are associated with high-performing projects. These patterns, as related to project types, are described here.

High-performing research projects showed extensive and decentralized communication patterns. People talked to many others and there were no rules prohibiting exchanges of ideas. Direct contacts and gatekeepers were used to acquire information from professional areas outside the firm. Within the firm, contacts were directed toward individuals who could provide effective feedback and evaluation. Projects were strongly connected to universities and professional societies. In general, there was less reliance on supervisory direction and more on individual initiative and peer decision-making and problem-solving [Tushman, 1982, p. 351].

High-performing development projects focused on communication patterns directed toward operationally oriented areas (how to get things done; what works, when) both within and outside the firm. Communication outside the firm was moderate and was mediated more often by gatekeepers than in the case of research projects. While there were some direct contacts within the firm, the supervisor mediated much of the communication. There were also widespread and direct communications with the user, for example, marketing and manufacturing [Tushman, 1982, p. 352].

High-performing technical service projects showed supervisor-dominated communication patterns both within and outside the firm. Communication outside the firm focused on suppliers, vendors, and customers. Communication within the firm related to marketing and manufacturing. In general, the supervisor served as a mediator for all external information sources and there was more supervisory-dominated decision-making and problem-solving than in research or development projects [Tushman, 1982, p. 352].

Experience shows that in the development and technical assistance projects of an organization there is an evolution of language, concepts, and values unique to the types of projects undertaken and, at times, unique to the organization itself. This local language and other characteristics make communications with the outside—that is, beyond the organization project boundary—difficult and prone to bias and misunderstanding [Tushman, 1982, p. 357]. Since communication external to the project (both within and outside the organization) is essential for high-performing projects, the acquisition of information can best be handled via "boundary-spanning individuals" whom Tushman calls "gatekeepers". A gatekeeper then is an individual who links the project to external information sources. Three types of gatekeepers (technology, marketing/manufacturing, and operations) are described in Chapter 10 on Technology Transfer.

Gatekeepers in an organization perform an informal but crucial function. Others working on the project have to feel sufficiently secure and comfortable psychologically to approach gatekeepers with their questions without fear of adverse consequences or personal evaluation [Katz and Tushman, 1981, p. 109].

To encourage gatekeeping, individuals performing this function can be rewarded without being given any formal title or status to their activity. Technology gatekeepers can be easily recognized since they are high technical performers and are able to interact harmoniously with others. For locally oriented projects, first-line supervisors act as gatekeepers for about 50% of the cases [Allen, 1977, p. 163].

A study was conducted to investigate the managerial roles and career paths of gatekeepers [Katz and Tushman, 1981, p. 103]. In a follow-up study 5 years later, it was shown that almost all gatekeeping project leaders had been promoted up the managerial ladder. In contrast, for the nongate-keeping project leaders, only one-half of the promotions were up the managerial ladder. The authors concluded: "This implies that higher managerial levels (in a technology-based R&D organization) demand strong interpersonal as well as technical skills" [Katz and Tushman, 1981, p. 103].

Allen et al. [1979, p. 707] suggest that, contrary to some earlier conclusions, the technology gatekeeping role is important for applied research and development projects where the technology is complex and external sources of information are relevant to the project concerned. For basic research projects and for technical assistance projects this role is not as critical. In the case of basic research, the problem is universally defined and contacts are best handled directly by the researcher working on the project. In the case of technical service projects, the technologies are well understood and stable; consequently, the organization is capable of providing the needed information internally.

Clearly, the main purpose of the communication network is the organization and processing of information. Also, as discussed above, different R&D activities require different communication networks. R&D managers, recognizing the importance of communication for the innovation process, should facilitate this process. Tushman [1982, p. 355] suggests that

1. The amount and pattern of communication within the project must match the information processing requirements of the research project.
2. The project must be linked to interdependent areas within the firm.
3. The project must be linked to external sources of information through direct contacts or through the gatekeepers.

To facilitate internal communication (within the work group and interdependent areas within the firm), one must pay attention to the architecture of the workplace and to ways in which socialization takes place. One commonly hears stories of how a scientist thought of an idea while having tea or coffee with a colleague. Americans joke about the sanctity of the British tea breaks. Maybe there is something to their tradition. Sir William Hawthorne of Cambridge University once remarked that institutionalizing (or encouraging) tea breaks or similar social interaction in an R&D organization is quite beneficial; such activities are not common in the United States but they should be fostered.

The effects of office architecture and the nonterritorial office on communication have been investigated by Allen [1977]. In managing an R&D organization, it is important to recognize the need for internal and external communication for the innovation process. A manager should facilitate this process to the degree that resources and organization policies permit. Questions are often raised by upper management as to why it is necessary to have researchers participate in technical conferences and symposia. An R&D manager should be able to justify these activities on the tangible contribution such activities make to the innovation process.

2.6 THE INNOVATION PROCESS

An invention is an idea, a concept, a sketch, or a model for a new or improved product, device, process, or system. Inventing is the creation of new knowledge or new ideas.

The innovation process is the integration of existing technology and inventions to create a new or improved product, process, or system. Innovation in the economic sense is accomplished through the first utilization and commercialization of a new or improved product, process, or system [Freeman, 1982, p. 7].

Various technology-based organizations look at the overall innovation process differently. In a general sense, the innovation process includes (1) identifying the market need or technology opportunity, (2) adopting or adapting existing technology that satisfies this need or opportunity, (3) inventing (when needed), and (4) transferring this technology by commercialization or other institutional means.

The innovation process integrates project need, invention and development, and technology transfer. Ideas and concepts are generated in each of these three major stages; the innovation process is accomplished when these three stages culminate in the utilization and commercialization of a new or improved product, process or system. Project need and what to research were discussed in Chapter 1. Inventions and development are discussed in this chapter. Technology transfer is one of the key issues in the innovation process. Indeed, the innovation process is never complete without this step. Although researchers are often ambivalent about technology transfer activities, utilization and commercialization cannot take place without them. Technology transfer is more fully discussed in Chapter 10.

2.7 FUNDS

While this topic is so obvious that it could be skipped, we have included it for balance. Funds are needed for personnel, equipment, office and laboratory space, libraries, computers, travel, supplies, and so on. This is not the place to discuss research budgets and the like. We wish only to make sure that the reader keeps this element in mind when thinking of the four equally important elements required by an R&D organization. It is important to emphasize the fact that conducting research requires considerable resources. It is indeed an expensive activity. To maintain research excellence, it is necessary to attract talented scientists and have well-equipped laboratory facilities. None of this is probable without sufficient funding support. Organizations that are successful in the technology transfer of their research outputs are more likely to generate customer support for future research. This is particularly true for applied research and development projects. In a way, the steps in the innovation process discussed in the preceding section provide a link to the customer or the sponsor via need identification and technology transfer.

One is always seeking ways to test user acceptance of research output and to determine organization effectiveness. Seeking funds for research can be one way to test the market and user response to the research output, and thus determine organization effectiveness.

Consider the following problems facing two R&D organizations.

Case 1. A premier private university experiences a substantial decline in the number of U.S. citizens applying to its school of engineering. Applications are down 55%. Factors such as high starting salaries for baccalaureate degree holders, rising cost of graduate training, and high opportunity cost of staying in the graduate school contribute to this decline. Increased competition from state universities offering quality graduate training at merely 25% of the private university tuition and a widespread impression that the private university is difficult to get into and lacks the many extramural social activities normally available at large state schools have contributed to that university's problem. Since much of the research at a university is conducted by graduate students with guidance from faculty, lack of graduate students makes it difficult for the university to obtain funding for research and to maintain research facilities.

Case 2. A federally funded environmental research laboratory finds that the national interest in environmental issues is waning. One senior official responsible for supporting such research states that of the many important issues facing the agency, the environment is now at the bottom of the list. In fact the sponsors assert that discovering better ways to protect the environment would only mean the agency would be required to spend yet more resources for environmental projects of little or no value to the main mission of the agency.

Clearly, often external factors beyond the immediate control of an R&D organization affect funding support. Carefully formulated programs and strategies that are user-oriented rather than sales-oriented have to be developed to overcome these problems. In the second case, for example, while the emphasis on environmental issues may have declined, environmental requirements are still there. Research that reduces the cost of complying with existing environmental laws and regulations still remains as vital as ever. Ultimately, the focus for securing research support shifts from solely meeting environmental requirements to including economic considerations as well.

2.8 A CULTURE FOR R&D ORGANIZATIONS

Culture is the human-made part of the environment. It consists of objective elements (e.g., research laboratories, equipment, office buildings, office furnishings, etc.) and subjective elements (rules, laws, values, norms). Among the most important elements of culture are the unstated assumptions concerning "the way things get done in this lab." Some of these assumptions become salient only when they are challenged—for example, is safety more important than production all the time? In some labs it is and in others it is not. It takes something like the January 1986 *Challenger* disaster to find out.

Some organizational cultures are more effective than others. For example, one experiment compared competitive (the highest producer gets all the reward), individualistic (to each according to contribution), and cooperative (equal share of the reward) conditions for building a tower. Participants randomly assigned to these three conditions had building blocks of different colors, so their contributions could be identified. Dependent variables included number of blocks placed, number of falls of the towers (often due to sabotage), and so on. The major finding: the highest productivity occurred in the cooperative condition. Of course, we do not know whether a team in a research lab working on some project behaves like a group of college students building a tower. Nevertheless, for at least some situations these findings must be applicable [see Rosenbaum et al., 1980 for details]. Competitiveness is certainly an aspect of some organizational cultures and this experiment questions its desirability. Other aspects of organizational culture worth noting are hard work, people emphasis, status emphasis, participative climate, tolerance for disagreement, and frequent rewards.

A word about each of them. One can see greater emphasis on hard work in some labs than in others. In some labs people work hard and very long hours, and usually take work home. There is no time for chatting. In other labs people chat a lot and stop their tasks when it is time to go home. In labs with "people emphasis" the lab comes to a stop if something significant happens to one of its members. Status emphasis is evident when titles, formal dress, or formal language are used. Participation is an important component if people are asked to contribute their ideas and to discuss major decisions, if they have some autonomy in those decisions.

Tolerance for disagreement can be seen when there is frank discussion, and when plans are critically evaluated no matter where they come from, whether from top management or from a lowly researcher. In some labs, rewards, recognition, and bonuses are frequent. It seems obvious that these qualities, with the exception of status emphasis, are desirable, but to what extent is every lab at an optimal point on these dimensions?

The first point, about allowing disagreement, deserves special emphasis. When important decisions are made, people often seek others who agree with them. They avoid or reject those who disagree with them. These tendencies result in *groupthink* [Janis, 1972] and in major mistakes. One of the most striking examples cited by Janis concerned a number of the decisions of the National Security Council (NSC) during the Vietnam conflict. Despite their own better judgment some of the NSC members who personally opposed certain policies contributed to unanimous decisions. People often feel unjustifiably optimistic about the way their research plan will turn out, they do not give sufficient weight to signals that something is wrong, they reject those who criticize their plans or their accomplishments, they censor themselves when they feel critical about actions of their team members, and they select their critics so as to receive a favorable review of their work. All of these behaviors are aspects of groupthink. Groupthink leads to poor performance. To avoid groupthink one needs to bring fresh perspectives into the group. That means tolerating those who disagree—the gadflies. It is even better to appoint a devil's advocate whose role it is to shoot down research designs, to reject drafts of papers, and to warn about disasters that could result from a particular course of action. In the case of very important projects, having several teams tackle the problem from different angles is not a duplication. It is the best way to get a solution. Finally, in the case of important decisions it is useful to allow a day or two between the decision and the start of the project, and to review the decision from other perspectives before committing major resources.

Experience shows that a manager has to watch out more for subservient researchers than for unruly ones. When critical analysis of a manager's proposals is not made early, much is lost. When suggestions made by the manager are taken as commands without discussion and analysis, research excellence is bound to suffer. Related to the groupthink phenomenon is the Not-Invented-Here syndrome.

2.9 NOT-INVENTED-HERE SYNDROME

The Not-Invented-Here (NIH) syndrome is defined as the tendency of a stable research group to believe it possesses a monopoly of knowledge in its field, thereby rejecting new ideas from the outside [Katz and Allen, 1982, p. 7]. As discussed previously, communication with the wider scientific community, other researchers within the organization, the user community, and marketing personnel within the organization is crucial for a successful and effective innovation process. The NIH syndrome, then, actually works to the detriment of organizational performance.

As the members of the research group work together longer, the group naturally forms a stable and cohesive project team. Individuals try to organize their work environments in a manner that reduces the amount of stress and uncertainty they must face [Katz and Allen, 1982, p. 17]. Project members then begin to work comfortably with each other and separate themselves from external sources of technical information and influence by reducing their communication level with the outside community.

It is important to note that it is not a mere reduction in this communication level that causes performance to deteriorate. More importantly, it is the project team's tendency to ignore and become increasingly isolated from sources of information and ideas that makes a crucial difference [Katz and Allen, 1982, p. 16]. As we discussed previously, communication patterns and the need for communicating with outside groups vary according to the nature of the research and development effort. When research and development organization groups are inflicted with NIH, overall performance will suffer. In such cases, research teams will fail to pay sufficient attention to new advances and information within the relevant external scientific community, technical service groups (as opposed to R&D groups) will fail to interact among themselves, and development project members will fail to communicate with individuals from other parts of the organization (for example, the user community, manufacturing, marketing,) [Katz and Allen, 1982, p. 16].

To ensure an effective and productive R&D organization, appropriate strategies need to be developed to circumvent and eliminate the NIH syndrome. In a general sense, the strategy needs to focus on keeping the individual research group members from reaching a complacent state, that is, finding ways of destabilizing and energizing the research groups within the organization. Some of the following activities might be helpful:

- Movement of new employees to the research groups.
- Active participation of outside researchers in the research group. This can be attempted by bringing in visiting professors and scientists from other organizations, by establishing a close relationship with premier research universities, and by bringing in graduate students to work with other tenured researchers in the organization.
- Encouragement of the research scientists to interact with the wider scientific community by participating in research seminars, scientific meetings, and professional society meetings.
- Encouragement and facilitation of interaction between development groups (product and process development engineers) and marketing, manufacturing, and user groups.

- Encouragement of interaction of members of technical services groups.
- Establishment of a sabbatical leave program. Though widely practiced in academic institutions, such programs are often looked at with a jaundiced eye by some research and development organizations. Clearly, implementation of a sabbatical leave program in an R&D organization requires considerable resources. Those individuals who are intellectually able to function at the cutting edge of technology in research and are able to provide technical leadership for an R&D organization would benefit immensely from the sabbatical leave program. Investing in such programs is well worth the cost.

Sabbatical leaves can be used to develop a new course or to pursue some new line of research. It provides an opportunity for scientists to take part in scholarly activities and research that they would not be able to do during the normal course of activities, and to interact with a scientific community outside their normal circles. Perhaps, to make the sabbatical program useful to the organization as well as to the individual, the individual should be given new roles and responsibilities to complement the sabbatical leave objectives.

Group members could present "new ideas," technologies, and perspectives acquired outside the laboratory to the group on a regular basis. Experience shows that some of these activities fade away after a while, and that a mechanism to stimulate interest in them is necessary. Inviting sponsors of other interested research groups and rewarding such activities may further stimulate participation and interest.

2.10 FIT OF PERSON AND JOB

A word should also be said about the fit of people and environment. A person whose abilities match the demands of the job will be most satisfactory to the organization. If the job makes greater demands than the person's ability the individual feels unable to cope; if it makes too few demands the individual becomes restless and bored. A close match between the individual's needs and the job's ability to satisfy these needs leads to job satisfaction. To some extent an individual's needs reflect expectations. People are most satisfied if the job provides what they expect the job to provide. There is empirical research showing that satisfaction is maximal when there is a match between expectation and realization. If one gets more than is expected, it can be disfunctional. It is a bit like receiving a $100 Christmas gift, when one expects a $10 one. Of course, when the expectation is higher than the realization, the person is disappointed or angry, and the effect on job satisfaction is most severe.

It is a good idea to pay attention to the match between personal attributes and organizational cultures. Some people are more competitive than others.

They would feel comfortable in a competitive organizational culture. Similarly, one can analyze each of the dimensions of organizational culture just mentioned and see if the individual would fit or not fit that culture.

Some R&D organizations compensate their employees with bonuses and profit sharing rather than with high wages. This is fine for achievement-oriented risk-takers but more conservative individuals will dislike this method of compensation. Another example is time perspective. If the organization has a long time perspective, requiring individuals to defer gratification for long-term successes, this will not be appreciated by individuals with a short time perspective.

2.11 CREATIVE TENSIONS: MANAGING ANTITHESIS AND AMBIGUITY

For a manager in an R&D organization, many questions related to the work environment arise. Answers to these questions are inconsistent and ambiguous. Examples of such questions are

- In general, what kind of climate in an R&D organization is conducive to technical accomplishment, excellence, and productivity?
- What is the optimum degree of freedom versus control?
- What should be the balance between basic research, applied research, development, and technical assistance?
- Should the scientist be isolated?
- How about the communication network? What is optimum in an R&D organization?
- To what degree is specialization of a researcher important?

Pelz and his colleagues studied 1300 scientists and engineers in 11 research and development laboratories, 5 industrial laboratories, 5 government laboratories, and 7 departments in a major university. Their findings shed light on some of the preceding questions. Based on this study, it was concluded that scientists and engineers were more effective when they experienced a "creative tension" between sources of stability or security on the one hand and sources of disruption or challenge on the other [Pelz and Andrews, 166c]. This study indicates that achievement often flourishes in the presence of factors that seem antithetical.

Specifically Pelz and Andrews found the following:

1. Effective scientists and engineers in research and development laboratories engaged in both applied and basic research, as well as a wide range of R&D activities (e.g. serving on review panels, providing technical services).

2. Effective scientists were intellectually independent and self-reliant; they pursued their own ideas and valued their freedom, *but* they also interacted vigorously with their colleagues. They did not avoid other people.

3. In the first decade of their career the effective scientists spent a few years on one main project, *but* they did not overspecialize. They developed several skills that they used well in the next decade.

4. Mature scientists were interested in both probing deeply *and* pioneering in new areas.

5. The best work occurred in environments that were not too tightly controlled, provided enough of a challenge as well as adequate security, and did not impose rigid goals of the organization on the scientists. Moderate coordination, allowing individual autonomy, usually resulted in finding the best solution. But effective scientists were strongly influenced by a variety of internal and external sources, including concerns about the goals of the organization.

6. The most effective scientists were those that influenced key decision-makers of the organization, but whose goals were highly coordinated with the goals of the organization.

7. High performers received personal support and stimulation from their colleagues, but differed from their colleagues in technical style or strategy. In other words, they had complementary talents with their colleagues, and were well respected and supported by them.

8. R&D teams change over time. As they get "older" they become more and more interested in narrow specialization and less and less interested in broad pioneering. The most useful teams are at a "group age" that has not yet become too interested in narrow specialization but has not yet lost interest in broad pioneering.

9. Effective older teams had members who preferred each other as collaborators, but remained intellectually combative and used different technical strategies.

Thus, in designing organizational cultures for R&D laboratories it is desirable to review some dimensions identified by Pelz and Andrews [1966c]. They emphasize balance between several extremes. It is not desirable to spend all of one's time on applied or on basic research, a mixture of the two is more effective. One should not emphasize extreme self-reliance in a lab; one also needs some interdependence. One should not overemphasize specialization; one needs to be good at many things. Supervisors should not provide too much structure; the subordinate needs some autonomy. Research scientists must find a balance between their personal research goals and those of the organization. Projects should not be too long or too short; a 3-year project is often optimal.

Jobs, particularly in research, should be designed so that they provide opportunities for autonomy, since research personnel is high on this need. They must also provide significance—that is, people should have the sense that what they are doing is important for the organization (1) for themselves, (2) for the profession, and (3) for society. Finally, jobs should provide feedback.

There is research suggesting that people who are in a good mood are more creative than people who are in a neutral mood [Isen et al., 1985]. Mood can be manipulated by having people think pleasant thoughts for a period of time. This experiment was done with college students, and requires replication in a research setting, but it is certainly worth trying to put people in a good mood if possible.

Stimulation by others requires that people be able to communicate easily. In some studies the elimination of physical barriers helped in the operation of R&D laboratories.

A desirable organizational culture allows employees to have a sense of control. In some experiments those without control became depressed. One increases the sense of control of employees by allowing them to participate in decisions that affect them, such as when to start work, what to study, and when to study it. Management by objectives is desirable since it enables the supervisor and subordinate to sit down periodically and agree on milestones, goals, or values. This review in turn allows for feedback, and discussion of why the goals were not reached and for congratulations when they were attained. Cultures that reward frequently are more effective than cultures that do not. That does not mean that one should get rewarded for every success. Rather, there should be uncertainty about getting a reward. However, when something major has been achieved the reward should be extremely probable.

Goals must be set in such a way that they are (1) specific, (2) difficult, but (3) attainable. There is research showing that this combination of goal attributes results in maximal motivation. This research will be reviewed in Chapter 6 on motivation.

A desirable culture has a family spirit, it uses slogans, myths, war stories, and has heroes that transmit the values of the organization. People need to feel that they belong to the organization and that they are important; they also need pride in being members of the organization.

A good R&D culture will accept failure. When all experiments come out as expected that indicates that the research is too conservative. "If you do not have several failures you are not doing a good job" should be the way R&D managers talk to their subordinates. Open communication (open doors), acceptance of suggestions, the assumption that there is always a better way, and that the better way does not constitute a criticism of the employee are important values and perspectives for the R&D manager.

The organizational culture should stress a win/win orientation, in resolving conflict. This orientation involves looking for a creative solution that will satisfy both sides in an argument. Chapter 8 on conflict will discuss this approach more thoroughly.

Develop a Climate of Participation. Participation is the right climate for the management of R&D laboratories. Participation makes especially good sense in the case of the management of research. Lawler [1986] argues that it makes sense in any organization, but the kinds of factors that make it desirable are found in particular abundance in R&D laboratories.

Lawler makes the point that participation means moving rewards, knowledge, power, and information flow to the lowest possible levels of an organization. He states: "My prediction is that for participative management to be effective it must put power, rewards, knowledge, and an upward and downward information flow in place at the lower levels of an organization. Limited moves in this direction will, according to this view, produce limited or no results" [p. 43]. Thus, he criticizes many of the proposed panaceas of contemporary U.S. management (such as quality circles, the employee survey feedback, job enrichment, work teams, union management teams, quality-of-work-life programs, gainsharing, and the new-design plants) as doing only some of the job and so achieving only part of the results. In his last chapters, he describes the kind of organization that he sees as optimally participative and successful in the way it deals with organizational change.

The most important point made by Lawler is that there must be congruence between the management actions in the areas of power, reward, knowledge, and information flow. If a management method reduces the level of decision-making in one of these ways but not the others, the effect would be much less desirable than if all four attributes (power, rewards, knowledge, information) were to change together.

The management philosophy that should characterize participative management is that:

- People should be treated fairly and with respect;
- People want to participate (this is particularly true in the case of highly educated samples, such as researchers);
- When people participate, they accept change;
- When people participate, they are more committed to the organization;
- People are a valuable resource because they have ideas and knowledge;
- When people have an input in decisions, better solutions are developed;
- Organizations should make a long-term commitment to the development of people because that makes them more valuable to the organization (this is particularly true in R&D organizations);
- People can be trusted to make important decisions about their work activities;
- People can develop the knowledge to make important decisions about the management of their work activities;

• When people make decisions about the management of their work, the results are high satisfaction and organizational effectiveness.

This perspective requires an organizational structure that has very few levels. A structure comprised of a director, a manager level, and researchers organized in functional or disciplinary groups is sufficient. The fundamental grouping should be organizational units that are responsible for a particular product or customer or research area. People should be able to identify with their work group. Each unit should serve some customer and receive feedback about customer satisfaction. Members of the unit should know precisely what the budget is and how it is being spent. They should know what is expected of them from various customers (e.g., funding agencies). They should receive feedback concerning their success in satisfying these customers. Ideally, information about the performance of the unit should be available at frequent intervals. Widespread use of computer networks should improve feedback.

The physical layout of the work group should be egalitarian, safe, and pleasant. The same informal dress should be worn by all. The physical layout should create team boundaries.

2.12 SUMMARY

The management of R&D organizations is quite challenging. It is difficult to coordinate numerous individuals who are socialized to work autonomously. However, one cannot leave them totally alone, since the organization has goals that its personnel must meet. It is hard to get ideas, funds, and the right climate at the right time and place, in order to produce a top quality research product.

In a real sense the job of the R&D manager is to create the right climate for research. A first-rate researcher, in the right climate, with adequate funding, is likely to come up with important ideas. But providing the right culture is complex. A manager must select people, match them with jobs, match them into teams, do team building, and help develop norms, roles, and standard operating procedures that will result in high levels of innovation. An organization must be developed that will allow people to be maximally creative. Rewards must be provided so that people will be motivated to work hard and to seek excellence. The manager must know how to lead, how to reduce conflict, and how to get maximum advantage of the resources that are available.

In this chapter we examined rather superficially, and at an introductory level, the people, ideas, funds, and culture that are required for excellence in R&D organizations. In the subsequent chapters we will focus in greater depth on the very same topics, and will also examine how to evaluate people and how to determine a laboratory's success. Technology transfer and satisfaction of the laboratory's clients are among the outcomes that are measurable and provide clues about the success of the laboratory. We will examine also how a manager can evaluate change in organizations and essentially learn to manage the culture of the R&D organization.

2.13 QUESTIONS FOR CLASS DISCUSSION

1 Discuss the kind of organization (bureaucratic vs. organic) that is likely to be most desirable in many R&D labs.

2 Define the gatekeeper in R&D labs. What are the functions associated with gatekeeping? How can these functions be performed best?

3 What is organizational culture? How can one develop an effective organizational culture for an R&D lab?

4 Discuss participation in decision making in R&D labs. What are the limits (too much; too little)?

5 Develop case studies related to:
- Staffing
- Communication networks
- Not-Invented-Here syndrome
- Creative tensions.

2.14 FURTHER READINGS

Allen, T. J. (1977). *Managing the Flow of Technology: Technology Transfer and the Dissemination of Technological Information with the Research and Development Organization*. Cambridge, MA: MIT Press.

Burgelman, R. A., & L. R. Sayles (1986). *Inside Corporate Innovation*. Free Press.

McGrath, J. E. (1984). *Groups: Interaction and Performance*. Englewood Cliffs, NJ: Prentice-Hall.

Pinto, J. K., & D. P. Slevin (1989). Critical success factors in R&D projects. *Research-Technology Management*. **32**, 31–35 (January–February).

Roberts, E. B. (1982). Generating effective corporate innovation. *Innovation/Technology Review*, pp. 3–9.

Root-Bernstein, R. S. (1989). Who discovers and invents. *Research-Technology Management*. **32** 43–50 (January–February).

Lawler, E. E., Ill (1986). *High Involvement Management*. San Francisco: Bass.

Pelz, D. C., and Andrews, F. M. (1966c). *Scientists in Organizations*. New York: Wiley.

Tushman, M. L. (1982). Managing communication networks in R&D laboratories. In M. L. Tushman and W. L. Moore (Eds.), *Readings in the Management of Innovation*. Marshfield, MA: Pitman.

_____3

CREATING A PRODUCTIVE AND EFFECTIVE R&D ORGANIZATION

In Chapter 2 we introduced the four key elements required for an effective R&D organization. In this chapter we will continue our discussion of these elements, emphasizing in greater depth those aspects that we believe are especially related to organizational effectiveness.

The productivity of an industrial operation usually includes the quantity of its output and its quality. However, in an R&D organization, many units of output are intangible and subjective in nature. Productivity also needs to relate to the objectives and goals of the organization. Consequently, to focus comprehensively on R&D productivity, the concept of "organization effectiveness" is proposed.

Organization effectiveness is a vector that includes quantifiable and nonquantifiable outputs and reflects the quality and the relationship of outputs to broad organizational goals and objectives. Organization effectiveness has a one-to-one correspondence to the general concept of productivity, but it also includes items not always included in productivity, for instance, quality and utility (i.e., relevance to organization objectives). Using this definition, if an organization is very effective, it is very productive, and if it is not very effective, then it is not very productive. Not only should an organization be productive but it needs to be viable over a considerable period of time. This in turn requires that members be satisfied with the organization.

TABLE 3.1   Criteria of Organizational Effectiveness in R&D Laboratories[a]

Criterion	Measurement Instrument
Quantity of output	Numbers of reports, publications, new products
Quality of the work	Number of patents obtained, number of times publications of lab members are quoted, number of refereed publications per member of lab
Increases in the size of organization	Obtaining more research funds
Absenteeism	Number of persons out of the total work force who are absent without a valid excuse on an average day (counted inversely)
Level of stress	Measured with physiological indexes, number of visits to hospital, frequency of peptic ulcers, etc. (counted inversely)
Level of job satisfaction	Measured with a standardized questionnaire, such as the Job Descriptive Index. Components: Satisfaction with pay, supervisor, organization or company, job, co-workers, working conditions
Pride in the organization	Feelings of pride measured via questionnaires
Congruence of individual and organizational goals	The extent individual goals are consistent with goals as they are reflected in employee and management statements
Profits	Direct profits or return on investment studies where returns are determined from implementation of research products

[a] A good case can be made for each organization developing its own criteria of effectiveness through participation of organization members in a debate that considers (1) different criteria, (2) how they should be measured, and (3) how they should be weighted. Such a debate has the advantage of involving the key members of the organization in the development of its goals. They become committed and ego-involved. The criteria that need to be debated are listed in Table 3.1. Other criteria might be suggested during these debates.

3.1   ORGANIZATION EFFECTIVENESS

Effectiveness can be determined by a number of different criteria. Table 3.1 lists some criteria that may be used: the reader will think of others. To some extent, the type of R&D organization will determine the criteria. The criteria listed in Table 3.1 are self-evident, but some comments are needed concerning the congruence of individual and organizational goals and the use of profit as a criterion.

First, consider the congruence of individual and organizational goals. If the individual's activities are quite consistent with the activities and goals of the organization, this will result in a better organization than one in which individuals try to do "their own thing" and are not really concerned with what happens to the organization.

Next, consider profit. For a profit-oriented organization, revenues or earnings may provide a good measure of its productivity or effectiveness. However, for a research organization (or for a non profit organization), other measures are needed. Nevertheless, a good way to integrate individual and organizational goals is to pay some bonus based on total organizational performance.

In summary, R&D organization output measures can be subjective or objective, discrete or scalar, quantitative or nonquantitative, and there can also be qualitative aspects associated with them. The relationship of output measures to organizational goals must also be included. An interesting categorization of output measures in terms of result, process, and social indicators has been proposed by Anthony and Herzlinger [1975, p. 141].

Different organizations (governmental, commercial, educational) will weigh the available criteria differently. It may be a useful exercise for the key teams of a lab to devote some time to a discussion of how the various criteria should be weighted. Agreement on how to do that is likely to increase the congruence of individual and organizational goals, and possibly reduce role conflict within the organization. Of course, in pure research the publication criterion is weighted more heavily and in applied research the product that has been invented or developed is the key output that must meet certain specifications. These specifications themselves can be stated as criteria (e.g., product should cost less than a certain amount, should weigh less than a certain amount, should have certain performance characteristics, and so on). Sessions that are devoted to goal clarification and how specific criteria will be used to determine their attainment by the individual or the organization will take time, but will be of great value in creating a good climate of cooperation within the organization.

Blake [1978, p. 260], commenting on organization effectiveness, suggests the criterion for evaluating the effectiveness of an R&D organization should be the record of its success or failure in meeting its objectives. He recommends a set of questions that would form a basis for determining R&D organization effectiveness:

- Are project cost schedules met?
- Are project time schedules met?
- Are time schedules kept that show both original estimated costs and actual costs of the projects?
- Are records kept that show both the estimated completion time and actual completion time for the projects?
- Is there clear delineation between overruns and cost increases caused by change in the scope of the projects or other proper causes?
- Is there significant scientific fallout?

Clearly, there are a number of ways of looking at organization effectiveness. Viewing organization effectiveness, and thus productivity, as a vector, the following relationship is proposed:

$$[Productivity] = [Effectiveness] = [Output] \times [Quality]$$

Output Measures

Output has three categories: *process measures, result measures*, and *strategic indicators*. A quantitative or a qualitative measure can be assigned where possible and these measures, where appropriate, relate to organizational objectives. Further description of these proposed measures follows.

Process Measures. These measures are process-oriented and relate to activities carried out by an organization or its subunit; they relate to short-term, day-to-day activities of the organization. Some examples in a research organization may be:

- Number of times technical assistance provided to an operational unit
- Number of responses sent to enquiries from outside scientific or internal unit
- Number of visitors to the organization
- Number of administrative types of actions handled.

Result Measures. These would be tangible, measurable outputs expressed in terms of an organization's objectives and goals. Some examples are

- Number of technical reports published
- Number of refereed papers published
- Number of patents generated
- Number of major innovations developed and adapted for commercialization
- Dollar amount of external research grants obtained
- Return on R&D investment.

Strategic Indicators. These indicators would focus on long-term and strategic aspects of the organization. Examples include:

- Reputation of the research organization
- Ability to attract highly qualified scientists
- The degree of customer (sponsor organization) satisfaction with research output
- Stability of research funding

- Ability to attract research support for new high-risk research projects
- Job satisfaction level of the employees.

It is clear that there are many ways in which one can assess the effectiveness of an organization. Thus, when thinking of an effective organization we should include all the variables because any one of them is likely to be biased or contaminated by extraneous ones. Any one criterion could be biased because of the way it is confounded with other variables of which we are not aware, or because the way it is measured may not be as accurate as possible. On the other hand, if we utilize many criteria and there is some degree of convergence across these criteria, then we are reasonably sure that we are dealing with a meaningful overall criterion (e.g., the weighted sum of the above-mentioned criteria), which can be used as a means of assessing the effectiveness of an organization.

3.2 WHO ARE THE INVENTORS AND INNOVATORS?

Individual capabilities, availability of resources to pursue research and development, and the ethos of a scientific community are all relevant to understanding inventors and innovators and the milieu in which they are likely to create and invent. The following are some ideas related to creativity and the characteristics of inventors.

Creativity

To invent or to innovate requires creativity. A very good account of creativity is given by Barron [1969], who discusses the majority of the tests that are available that purport to measure creativity. These tests do not specifically focus on R&D personnel; however, the attributes are those that Barron and others have discovered in their research with creative people. In doing the study, Barron and others obtained nominations of creative people from different professions and studied these individuals. They found a number of attributes frequently associated with creativity. Of the more than 30 attributes, the significant ones are:

- Conceptual fluency (that is, being able to express ideas well and to reformulate the ideas as one proceeds)
- The ability to produce a large number of ideas quickly
- The ability to generate original and unusual ideas
- The ability to separate source (who said it) from content (what was said) in evaluating information
- The ability to stand out and be a little deviant from others
- Interest in the problem one faces

- Perseverance in following problems wherever they lead
- Suspension of judgment and no early commitment
- The willingness to spend time analyzing and exploring
- Genuinely valuing intellectual and cognitive matters.

As mentioned briefly in the previous chapter, an interesting study by Isen et al. [1985] suggests that people can become more creative if they are in a "good mood." Subjects were randomly assigned to experimental groups (where manipulations of good mood were provided) and to control groups (where a neutral or negative mood was created). The mood manipulation was achieved by asking the subject to give associations to specific words. For the positive mood, the words were positive; for the negative mood, they were negative. The experimenter then scored the extent to which the associations were "unusual." Previous work has shown that creativity is higher when people make unusual associations. Standardized norms were available to obtain an objective measure of "unusualness" (i.e., if a response is frequently given by similar samples, it is not unusual). Thus, if the study were generalized to R&D laboratories, it would seem that managers in such laboratories must be particularly concerned when their subordinates suffer from poor morale. Such a condition may be particularly detrimental to creativity.

Characteristics of Inventors and Innovators

Views on characteristics of inventors and innovators naturally vary. Commenting on inventors and innovators, McCain [1969, p. 60] has suggested that the amateur scientist is nearly extinct and that formal training is almost a prerequisite for inventions and new scientific concepts. The individual normally has spent a very substantial amount of time and effort absorbing existing knowledge in his/her particular discipline while obtaining a graduate degree. These individuals tend to be above average as measured by ordinary testing methods.

However, even these highly trained, intelligent individuals with backgrounds in a scientific discipline are not very likely to make any substantial new contributions. In some fields, the average number of publications, during the lifetime of a person with a doctorate, is just a bit over one! Of those who make some contributions, only about 10% contribute more than half the scientific publications in a given field [McCain, 1969, p. 60].

Education and aptitude then form the first signaling mechanism in identifying inventors and innovators. Among this select group, however, only a small proportion will produce many inventions and innovations. Empirical studies [Charpie, 1970, p. 7; Twiss, 1986, p. 17] further suggest other characteristics that contribute to innovation. Focusing on the individual, some characteristics of a successful innovator and inventor are [Charpie, 1970, p. 7]:

- Strong technical background
- Able to deal with *"things"* rather than people
- Fluency in discussing ideas rather than handling processes in a formal organization
- More at home with technical products than with marketing problems
- Inclined to be disdainful of the professional judgments of others
- Committed to innovative concepts and product notion.

Recall, as discussed earlier, the distinction between inventors (basic research) and innovators (applied research). At the University of Sussex, U.K., 29 pairs of similar innovation projects were examined. In each pair, one project was successful and the other less so. There were clear differences within pairs that fell into a consistent pattern of successes. The characteristics of a successful innovator and the related organization structure that was implied can be summarized as follows [Twiss, 1980, p. 17]:

- Successful innovators are seen to have a much better understanding of *user* needs.
- Successful innovators pay much more attention to *marketing*.
- Successful innovators perform development work more *efficiently* than those who failed, but not necessarily more quickly.
- Successful innovators make more *effective use of outside technology and outside advice* (even though they perform much of the work in-house).
- The responsible individuals in their successful attempts are usually more senior and have *greater authority* than their counterparts who fail. This could be because of the successful individual's previous record.

None of these factors can be taken in isolation, but clearly, individuals working together on a research and development project who exhibit these characteristics are likely to show a higher degree of success.

Characteristics of inventors and innovators discussed here cannot be measured precisely and they represent a rather subjective evaluation of human capabilities, behavior, and accomplishments. Consequently, any rigid formalization of these characteristics is likely to lead to their misuse and thus be counterproductive. For example, many individuals without extensive formal education or other characteristics mentioned here have made important contributions to inventions and innovations in the past and they will continue to do so in the future.

3.3 ODD CHARACTERISTICS OF INVENTORS AND INNOVATORS

Rosovsky [1987] raised the question: Is there any substance to the theory that a significant proportion of scholars possess difficult and childish personalities, that is, The Amadeus Problem? While it is not prudent to generalize on personality traits, many R&D managers would agree with this assertion. In the film "*Amadeus*," Mozart was characterized as infantile and fundamentally unpleasant. While his behavior was atrocious, his musical gifts were divine. A manager may have to deal with the Amadeus Problem or Complex when a researcher displays exceptional scientific talent, but is a difficult, inconsiderate, and unpleasant person to work with.

Some inventors and innovators—men and women of science—are the essence of modesty and kindness. Many of them, however, are not likely to be so characterized. Few have the fine human qualities of Einstein. Many inventors and innovators have well-developed egos and incredible hubris. Some cases described below will give the reader a better understanding of the problem.

Let us take the case of Wolfgang Pauli at the Institute for Advanced Study, Princeton University. Pauli, of course, was a brilliant physicist, discoverer of the "Pauli Particle," and inventor of the "Exclusion Principle," which is one of the pillars of new physics. Pauli used to put people down at physics conferences whenever presenters were not being clear or correct according to his own thinking. This once happened to Robert Oppenheimer at a seminar in Ann Arbor, Michigan [Regis, 1987, p. 196]. While Oppenheimer was lecturing he covered the blackboard with equations. All of a sudden, Pauli jumped up, grabbed an eraser, and cleaned the whole blackboard off, saying it was all nonsense!

Pauli's uncontrolled behavior continued 20 years later when Frank Yang was lecturing at the Institute for Advanced Study on the topic of Gauge invariance [Regis, 1987, p. 196]. Yang, a Nobel laureate, had barely started when Pauli interrupted him with a question: "What is the mass of this particle?" Yang replied that it was a complicated problem and that he had not come up with a definite answer yet. Pauli retorted that this was not a sufficient excuse. Yang, who was a model of politeness and reserve, was so stunned that he had to sit down and collect himself [Regis, 1987, p. 196]. Pauli did not feel he had done anything wrong, instead he thought that it was Yang who was not responding appropriately. Pauli left a note in Yang's mailbox suggesting that Yang had made it almost impossible for Pauli to talk to him after the seminar.

Pauli was not a modest person. He often complained to his colleagues that he was having a hard time finding new physics problems to work on, because he knew too much [Regis, 1987, p. 196].

There is also the case of Kurt Gödel, the brilliant logician, probably the greatest since Aristotle, who was also at the Institute for Advanced Study. Gödel published his work on general relativity in 1949 and at the Institute he was regarded as utterly profound and inexpressively deep [Regis, 1987, pp. 63, 47]. This great logician and mathematician, however, believed that his food was being poisoned and that his doctors were trying to kill him. He died of malnutrition.

3.4   RESEARCHER'S RELATIONSHIP WITH MANAGEMENT AND PEERS

Many researchers have a rather negative view of managers or directors of research organizations. As an example, at the Institute for Advanced Study, Oswald Veblen, the famous physicist, suggested that the Institute did not need a director. Instead, he proposed that the Institute should have a rector, who would not have any power or authority to hatch forward-looking plans or schemes or develop any new institutional policy [Regis, 1987, p. 128]. Some scientists at the Institute joked that a good director should be "a little stupid" so that he would not come up with new ideas that might change the status quo of the institution. When Oppenheimer was being considered for the position of the Director of the Institute, some scientists advanced the truly shocking notion that perhaps the faculty could manage quite well on its own with only an administrator to manage business affairs. Later on when Oppenheimer became the Director of the Institute, he quite seriously suggested that the Institute could probably function quite well without a faculty [Regis, 1987, p. 129]!

One of the directors of the Institute for Advanced Study stated that many of the scientists claimed that they wanted to be free of routine administrative matters so they could focus their energies on research and scholarship. The director suggested that they did not mean a word of it, that is, although they want opportunities for research and scholarship they also want managerial and executive powers [Regis, 1987, p. 38].

Power sharing is essential in an R&D organization. Yes, researchers do, in fact, want to share the managerial and executive authority with the administrative structure. Researchers, in particular, want to share those aspects of managerial and executive authority that affect their research activities. Researchers on the other hand need to understand that accountability and some administrative duties also go with such sharing. This simply cannot be avoided. In sharing these powers, researchers will have to do some administrative work, meet scheduled deadlines, listen to the views of others, compromise where there are differing views, and not engage in guerrilla warfare after the decisions are taken.

Some of the negative views that researchers have about management are based on their experiences with organizations. There are cases at universities and research organizations where the administrative structure seems to grow at a proportionally higher rate than the size of the research group or faculty. As an example, at the Institute of Advanced Study, when Oppenheimer was the director he did not spend all of his time running the place. He even used to do some actual research. He had only one secretary, a business manager, and another administrative person. A few years later after he left, the Institute had an Associate Director and several assistants and secretaries [Regis, 1987, p. 285]. The size of the administrative staff seems to grow geometrically and thus many scientists in R&D organizations and faculty members at universities feel that the administration lives for itself and research and teaching activities become side issues. Managers would be well advised to look periodically at the administrative structures in their own offices and question the necessity for every job.

3.5 FORMATION OF TEAMS

There are many attributes that need to be considered when forming a team. The work of Pelz and Andrews (1966b) has already indicated that effective teams are characterized by support of members for each other's work, great respect for other members, and complementary skills, strategies, and approaches. Respect requires similarity in level of ability, and basic attitudes and values. Yet team members must have varied skills and specific attitudes that are different and complimentary. For example, they may all be top level scientists with similar values toward autonomy, yet differ in their disciplines and in their attitudes toward specific methods of data collection. Empirical support for this point has been obtained in laboratory studies [Triandis et al., 1965] indicating that creativity was highest when team members were similar in their abilities but different in their specific attitudes.

Similarity in ability is important because it is undesirable for people to look at their co-workers as being intellectually too different. A person feels uncomfortable with co-workers who are either "dummies" or "geniuses," and thus cooperation will suffer. At the same time, complementarity is desirable for many personality attributes. For example, a person who would like to dominate a team can get along much better with people who like to be dominated than with others who also want to be in charge. A person who is talkative gets along better with people who like to listen. A diversity of viewpoints on how to approach a research project and different skills concerning its actual operation may result in a better research project [Janis, 1972]. If members of the team are too different, cooperation will suffer; if they are too similar in perspective, one gets *groupthink* (see Chapter 2).

What is the optimal team number? There is research suggesting that five is the best number for a discussion group. In larger groups people feel they do not have enough time to present their ideas, the leader becomes more autocratic and monopolizes the available time, and competing subteams may develop. Smaller groups often lack a definite leader, and may not develop clear goals, or have enough different perspectives to avoid groupthink.

The effectiveness of a team depends on the quality of the people in it and the coordination of its activities. However, how these variables impact on team effectiveness depends on the task. There are three types of tasks that need consideration:

Divisible vs. Unitary Tasks. Divisible tasks can be done by different people, for example checking the references in a reference list (one could divide the checking across as many clerks as there are pages of references to be checked). Unitary tasks cannot be divided, for example, understanding this paragraph.

Maximizing vs. Optimizing Tasks. Maximizing tasks have a criterion with no limit, for example, find as many references as you can; optimizing tasks have a criterion with an optimal level, for example, determine how much space you need for this project (too much space is wasteful and too little results in an ineffective project).

Disjunctive vs. Conjunctive Tasks. In disjunctive tasks, if one member has the correct solution the others will necessarily agree; for example, the root of a quadratic equation. In conjunctive tasks, every member must agree, for example, a jury, or in a committee in which everyone has veto power.

In disjunctive tasks, if the probability that one member has the correct solution is P, and the probability that no one can solve the problem is Q, where $Q = 1 - P$, the theoretical probability that the group will solve the problem is $1 - Q^n$, where n is the number of members. Clearly, the more members you have the better the group's chances of being successful. In the case of conjunctive tasks the opposite is true. A solution is more likely if the group is small than if the group is large.

Incidentally, empirically, groups do less well than the theory ($P_g = 1 - Q^n$) predicts, primarily because there are losses in efficiency that occur when people discuss various solutions. Similarly, in divisible tasks, one would expect n people to produce n times the output of one person, but empirically this does not happen. The group often produces less. This lack of individual responsibility, called "social loafing," results when there is no clear identification of each person's output. Usually when one can identify the output of each individual, social loafing is small or nonexistent. Finally, unitary tasks are better done by individuals than by groups.

Osborn [1957] advocated the use of "brainstorming" to increase the creativity of small groups. According to his theory, when people generate ideas in the nonevaluative climate of a group and get stimulated from each other they produce more ideas. However, the evaluation of this proposal has not supported this idea. For example, Dunnette et al. [1963] arranged for 48 research scientists and 48 advertising personnel to either do brainstorming or work individually. In 23 of the 24 groups a greater number of different ideas was produced by the individuals than by the groups. Individuals not only produced more ideas when working alone, but also the quality of these ideas was not inferior.

An important aspect of good group problem-solving is the development of a wide range of alternatives. This can best be done when people think of a variety of courses of action independently of others. However, when it comes to evaluating these alternatives there is an advantage in having many different critics, who examine the solution from as many points of view as possible. This critique also can be done individually, but groups can be more effective when the evaluation requires memory for previous events. Groups are better in remembering complex material than are individuals, who often forget some fact that others remember and can supply during the evaluation.

3.6 GENERATING NEW IDEAS

Precise definition of how new ideas are generated and how results from R&D are converted into innovation are hard to articulate. In an article entitled "Serendipity or Sound Science?" Sutton [1986] points out that the Nobel Prize to Burton Richter and Samuel Ting resulted from discoveries that though unexpected, were nonetheless the result of a lifetime of careful research. Sutton shows that the way to unexpected results lies not in accidents, but in excellence and in thorough scientific investigation with the best possible intellectual and laboratory resources.

An article entitled "The Acid Test of Innovation" provides several examples of innovation; it concludes [Bell et al., 1986, p. 32]:

> Serendipity, self-interest, concentrated and coordinated work: all these are characteristics of successful innovation. But the single most important lesson of these examples is the importance of keeping in touch. Academics need to know what their local industries can do and what they might be interested in making and marketing in the future. Companies, large and small, benefit by having key personnel who can keep up with scientific literature and what is going on in university departments to which they have easy access.

Many innovations occur when facts from previously unrelated fields of knowledge are brought together in a creative solution. For example, a process used in the chemical industry may prove useful in the textile industry. Many other innovations require the redefinition of the problem. For example, for thousands of years horses were used to draw chariots, until it occurred to some warriors that they could ride them, giving them speed not available until that time.

Since such redefinitions are inhibited by conventional wisdom, people without such wisdom (e.g., the newcomer) are often more creative than those steeped in conventional ideas.

MacKinnon (1962) has summarized research on creativity that suggests that creative people are more open to their own feelings, have a better understanding of themselves, have a widerange of interests, and many interests that U.S. culture classifies as feminine (e.g., an interest in the arts). They tend to be uninterested in small details and more interested in the broad picture and its implications. They possess cognitive flexibility and verbal skills, are good communicators and intellectually curious, but are not interested in policing their own impulses.

Intelligence and creativity are not correlated for IQs in the 120 (ability to do college level work) to genius range. In other words, there are many examples of modestly intelligent individuals who are extremely creative and extraordinarily intelligent individuals who are not.

Creativity depends on both people and environment. A creative environment allows the creative scientists to feel free to work in areas of their greatest interests, provides them with many rewards and recognition, allows them to have broad contacts with stimulating colleagues, encourages them to take moderate risks, and tolerates some failures and nonconformity.

Numerous techniques have been suggested that supposedly improve creativity. Among them we will mention teaching the scientist to ask questions such as "Should I adapt, modify, reduce, substitute, rearrange, reverse, or combine the processes under consideration?" Brainstorming [Osborn, 1963], synectics [Gordon, 1961], lateral thinking, need assessment [Holt et al., 1984], and combinations of the above [Carson and Rickards, 1979] have been suggested. There are also analytic techniques [see Twiss, 1986 for a review], which follow logical analysis, the analysis of the attributes of the products that need to be developed, morphological analysis, the study of the needs of customers, technologists and marketers, as well as the systematic monitoring of technological developments.

Each of these techniques has enthusiastic proponents, but systematic evaluations of the effectiveness of the techniques are lacking. In the few cases where careful evaluation was done it did not support the claims of the proponents. However, one could argue that careful evaluation in laboratory settings may not generalize to the field.

The general idea of most of these techniques is to involve many people in the creative process, to use a number of different ways of generating ideas, to find ways to systematically eliminate those ideas that are unlikely to be workable, and to keep eliminating until one idea survives. This new product would be one of a myriad of potential ones, but many perspectives will converge in support of it.

In many of these techniques one is supposed to "suspend criticism" during the idea-generation phase. Thus, in brainstorming one is allowed to suggest any idea, no matter how unworkable. In synectics one is supposed to link apparently irrelevant elements and be free from the constraints of critical judgment and the boundaries of orthodox ideas. One states and restates the problem, makes analogies, uses fantasy, and is encouraged to produce paradoxical ideas, such as "dependable unreliability" or "living death." In lateral thinking one is supposed to challenge assumptions, focus attention on different aspects of the problem, generate many solutions, and introduce irrelevant ideas and even discontinuities in thinking about the problem. In need assessment one examines the existing, future, emotional, and rational needs of customers, technologists, and marketers with respect to a particular product.

Since systematic evaluation of these techniques is not available, we offer this advice. Speak to several "expert" trainers who advocate each of these techniques. Select two or three of these techniques on the basis of how promising they may be in relation to your particular products or problems. Randomly assign problems to techniques, and have experts lead your groups through the creativity phase utilizing each technique. Evaluate the results by examining which technique produced the best set of results.

This approach seems wise because it is likely that *your* products or problems can be better solved with one approach than with another. In short, it is not clear that a particular technique will prove effective for all problems. Your problems may well have some industry-specific characteristics. Thus, by experimenting, you should be able to identify the unique combination of techniques that is most helpful in solving your particular *kind* of problem.

Successful innovators pay close attention to their users' needs and desires [Quinn, 1985], avoid detailed early technical or marketing plans, and allow entrepreneurial teams to pursue competing alternatives within a clearly conceived framework of goals and limits. A number of important patterns contribute to innovation [Quinn, 1985, p. 77], as discussed below:

Atmosphere and Vision. This includes providing the proper environment, value system, and atmosphere (perhaps culture of the organization) to support the innovation process. Perhaps an executive vision (having goals that move the organization toward societally valued achievements) is more important than a particular management background. Managers with executive ability project clear long-term goals for their organizations that go beyond simple economic measures. Such vision, combined with a creative organizational culture, is likely to lead to an innovative organization.

Orientation to the Market. Since innovation involves doing research and development activities that are commercially useful, innovative companies inevitably have to tie their activities to the realities of the marketplace. This means keeping in touch with the user.

Small, Flat Organizations. This means an organization with two or three levels and project teams that are small (fewer than seven).

Multiple Approaches. Since many positive results might come from unexpected approaches, it is important not to narrow the investigation too early. Thus, management should not overdirect the approach used for research and development activities, at least early on.

Developmental Shootouts. It may be desirable to use parallel and competing developments for an activity. While the cost of such an activity may seem high, this duplication may provide the most efficient and effective output. These developmental competitions or shootouts among competing approaches perhaps can be handled best when the project reaches a certain prototype stage. Quinn [1985] points out that one of the problems associated with such an approach is the issue of managing the reintegration of the members of the losing team.

Skunkworks. According to Quinn [1985, p. 79], for every highly innovative enterprise in the research sample he studied, a small-company environment was emulated by using groups that functioned in a "skunkworks style." In this approach, small teams of engineers, technicians, designers, and others were placed together with no other intervening organizational or visible physical barriers to developing a new product from the idea stage to the final commercialization stage. This approach has been used successfully in many Japanese companies. Quinn [1985, p. 79] gives the example of Soichiro Honda, who was known for working directly on technical problems and who emphasized his technical points by personally working with other members of the "skunkworks team."

Interactive Learning. While "skunkworks" emulate the highly interactive and motivating learning environment that characterizes many successful ventures, there is also the need for interactive learning achieved by close contact with the wider scientific community. Even the largest research organization represents only a small fraction of the total research investment internationally and, in turn, only a small fraction of the enormous intellectual and technological resources available and necessary for generating new ideas and innovation.

3.7 EMPHASES ON ASPECTS OF ORGANIZATIONAL CULTURE

Culture includes values, that is, conceptions of the desirable. For example, values specify how much freedom people should have to determine the kinds of research problems they will tackle or what level of equality there should be within the organization (i.e., whether people should feel "great respect" and distance from their supervisors or be able to walk into their offices and feel close to them).

Related to values are norms, which are ideas about desirable behaviors for members of the organization. Organizations have norms about many things (for example, how much to produce). A norm many research organizations have is that its members should try to publish at least one paper in a refereed journal every year. Members of cultures also have ideas about rewards. Who should get rewarded, when, and under what conditions? What kinds of activities should get rewarded and what activities should not be rewarded? What kinds of schedule for these rewards should be adopted and used? How should people be socialized in the organizations so that they become "good" members of the organization? How should they keep up to date? What sorts of norms should one have about attendance at scientific conferences? How should one develop new skills? Should one take courses? Should one go back to a university?

An organizational culture that fosters excellence in R&D work, that is internally coherent and dominates a laboratory is highly desirable. No specific or comprehensive list of cultural elements is possible. In what follows, we propose some crucial areas a manager may want to consider:

- Nurturing the ethos of modern science as an important aspect of organizational culture as postulated by Merton [1973] and discussed in detail in the section on "Who are the Innovators?" When the ideal ethos (universalism, sharing of scientific knowledge, disinterestedness in terms of commercial or financial benefits, organized skepticism involving detached scrutiny of scientific discoveries) becomes part of the culture of the organization, science and innovation can flourish.
- Tolerating an innovator who may not always work well within the existing administrative procedures.
- Providing meaning to every person's contribution in terms of organization goals–personal goal congruence.
- Recognizing the importance of interaction with the wider scientific community and users (who can play an important role in the innovation process) and encouraging such interaction.
- Encouraging the various gatekeeper roles, as further described in chapter 10 on Technology Transfer.
- Recognizing and rewarding excellence—both technical and managerial.
- Finally, developing a culture with a "can-do" attitude directed toward the needs of the customer.

3.8 ETHOS OF A SCIENTIFIC COMMUNITY

Robert Merton [1973, p. 270], commenting on the normative structure of science, stated that "the institutional goal of science is the extension of certified knowledge. The technical methods employed towards this end provide the relevant definition of knowledge: empirically confirmed and logically consistent statements of regularities." He further stated that the ethos of modern science includes universalism, communalism, disinterestedness, and organized skepticism [Merton, 1973, p. 270].

Universalism. This expression suggests that scientific discoveries, whatever their source, are subjected to preestablished impersonal criteria. The truth and scientific value of a scientific discovery is independent of the personal or social background attributes of the individuals. Merton further stated that "universalism finds further expression in the demand that careers be open to talents . . . to restrict scientific careers on grounds other than lack of competence is to prejudice the furtherance of knowledge. Free access to scientific pursuits is a functional imperative" [Merton, 1973, p. 272].

Communalism. Communalism implies that scientific findings should be shared equally among all members of the scientific community. Since findings of science are a product of social collaboration within the scientific community, the ownership of such discoveries is a property of the commons and the rights are assigned to the wider scientific community. Merton [1973, p. 273] suggests that scientific discoveries

> . . . constitute a common heritage in which the equity of the individual producer is severely limited . . . . Property rights in science are whittled down to a bare minimum by the rationale of the scientific ethic. The scientist's claim to "his" intellectual "property" is limited to that of recognition and esteem which, if the institution functions with a modicum of efficiency, is roughly commensurate with the significance of the increments brought to the common fund of knowledge.

Disinterestedness. Merton [1973, p. 276] has stated:

> A passion for knowledge, idle curiosity, altruistic concern with the benefit to humanity, and a host of other special motives have been attributed to the scientist. The question for distinctive motives appears to have been misdirected. It is rather a distinctive pattern of institutional control of a wide range of motives which characterizes the behavior of scientists . . . , The demand for disinterestedness has a firm basis in the public and testable character of science and this circumstance, it may be supposed, has contributed to the integrity of men of science.

Scientists make few spurious claims and, in fact, they would be ineffective since much of what is produced by scientists undergoes scrutiny, replicaton, and review by fellow scientists. Since scientists do not personally benefit from many of these discoveries, disinterestedness (in terms of commercial or financial benefits) forms an important characteristic of the scientific community.

Organized Skepticism. Organized skepticism is interrelated with other characteristics of a scientific community. It is both a methodological and institutional mandate. This involves a temporary suspension of judgment and the detached scrutiny of scientific discoveries. Numerous scientific conferences and meetings held throughout the world embody many of the characteristics described here.

In many ways, in a modern society, it has become possible to further strengthen these characteristics due to the ease of communication among scientists. Fostering this ethos is essential for productivity and excellence in an R&D organization.

The ethos of the scientific community, as is the case with such principles, can never be universally achieved in practice. As Bok [1982, p. 151] has stated, the force of competition, lure of prizes, and fame, among other things, can have some negative effects on this ethos. Over the years, nonetheless, the peer review and refereed publication process and the universal nature of science has helped to make these aspects of ethos the norms of the scientific community.

Discussing the rationality of science, Newton-Smith [1981, p. 44] states: "According to Popper, truth is the aim of science. But the scientific condition is one of ignorance. . . . Popper's thesis of the utter inaccessibility of truth leads him to reconstrue the goal of science as that of achieving a better approximation to the truth, or as he calls it, a higher degree of verisimilitude." For Popper, when an experiment turns out as the hypothesis predicted, this only means that the hypothesis has not been refuted. Popper asserts that positive evidence favoring a hypothesis does not necessarily constitute evidence in its favor [Newton-Smith, 1981, p. 45].

Some science historians would argue that science does not and cannot get hold of the "truth" in any objective and impersonal sense [Regis, 1987, p. 217]. Ed Witten, one of the inventors of the superstring theory, suggests that whether we get to the "truth" or not, we learn new things as we develop new theories. He suggests that as we learn new things, "We develop more powerful laws, laws that unify principles and give us more accurate descriptions of more and more phenomena. It doesn't mean that the old stuff was wrong. It just wasn't complete" [Regis, 1987, p. 211]. Basically, new discoveries mean we know more than we did before, and it is a step forward.

3.9 SUMMARY

In summary, this chapter has comprehensively defined organization productivity in terms of organization effectiveness, and presented suggestions regarding what might constitute organization effectiveness. Creating such an organization, its team structure, and its culture have been discussed. Further information on creative tensions and staffing was included in Chapter 2 on Elements Needed for an R&D Organization. We have tried to focus on such interesting questions as the way in which new ideas are generated and who are the inventors and innovators. Ideas and empirical data available on such issues cannot be precise. Thus, rigid formulation of information about the characteristics of an innovator or inventor is treacherous ground and should be avoided. Instead, in managing a productive and effective R&D organization, a manager should foster the environment so it will be conducive to the characteristics of successful innovators and inventors.

3.10 QUESTIONS FOR CLASS DISCUSSION

1 What are the criteria of R&D lab organizational effectiveness?

2 What kinds of people are most creative?

3 What can be done to increase lab creativity?

4 How should unique characteristics of inventors and innovators be handled by research managers? Develop a case study to focus on the issues.

3.11 FURTHER READINGS

Carson, J. W. and T. Rickards (1979). *Industrial New Product Development: A Manual for the 1980s*. New York: Gower Press.

Gordon, W. J. (1961). *Synectics*. New York: Harper & Row.

Holt, K., H. Geschka and G. Peterlongo (1984). *Needs Assessment*. New York: Wiley.

Merton, R. K. (1973) In N. W. Storer (Ed.), *The Sociology of Science: Theoretical and Empirical Investigations*. Chicago: The University of Chicago Press.

Osborn, A. F. (1963). *Applied Imagination*. New York: Charles Scribner.

Root-Bernstein, R. S. (1989). Who discovers and invents. *Research Technology Management*, **32**, 43–50 (January–February).

Twiss, B. C. (1986). *Managing Technological Innovation*, 3rd ed. London: Pitman.

____4
JOB DESIGN AND ORGANIZATIONAL EFFECTIVENESS

A major consideration in designing jobs is the match between the requirements of the organization and the requirements of individuals. To design a job optimally one needs to consider the abilities, interests, and personality of the individuals as well as the needs of the organization. For example, the organization may find it optimal to have people follow precisely the rules and regulations that the organization develops, but individuals often find it much more satisfying if they have considerable freedom in deciding how to behave within the organization. The individual's freedom, on the other hand, cannot be unlimited, so jobs have to be designed in such a way that a balance is achieved between the needs of the organization and the needs of individuals. Some individuals, because of their personality, have an especially strong need for autonomy and will require a job that is designed with even greater autonomy than for the majority of individuals.

The organization must be concerned with the compatibility of individual goals with those of the organization in order to maximize the motivation of individuals and to minimize friction among them. However, individual needs can be satisfied in a number of ways, and they tend to change with experience, maturity, and the individual's stage in life. For example, security may be less important to an unmarried 20-year-old than to a married 45-year-old. Security can also be satisfied in different ways (e.g., a social security system that operates over a long period or a high salary for a short period of time). In matching individual and organizational goals there is necessarily some give-and-take in both directions, probably with the individual giving more than the organization, simply because the organization cannot bend as easily as can an individual.

Managers can accomplish the melding of individual and organizational goals by selecting people whose personal goals are already compatible with those of the organization, and second, through participative management, which sets goals in such a way that individuals can accept them and the organization can attain its objectives. Some "negotiation" of such goals is healthy, since the organization can reach its goals by a large number of paths. For example, commercial organizations can make a profit in many ways, and it is more likely that they will do so if they use goals that are compatible with the goals of their employees.

In dealing with job design, we need to consider the match between the person and the job in greater detail. On the individual's side, we have the person's abilities as well as needs. On the job's side, we have requirements that can be conceived both in terms of ability requirements and job attributes that satisfy needs. When there is a good match between the job ability requirements and the individual's ability, the individual is more likely to be satisfactory from the point of view of the organization. In that case, the individual is also more likely to be promoted and achieve his goals within the organization. When there is a match between the needs of the individual and the job's ability to satisfy those needs, the individual is more likely to be satisfied with the organization, to find the job enjoyable, and, as a result, to stay with the organization and participate in its activities more frequently. For example, low absenteeism is likely to be associated with such satisfaction.

Jobs should be designed so that people can define the functions. It is a mistake to think in terms of the traditional bureaucratic structure, in which the organization writes the job description. Those who are members of a team should write their own job descriptions, and the team must do some of the job defining. Of course, the team leader has to provide some guidelines, and ensure that the jobs that are so defined are consistent with corporate goals. But the details can be left largely to the job holders. Once a talented scientist is given a broad objective, compatible with the goals of the organization, a lot of job designing can be done by the researcher.

An organic organization allows job incumbents to develop job definitions, and the research team to define the jobs of its members. Competence is used as the main determinant of status in the hierarchy of the organization. Peer review of projects and job definitions proposed by job incumbents can shape the job definition better than management review.

4.1 JOB ATTRIBUTES

There is considerable literature that is consistent with the Hackman and Oldham [1980] analysis of job attributes and how they are related to satisfaction. The general argument in this literature is that jobs that provide sufficient variety, autonomy, task identity, and feedback are more satisfying than jobs that do not have these attributes. Variety refers to the ability to do different jobs at the particular job site. *Autonomy* refers to the ability to decide for oneself what should be done. *Task identity* refers to having a job that can be identified as a distinct unit. For example, completing a particular research project, or saying that this particular discovery is associated with this particular individual, gives the specific activity more task identity because the activity can be associated with the name of the investigator. On the other hand, in a research job involving many investigators, where the complete job is done at different organizational levels and locations, the situation reduces the identity of the job. *Feedback* refers to knowledge of how well one is doing the job.

Hackman and Oldham's theory argues that a job is high in meaningfulness when it has task variety, task identity, and task significance, so that people think that what they are doing is important. High meaningfulness in turn creates satisfaction. Similarly, they argue that autonomy, which allows a person to be more responsible for the job activities and outcomes, also leads to satisfaction. Finally, feedback is very important. People should know how well they are doing and whether what they have been doing is having an impact. A person who works for years on something without receiving any attention, for example, if nobody quotes his/her scientific work, is not receiving feedback.

So, in research, as in other kinds of work, the best possible job is one that is designed so that it is variable, has significance and identity, allows the investigator considerable autonomy, and gives him or her feedback.

There is a substantial literature that deals with these issues [Loher et al., 1985]. Thus, in designing research and development jobs, it is well to remember that maximizing variety, autonomy, and feedback, as well as the meaningfulness of the work, is likely to be associated with satisfaction.

4.2 PHYSICAL LOCATION AND COMMUNICATION

Another aspect of job design concerns the way jobs are physically located in relation to each other. There is a considerable literature that indicates that arranging jobs in such a way that communication is either increased or decreased can result in improved performance in research and development jobs. For example, Allen [1977], and Szilagyi and Holland [1980] have indicated that the probability of communication increases rather sharply with a decrease in the distance between co-workers. Moreover, Szilagyi and Holland [1980] have reported that increased social density (a situation in which there were many employees per square foot who were able to talk to each other quickly) resulted in such employees experiencing task facilitation. Co-workers exchanged information much more easily, and, as a result, they were more effective and also more satisfied with their jobs. There is also a study by Morton [1971] that found that removing spatial barriers improved communication between innovators and their customers.

On the other hand, one should not oversell these ideas because there are some studies, such as Thompson's [1967], that indicate that there are situations when barriers are desirable. For example, if one has a rather creative group in a bureaucratic organization, physical barriers between that group and the bureaucratic organization can be extremely desirable.

There are differences also between scientists and engineers in the way they communicate [Allen, 1977]. Scientists communicate through the literature and through professional meetings. They spend a good deal of time talking with outsiders and exchanging experiences. On the other hand, engineers spend most of their time communicating with customers, vendors, and doing actual experiments within the laboratory. The motivation of the two groups is to some extent different because the scientists are much more individualistic and require recognition as individuals by the scientific community. Publishing is vital for them. In contrast the primary concern of engineers is the success of the organization. For the scientist, the number of colleagues in the same discipline who are working on the same problem is associated with success; for the engineer the number of colleagues in the same laboratory is related to success. In other words, we need to distinguish between scientists and engineers. The motivational and organizational courses of their success are not identical. This has implications for the effective management of an R&D organization, as well as for job design.

In designing jobs, we also ought to consider the flow of information. Research and development jobs are particularly susceptible to this factor because there is so much task uncertainty and novelty associated with such jobs. There is also the need to communicate with the wider scientific community. We must consider the conditions under which jobs will be better performed because they are designed so that people can exchange information that clarifies and improves the task. To some extent this has to do with the way we organize the job in relation to other jobs. For example, how we place one job next to or away from another, or the arrangement of the desks of particular scientists or engineers, may be crucial in determining how effective they are going to be. Some of the research literature, such as Cheng [1984] and Katz and Tushman [1979], discusses these matters and points out that on jobs for which there is no organized body of literature to which technologists and engineers can turn when they face a new problem, new information is obtained from others who have had similar experiences. Thus oral communication is extremely helpful to them.

Oral communication permits rapid feedback, decoding, and synthesis of complex information, and fits especially well in scientific settings where most of the research ideas are as yet unformed and difficult to articulate [Katz and Tushman, 1979].

However, the literature suggests that too much communication may be disfunctional if the actors who exchange information do not share a common language. In one study [Katz and Tushman, 1979] that involved 350 academic research units located in six countries, the researchers found that in those situations in which there was low uncertainty about how to do the job and high ambiguity about the long-term goals of the job, there was a positive relationship between communication within the unit, but a negative relationship between communication outside the unit and performance. If people started talking with others outside their units, and lacked a common language, the greater the amount of communication frequency the lower the performance. In short, people spent so much time clarifying what they meant that they were not effective in performing their tasks.

These findings are not consistent with the points made by Pelz and Andrews [1966b], who found that among 1130 scientists in academic and industrial laboratories *both* intra- and interunit communication was highly desirable. However, an explanation of the discrepancy between the findings by Cheng and Katz–Tushman on the one hand, and Pelz–Andrews on the other , may be that Pelz–Andrews dealt primarily with applied scientists. In their case, perhaps the difficulties in not having a common language are not as great as is the case with those doing more basic research, who are trying to develop new concepts and a new language at the same time that they are communicating.

A comment about the physical work environment of the R&D personnel might be in order. As discussed previously, scientists have a tremendous need for autonomy. In addition to providing a formal and informal supportive management environment, R&D personnel should be given considerable freedom to modify and personalize their office environment within the resources available for such improvements. In the case of R&D personnel, more than in other professional groups, one may find some office modifications and arrangements unusual and bordering on the grotesque. Our experience indicates that some of these problems may seem trivial, but in practice they are much more difficult to resolve. Exhorting a researcher to change his office arrangement or keep his office better organized simply does not work. Unless the physical situation in the office is clearly adversely affecting job performance or safety (for example, creating a fire hazard), it is best to tolerate such idiosyncrasies.

4.3 CAREER PATHS

In designing jobs, it is also desirable to think of the total career path of the scientists. One of the problems in a research and development setting is that there are not sufficient opportunities to reach the top of the organization in terms of pay and prestige for those engaged in purely technical activities. The jobs are designed in such a way that administrators receive higher compensation, but this is inconsistent with many of the values and needs of technically gifted individuals. To the extent that the engineer or the scientist is dissatisfied with his job definition, he is more likely to turn to other sources of satisfaction, for example, family or civic matters. There is evidence [Bailyn and Lynch, 1983] that indicates that this is exactly what happened to those engineers who were less satisfied with their careers. Keenan [1980] reports a study by Gorstel and Hutton that indicates that many engineers who became part of the management team did so rather reluctantly and because of the absence of sufficient opportunities for technical careers, rather than because they enjoyed the management position.

In other words, we have a situation in which the role a person really wants (a top level technical job) is not available in the organization. Furthermore, only the managerial jobs pay well. This situation results in low morale and inefficiency. It is a problem that most organizations must face squarely and try to solve. It is often necessary to design jobs to fit the needs of employees to some extent.

When thinking about job design we should also realize that engineers go through various stages in the development of their careers. For example, Thompson and Dalton [1976] interviewed over 200 scientists, engineers, and managers and identified several stages for the development of an engineer's career. They argue that in order to perform well an engineer should go through four different stages.

1. The engineer should work with a mentor, who can teach him/her how to design and carry out projects and how to be successful in relating to clients and upper management. During this stage, the mentor obtains the projects, designs the broad outline of the project, and fits the project into the activities of the organization. The apprentice does the detailed work, makes sure that everything is accurate, and follows up on all details. It is obvious that during this stage the definition of the job makes the apprentices appendages of their mentors, and so they must be physically located very close to each other in order to develop the proper interpersonal relationships.

2. The engineer assumes responsibility for a definable portion of a project or process, works independently, and produces results that are significantly identifiable with him/her. The professional begins to develop credibility and a reputation as a person who knows a great deal about a particular area. The professional now manages more of his/her own time and accepts more responsibility for the outcomes. Relationships with peers and fellow professionals now become very important, while the relationships with the supervisor or mentor are less significant. This requires a different kind of job definition and a different kind of physical arrangement. For example, the professional, in this case, could be located far away from the supervisor.

In general, organizations consider Stage Two valuable, but not especially desirable. If a person stays in Stage Two for a very long time, the chances are that he will be fired or moved to some other job that is not very important. In other words, the expectation is that the engineer will get out of Stage Two and into Stage Three if he is going to be considered "successful."

3. This stage is somewhat different. Here the engineers apply their technical skills to several areas rather than to a specific project. They get involved in external relationships with suppliers, with clients, and with new business ventures, and they begin to do things that benefit others and the organization in general. They become involved in the development of other people. Many engineers stop at this point, and are considered very successful.

4. In Stage Four the manager exercises a significant influence over the future direction of a major portion of the organization. He tends to engage in wide and varied interactions both outside and inside the organization; he is also involved in sponsoring and developing promising people who might fill future key roles in the organization. Generally, people in Stage Four spend their time in three ways: (1) they are innovators who contribute to the future of the organization by supplying innovative and original ideas that might shape the organization; (2) they are internal entrepreneurs who bring together resources, money, people, and ideas in order to pursue new developments (for example, new research projects); and (3) they are upper level managers who form policy, initiate programs, and monitor the progress of the organization.

It appears clear from this discussion that there is an increasing managerial component in the activities of the engineer as he/she moves from Stage One to Stage Four. However, it is important to remember that the technical side of the activities can remain a very substantial component of the engineer's total activity. It seems appropriate, then, to reward people who do purely technical work in spite of the fact that they are not supervising a large number of people. In other words, the managerial career and the technical career should not be viewed as inconsistent. On the contrary, sometimes professional employees in a managerial position can take better care of their interests as professionals by increasing their decision-making latitude concerning research and by their control over resources relevant to their scientific work.

Roberts [1978, p. 6] asserts that "even with academic scientists, some of our own studies here at MIT show that faculty are more productive when they have a mix of work activities. There's even a finding that mixing research with administrative work helps increase creativity and idea generation!"

It would seem, therefore, that technical competence and management responsibilities are not inconsistent. Nonetheless, in job design and in structuring an organization, the problem still remains of providing promotion opportunities for technical personnel, who may not want management responsibilities at higher levels where they can no longer contribute directly to R&D. A mechanism—using multiple hierarchy—for addressing this problem is discussed in the next section.

4.4 DUAL AND TRIPLE HIERARCHIES

One of the ways of dealing with the problems outlined above is to develop a dual or even a triple hierarchy within the organization. In the dual structure, organizations develop an additional hierarchy with technical positions that parallel the positions in the management hierarchy. These technical positions comprise a professional hierarchy that has the same degree of control, authority, and compensation as the corresponding positions in the management hierarchy. However, Schriesheim et al. [1977] reviewed the literature and concluded that dual hierarchies have been generally unsuccessful at resolving conflicts between professionals and their employee organizations and at providing alternative career opportunities and reward systems.

Apparently, the most important reason that these organizational structures failed is that promotion in the professional hierarchy was, by definition, "a movement away from power." In addition, there were signs of failure among those who followed the professional hierarchy because they felt they lacked parity with the managerial hierarchy and because evaluative criteria used were inequitable. For this reason, Schriesheim et al. [1977] suggested a triple hierarchy as an alternative structure for managing professional organizational conflict.

The triple hierarchy provides three different advancement opportunities. The managerial hierarchy is available to those who desire advancement to managerial positions. For those professionals who desire only professional duties (here "professional" implies scientific, research, and technical duties) the professional hierarchy remains a viable option.

The third hierarchy is occupied by professionals who have key administrative jobs, as well as regular professional duties. They have hierarchical authority in those areas where professional values and organizational requirements are most likely to diverge.

This type of organization is similar to the organization of major research universities. In such universities the administrators are usually individuals with a good research record. Thus, they are able to relate to the faculty. At the same time, they have other attributes that enable them to interact successfully with government officials, trustees, alumni, major donors, and so on. Some administrators are closer to the research process while others are closer to the political activities needed to run a university. A successful university has the right mix of administrators. Similarly, R&D organizations need some people who will deal with the politics, some with the technical aspects, and some with both. The right mix results in the best R&D organization.

We will use the terms *technical, professional–liaison*, and *management hierarchy* to discuss the advantages of the triple hierarchy. In the university setting, these terms might correspond to the head of a department, a dean, and a university president. The head of the department is able to evaluate a faculty member's professional qualifications; a dean is able to evaluate a head of department; a president is able to evaluate a dean. Usually, the head of the department is technically very competent, and even does research. The dean is also technically competent and in some cases does research. The president is often a generalist and rarely does research.

The argument is that the triple hierarchy can deal with all three of the problems: the domination of the organization by the management hierarchy, miscommunication, and inadequate evaluation procedures. In the triple hierarchy, managers have less power, since much of it has been taken away by those in the professional-liaison hierarchy. While managers and professionals in the dual hierarchy have different perspectives and often miscommunicate, in the triple hierarchy the technical people interact mostly with those who are in the professional–liaison hierarchy rather than with those in the management hierarcy. As a result, they are able to communicate and get along better because they share the same values. In the dual hierarchy, the managers judge the technical people, whereas in the triple hierarchy, the professional-liaison hierarchy individuals, rather than the managerial structure, evaluate the professionals. The result is that those who best understand their perspective are the ones who are judging how well the technical people are doing. There is some evidence that the triple hierarchy is effective. For example, Baumgartel [1957] and Pelz [1956] found that when the positions of research director or administrator were held by individuals with professional or scientific backgrounds, researchers felt more protected and work units had higher productivity and morale. Additional support came from studies by Lawrence and Lorsch [1967], Likert [1967], Marcson [1960], and Mintzberg [1973].

Can this triple hierarchical approach be successfully implemented in an organization and is it really practical? In formal organizations, by necessity, both the organizational structure and individual responsibilities are rigidly defined, while the triple hierarchical organizational structure requires more flexibility and cross or parallel communications. When this triple hierarchical approach is successfully implemented, many unintended and secondary benefits have occurred, such as retaining highly qualified technical staff and minimizing the complacency process of the organization. (For the purpose of this discussion, *complacency* is defined as a state of being uncreative, stale, and aging.)

4.5   CENTRALIZATION AND DECENTRALIZATION

Another broad issue of job design is whether to use centralized or decentralized structures. According to Allen [1977], in a centralized project or project structure a majority of the people working on a particular activity report to one project manager, who makes the assignments. They receive management reviews from this particular individual and are also physically located near that person. On the other hand, if fewer than 50% of the personnel are reporting to this one person, then the project is considered decentralized.

Allen [1977] and Marquis and Straight [1965] suggest that both the decentralized and the centralized structures can be effective, but under different conditions. In decentralized structures all the information needed to do the job is available to most members. In centralized structures the information must be obtained from one or two specific individuals who have most of the relevant information. The decentralized structure is effective when the flow of knowledge has to be relatively fast and the projects are of long duration. On the other hand, the centralized structure is more effective when the projects are short-term and the flow of knowledge is not especially rapid. The decentralized structure is better when a lot of new information comes in and out of the project area, requiring a flexible system of organizing as well as a great deal of communication and cooperation among people participating in the project.

According to Peters and Waterman [1982, p. 15], excellent companies combined centralized and decentralized structures. These companies have given autonomy to many aspects of the organization down to the lowest level. However, when it comes to the core values that are dear to the company, they are fanatics about being centralists. Peters and Waterman [1982, p. 314] suggest that the hybrid alternative for organization structure responds to three crucial needs: a need for efficiency, a need for innovation, and a need to avoid rigidity.

Many other aspects of centralization and decentralization for large organizations are beyond the scope of this book. As organizations become larger, the hybrid (centralized and decentralized) approach is quite appropriate at the lower levels. There still is a need to provide some further division of the large work force. Divisions based on product line, geographic location, or specific project are among the possibilities.

4.6   KEEPING THE RESEARCHER AT THE INNOVATION STAGE

An individual goes through a number of stages in a given position. One first goes through a socialization stage, then an innovation stage, and, finally, the stabilization stage. In the stabilization stage the individual is less creative, less risk-taking, and less productive. While individual differences exist, the stabilization stage is normally reached by an individual after 6–8 years of being in a given position. How a person is socialized into an organization makes a lasting impression. Thompson and Dalton [1976] have presented a suggestion that might be helpful in keeping a researcher at the innovation stage and minimizing the stabilization process.

The idea is to limit the tenure of supervisory personnel to approximately 5 years. In such a case, after the 5-year period, the individual will have to return to a technical function. The individual will thus have a strong incentive to remain current on the technical side of activities. In addition, there will be an opening so that another person can move into that particular managerial activity. There should be a budget that allows the retraining of personnel, so that senior people who are not aware of the new technologies can have sabbaticals that allow them to catch up with new developments in their fields.

Lateral transfers can also be used to motivate technical personnel. The idea of working on a new project every now and then can be quite refreshing. It provides an opportunity for the person to become motivated and avoid becoming stale. Many managers are against such transfers because they do not want to lose good people, but if these transfers become the norm for the laboratory, then managers should be able to get their share of good people in the course of the total change occurring in the laboratory.

Some organizations use a matrix structure in which the employee has two bosses: one who is responsible for a particular project and another who is responsible for a particular function. For example, there might be a project manager to whom the individual reports, plus another person in the same technical field (functional manager) as the individual, who looks after the development of his career and makes sure that high standards of professional activity are maintained. In such a case, the functional manager may undertake to transfer a person from one project to another in order to increase his skill. It is important to note that Peters and Waterman [1982, p. 307] state that "virtually none of the excellent companies spoke of itself as having formal matrix structures, except for the project management companies like Boeing." They further point out that even at Boeing, where many of the matrix management ideas originated, what is meant by "matrix management" is not what is generally thought of. In an organization like Boeing, people operate in a binary fashion. Individuals are either part of the project team and responsible to that team for getting tasks accomplished, or are a part of a technical discipline almost all of the time. There is no day-in and day-out confusion as to which team they belong to. One responsibility has clear primacy. A matrix organization where a person reports to two different bosses complicates the organization and should be avoided.

Another approach has been to institute manpower reviews designed to increase the skills of employees. The idea is that every 6 months the employee discusses with second- and third-level supervisors his or her activities and reviews career progress. Decisions are then made concerning transfers and current assignments so as to maximize the development of skills.

Another idea is "career monitoring." This system assigns an engineer or scientist to a new project not less than every 4 years. Anyone in the same job for more than 4 years has his or her name sent to the chief engineer or the technical director of the laboratory, who checks to see what is happening and then makes a judgment concerning whether the particular individual should continue to remain in that job. The general idea is to make sure that assignments are such that repetitiousness and overspecialization do not occur.

Bailyn [1984] suggests that research and development organizations should develop career programs based on relevant information about the employees working in these organizations. This information would take into account the orientation of each scientist. If, for example, his/her orientation is quite academic, there would be more opportunity for the scientist to participate in professional activities and to undertake activities that maximize scientific growth. On the other hand, if the engineer or scientist is not that concerned with academic work, a career that emphasizes support of ongoing research might be more appropriate.

Company or college courses or exposure to professional journals can be used to promote the career of a scientist or engineer. However, Thompson and Dalton [1976] report that they do not find any correlation between high and low performance on research and development jobs and the level of education of the individual. This may be due to the fact that to begin with, most R&D personnel are highly trained and are high achievers. In a modern R&D organization, a doctoral-level education is the norm for R&D personnel. Undoubtedly, some unique individuals without this advanced training have made, and should be given opportunities to make significant contributions. Thompson and Dalton found that the complexity and the challenge of the job were much more strongly linked to job performance than the educational level of the researcher. Such findings would suggest that an individual's success is related to how the organization structures the job rather than the educational preparation of the individual.

Providing a sabbatical leave, though routinely practiced in many university environments, has not been as widely used by R&D organizations. Those individuals who have the motivation and the ability to take advantage of such opportunities should be encouraged to do so. If the managers really believe and want to practice the dictum that "people are our most important resource," then the cost of providing sabbatical leaves should be worth the investment. There should be no confusion about the extensive resources and organizational flexibility needed to allow such leaves. Excellent research organizations can and have successfully implemented these sabbatical leave programs.

4.7 JOB DESIGN AND CONFLICT

Sometimes the design of jobs increases the chances of conflict in organizations. This is particularly true because the goals of scientists are sometimes not the same as those of the organization. The goals of scientists are more likely to reflect scientific values, while the goals of the organization often reflect concern for profitability [Keenan, 1980; Souder and Chakrabarti, 1980].

An important attribute of job design is the degree of autonomy that is allowed on the job. There are two kinds of autonomy [Bailyn, 1984]: *strategic autonomy*, the freedom to set one's own research agenda, and *operational autonomy*, the freedom to implement the agenda in different ways. Bailyn discovered through empirical studies that at the beginning of a technical career operational autonomy is more important than strategic autonomy. As the employee becomes more and more experienced, it is essential for the employee to have a certain amount of strategic autonomy. Thus, in the design of jobs we ought to assume that the employee will have a certain amount of autonomy. However, the kind of autonomy that we design for the job may differ depending on the level of the incumbent in the particular job.

There is a considerable literature that discusses the conflict between professional values and organizational goals. Professional values reflect concerns for scientific development. To the extent that scientists regulate their behavior to reflect such professional values, they are likely to remain up-to-date. Thompson and Dalton [1976], however, point out that this emphasis on keeping up with professional development often clashes with basic organizational goals (see also Marcson [1960], Souder and Chakrabarti [1980], and Pelz and Andrews [1966b]).

LaPorte [1967] describes the main sources of conflict between professional and organizational goals:

(1) There is often a clash between profit and technological innovation, since an interesting technological development may not necessarily be profitable.

(2) The expression of professional desires and goals is often different from management goals because the individual wishes to be autonomous, while management wishes to integrate the organization.

(3) Professionals seek freedom from procedural rules, while managers emphasize them.

(4) Professionals seek authority relations based on professional status, whereas managers rely on bureaucratic position and power.

(5) Professionals seek rewards contingent on professional status, while managers emphasize rewards that match the organization in strength and status.

Pelz [1956] identified four types of conflict that occur in technical organizations. Type I is mostly technical conflict that occurs with peers and is related to such things as technical goals, milestones, means of achieving a particular goal, and interpretation of data. Type II is interpersonal conflict with peers (for example, likes and dislikes, trust and apprehension about the goals of peers). Type III is conflict that occurs between supervisor and subordinates about technical or administrative matters such as technical approach, milestones, and schedules, while Type IV is conflict that occurs between the supervisor and the subordinate about interpersonal matters such as power, authority, rules, and procedures. Evan's [1965a and b] empirical research discovered that technical conflict is twice as prevalent as interpersonal conflict in governmental and industrial laboratories.

A rather common type of conflict occurs when different parts of the organization have different mandates and, as a result, try to maximize different criteria. An example is the conflict between marketing and research and development groups. The research and development groups are likely to wish to develop products that meet certain technical criteria, while the marketing groups are likely to wish to develop products that will sell well. While the two sets of goals are not incompatible, there are situations when the coordination of the activities of these two groups is complicated and requires very careful attention by management.

The problem has been analyzed by Souder [1975] and Souder and Chakrabarti [1980], who have identified three possible approaches or mechanisms for the coordination of the research and development groups and the marketing groups. The three approaches, which Souder has named "state-dominant," "process-dominant," and "task-dominant" are described below.

In the *state-dominant approach*, the research and development, as well as the marketing groups, create formal structures that have specialized functions; these groups have narrowly defined responsibilities and specifically limited activities. People in such an organization have responsibilities that are directly tied to their functional specialities. For example, the engineers limit their activities and their responsibilites to the technical side, while the marketing people, who are concerned about the way the public reacts to products, have specific responsibilities that deal with the way the product is likely to be received by the public. These formal structures are also reflected in the way the particular job is transferred from one group to another. There are formal and institutional transfer points where the research and development people hand the job to the marketing people, or the marketing people hand it back to the research and development people, with a special ceremony.

In the *process-dominant approach*, there are no apparent transfer points and the parties hand the job to each other, back and forth, without any kind of ceremony. There are no apparent cases where one group builds up and another builds down in order to get extra manpower to complete a particular job during a particular phase. Rather, people move in and out of the activities and the groups as needed. The interaction between the technical side and the marketing side is almost continuous and people do not have points at which they say "that is your job" and "I am not going to deal with that," but rather they are continuously involved in the development of the product. The incumbents in this process are specialists, of course. However, they do understand what is happening in the jobs of the other group. The engineers, for example, understand a fair amount about the marketing situation, and the marketing people understand quite a bit about the technical aspects of the project. There is no paperwork that is filed to indicate transition points where the job goes from the research group to the marketing group, or from the marketing group to the research group. The products are expected to and do oscillate from one group to the other.

The *task-dominant approach* is characterized by even greater flexibility. Here the incumbents have a strong orientation and focus toward the task and the end product, and they talk in terms of "our" product rather than "our" and "their" functions. It is not "I am the technical person" or "I am the marketing person," but rather "I am the person who is interested in that product." There are no transfers of authority in this case and personnel do not go on and off the team as the product is developed. People are specialists, of course, but they do not function as specialists. They are part of the team that is developing the product, and the fact that they happen to be scientists or engineers, economists, or public opinion experts is irrelevant. All they are doing here is participating in a project-oriented team. Thus, in the task-dominant approach the individuals are in continuous contact with each other as a team. This is very different from the situation in which there are formal structures where the research group meets with the marketing group and where people have identities as a "research person" or as a "marketing person."

Souder argues that each of these approaches has some advantages under some conditions, so that one should not generalize and say that one of these three approaches is better than the others under all conditions. Obviously, when you have an organizational structure that allows people to be specialists, they can practice their special skill and become very good at the particular functional activity.

Unfortunately, while the specialists can be especially good in their activities they may not have very much understanding of what is going on in the other group. The advantage of high specialization is that specialists can do some tasks very fast and extremely well. At the same time, a disadvantage is that there is little coordination with other activities.

Souder has outlined a number of factors that are relevant to maximizing the effectiveness of one or the other of these three organizational structures. Those who are facing the specific question of how to organize teams should consult the original publication [Souder and Chakrabarti, 1980], which shows that the criteria that one wishes to maximize will influence the type of organizational structure likely to be optimal. These criteria include environmental factors (e.g., environmental uncertainty, dynamics), tasks factors (type of technology, the type of innovation), and organizational factors (the nature of the organization, the complexity of the organization, the kinds of communication patterns, and the division of responsibilities).

4.8 SUMMARY

In this chapter we have examined job design, broadly defined, as it contributes to organizational effectiveness. We have considered how managers can interrelate individual and organizational goals for effectiveness, how job attributes suggest that certain people would be more or less effective doing some jobs, and how physical layout can help communication. Jobs should be designed to promote the interrelationship of personal and organizational goals, match available personnel, and be consistent with the physical layouts that are good for communication. We then turned to career paths, which inevitably have implications for the organizational structures that are likely to be effective in an R&D laboratory, and that discussion resulted in an examination of the advantages and disadvantages of various organizational structures. Keeping the researcher on the path of innovation and designing the job so as to take advantage of productive conflict and avoid destructive conflict were also discussed.

4.9 QUESTIONS FOR CLASS DISCUSSION

1 What kinds of hierarchy are ideal for an R&D lab?

2 What are the advantages and disadvantages of a matrix form of organization?

3 How should jobs be designed in an R&D lab?

4 How can a lab minimize destructive conflict and maximize productive conflict?

4.10 FURTHER READINGS

Schriesheim, J., M. A. von Glinow and S. Kerr (1977). Professionals in bureaucracies: A structural alternative. In P. C. Nystrom and W. H. Starbuck (Eds.), *Perspective Models of Organizations*. New York: North-Holland.

Souder, W. E. and A. K. Chakrabarti (1980). Managing the coordination of marketing and R&D in the innovation process. In B. V. Dean and J. L. Golhar (Eds.), *Management of Research and Innovation*. Times studies in the management sciences, Vol. 15, pp. 135–150. New York: North-Holland.

____5
INFLUENCING PEOPLE

An important aspect of a manager's job is influencing others. Top management often needs to influence the rank and file, lower management to influence middle management, and so on. In this chapter we will consider how attitudes are formed and changed, and how a person can influence others.

"Influence" may sound like manipulation, and some people may find it objectionable on moral grounds. Yet the evidence is clear from several studies that managers who are influential with their bosses are better managers and can be more helpful to their own subordinates. For example, some studies show that those managers who are influential with their supervisors have subordinates who are more satisfied with their jobs.

Furthermore, an important aspect of lower or middle management is to get resources from top management. Such resources in the form of budget approvals, space allocation, and the like are vital for the unit the manager is administering. Since research output can never be completely predicted and since considerable time lapse exists between resource inputs and research outputs, R&D managers' ability to influence upper management and sponsors could be crucial in acquiring needed resources for research. This ability of influencing people could be important for an R&D manager for internal purposes as well. For example, many research projects require the collaboration of researchers in the manager's own group as well as periodic assistance from external groups. The manager's ability to influence people should give him or her the necessary tools to provide order, and purpose, and to integrate the contributions of different participants to the research effort.

A principal investigator, on the other hand, often has to deal with researchers within her own team and also has to work with the immediate supervisor, the sponsor, and many individuals in the support offices of an R&D organization. The ability of a principal investigator to understand the attitudes and motivation of different people and to influence these people could make a crucial difference in getting the job done.

In influencing people, some important aspects deal with attitude and attitude change, and communication alternatives and outcomes. These two major topics along with a case study and its analysis are discussed in this chapter.

5.1 ATTITUDE, ATTITUDE CHANGE

A central construct for understanding influence is the construct of attitude. An attitude is an idea, charged with affect, predisposing action. For example, Mrs. Top Manager's attitude toward Department X getting additional space is based on several beliefs about the space problems of Department X, how well Department X is doing, the future of Department X research, and so on. Each of these ideas has some emotion, positive or negative, attached to it. For instance, if Mrs. Top Manager thinks that Department X is doing well, she is also likely to feel more positively about Department X getting additional space. Such feelings become intentions (e.g., self-instructions to approve the extra space), which often lead to action (approval of the space).

To change an attitude one needs to consider the phases of the attitude change process. These are *attention, comprehension, yielding, remembering*, followed by *action*. For example, if top management wants to change the attitude of the rank-and-file toward a new policy it must produce a communication that will be attended. If the employees place the memo describing the new policy in the waste paper basket, unread, it will obviously have no effect. But even if it is read, it must be understood. Comprehension is the phase when the attitude change message is understood. However, understanding does not necessarily mean acceptance. The reader might understand it and reject it. So, *yielding* refers to the phase in which the reader not only understands but goes along with the suggestion or the message. While yielding is very important in attitude change, if one is interested in action one needs two more phases: first the person must remember yielding, and second, the factors involved in the action (norms, roles, previous habits, affect toward the behavior, perceived consequences, and so on, as discussed in Chapter 6 on motivation) should not cancel out the intention to act. In other words, the analysis of attitude change shows that it is a complex process in which the attempt to change attitudes and behavior can be "derailed" by many factors. In thinking of the best means to change someone's attitude it is useful to be analytic, and to consider and anticipate all those factors, and, if possible, make them favorable to the change.

The analysis of attitude change also requires thinking of the factors that are important in this change. There are four factors to be considered: the source of the attitude change, the message, the medium, and the audience. The source is the person or group that produces the attitude change message. For example, if Department X wants to get more space it could send its manager to talk to the top management, or it can send a departmental resolution to the top management, or ask some allies to suggest to the top management that more space is needed. In each of these examples both the source (manager, department, allies) and the message are different. One must also consider the medium. For example, one might attempt to influence face-to-face, through a written document, or a video presentation. Finally, one must consider the characteristics of the audience. Who are we trying to influence? Depending on our analysis of audience attributes, we can develop different strategies for attitude change. If the audience is very intelligent research shows that we must produce a message that presents the position we advocate, and also convincingly deals with any objections to that position. This has special implications for an R&D organization whose participants are relatively intelligent.

5.2 FINDINGS FROM ATTITUDE RESEARCH

There are many experimental findings about attitude change (for further reading see Triandis [1971] and Cialdini [1985]). We will summarize a few that may be of special interest to managers.

Sources. What kinds of sources are most effective? Those sources that the audience trusts most and finds most attractive and most similar to itself. It is good to use a source that has high credibility based on past support for successful change.

Message. What kind of a message is best? Here we need to consider whether we are going to have the greatest difficulties changing the audience at the level of attention, comprehension, yielding, remembering, or action. If the level of attention is the weak spot, we need a message that is dramatic and includes a simple slogan. If the level of comprehension is the weak spot, we need a message that is clear and draws a definite conclusion. If the message needs mostly to influence the yielding stage, it must link the goals of the audience with acceptance of the central ideas of the message. If remembering is likely to be the weak spot, then repetition is useful (as in advertising). If action is the weak spot, the message needs to address issues that may detail the intention to act such as incompatible norms, roles, or perceived consequences.

A good message starts with the good news, since people open up when they hear good news. The amount of change advocated must not be too great or too small. That is a very tricky point. If one asks for too much change one loses credibility; if one asks for too little one will not get as much as is feasible. So, it is important to know something about the audience's "range of noncommitment."

An example about buying a car may be helpful in explaining this idea. When the average manager goes to a car dealer, the chances are that he has a range of prices in mind, for example, $12,000 to $15,000. If the dealer were to show him a $10,000 car that the buyer likes, the salesman would not make as much profit. If he were to show him a $25,000 car, he would not make a sale. So the trick is to know the range, and to present a car that is just a little higher than the range, say $16,000. There is a phenomenon in perception known as "assimilation and contrast." Stimuli that are similar to a given category are assimilated into that category, because they appear to be more similar than they really are, while stimuli that are different from the category are contrasted, that is, they are seen as more different than they really are. So, the $16,000 car will appear not too different from the $15,000 car while the $20,000 car may well appear as different as the $25,000 one. The $16,000 car is thus assimilated into the range of noncommitment, while the $20,000 car is contrasted from it.

There is another way to change the range of noncommitment, and that is to change the audience's "level of adaptation." The level of adaptation is a kind of neutral point. It separates "expensive cars" from "inexpensive cars." Obviously what is expensive for one buyer might well be inexpensive for another. This neutral point turns out to be the geometric mean of all the stimuli that are salient at the time of the particular judgment. Some of these stimuli will influence the judgment more because they are most recent, and some will influence it more because they have occurred very frequently. If we take all these stimuli into account, and take the geometric mean, we get the level of adaptation for a particular judgment. Therefore, if 10 stimuli are salient in somebody's head, we multiply their values and take the 10th root, and the result of that calculation is the level of adaptation.

Now, obviously, one can change the level of adaptation by exposing a person to stimuli. For example, a salesman may say: "I know you do not want to spend that much money, but let me show you this beauty of a car here. Is it not a work of art?" The car turns out to be worth $18,000. The customer does not buy it, but it goes into his calculation of the level of adaptation. If the customer, at the start, has cars in mind worth $12,000 to $15,000, his level of adaptation would be 13.45. Now if in addition, he has been exposed to a $16,000, a $16,500, a $17,000, and an $18,000 car it would be 15.06. So, now his upper limit has become his level of adaptation! A $15,000 car would now appear "quite inexpensive"!

A good message links the proposal to the rewards that will be received by the audience if the proposal is accepted. For example, if the manager asks for a new building, a good message might mention that the new building eventually will be named the (Mrs.) Top Manager Research Center!

An effective message anticipates objections and shows that they can be overcome. As an exercise, the reader might think of objections based on various components of the model discussed in Chapter 6 on motivation and think how they might be dealt with. Perhaps the best way to do this is to read the case that follows.

5.3 BEHAVIORAL SCIENCE DIVISION CASE*

The Laboratory for Behavioral Sciences at Government R&D Lab (GRDL) has been under attack by the Scientific Director, Dr. Brown, because it has experienced substantial reductions in grants and contracts. Much of this reduction is atttributable to an unfavorable climate for support of such research by the federal government. However, a team of managers from other divisions of GRDL who inspected the laboratory identified several internal problems as well.

The laboratory used to have a sizable research program consisting of $2–$3 million a year, but in recent years grants and contracts amounted to only about $750,000. The director, Dr. Park, formed the laboratory 15 years ago and has been highly instrumental in obtaining outside grants and contracts. Four researchers from various behavioral sciences are also connected with the Laboratory. Dr. Link, a psychologist, deals with artificial intelligence. Dr. Henson, a sociologist, deals with public opinion sampling. Dr. Duff, a geographer, employs aerial photography to develop information about economic geography. Dr. Barron, an economist, conducts market surveys.

In addition to these four researchers, three researchers work at GRDL: Dr. Clay, a political scientist; Dr. Goa, a sociologist; and Dr. Harden, a geographer. The laboratory provides substantial space for the offices of these associates and their research assistants, for computer outlets that link the laboratory with a main computer of GRDL, and for a library that has a full-time librarian. The central administration of GRDL feels that the current rate of activity does not justify the space that it occupies, and has announced that the laboratory should confine itself to about one-half of its

---

* From the files of H. Triandis and David Day. The events are true but all the names of people and laboratories are fictional.

present space so that the other half might be used by another laboratory that is expanding.

The visiting inspection team, which consists of division managers, has identified numerous problems. For example, there is conflict between Dr. Park, the director of the laboratory, and Dr. Link, who is working on a problem that has occupied him for 7 years but has not yet produced any publications. However, Dr. Link is very optimistic that the problem will eventually lead to a major publication of high theoretical value. The inspection committee estimates that the probability is around 0.3 that such a publication might be forthcoming. Dr. Park has identified an interest by the Office of Naval Research (ONR) in work related to the research that Dr. Link has been doing, and is pressuring Link to drop his current activity and try to obtain a contract from ONR. The work that the ONR contract would pay for is estimated to have a high probability (around 0.8) of resulting in several publications. However, because this work is going to be applied, these publications may not make an impact on the writer's whole scientific field, and may, instead, only solve a specific problem. Current income in the form of overhead received by the laboratory from the work that Link does is very small, whereas the work that would be done under the ONR contract is expected to bring in considerable amounts. Although Link's current traveling, which causes him some concern, could be reduced significantly if he were to work on the ONR project (the new project would employ a research associate to do most of the traveling), he is resisting pressure from Park.

The visiting committee identified many other cases of conflict between Park and his co-workers. Park was critical of Harden for spending too much of his time repairing antique cars instead of doing research. Harden, however, says that his publication record is at least as good as the upper third of the members of the laboratory, and therefore it is none of Park's business how he spends his time. The laboratory has no clear standards concerning either the number or the quality of the publications of its associates. For example, Park criticized Henson's publication record for 1985. Henson, however, feels that his record is satisfactory and improving, and that in his field it is pretty good. In any case, 1986 was better than 1985. Park was also critical of Henson and Duff because they failed to collaborate in the bidding for a contract with the National Institute of Education (NIE), which required the skills of these two researchers. Because Henson and Duff do not get along and prefer to work independently rather than collaboratively, the opportunity of an NIE contract was lost.

In talking with Goa, the inspection team learned that he felt isolated and found his colleagues uncooperative. He tended to attribute this to the fact that he was Portuguese, and that, in his view at least, there was some discrimination towards foreigners in the laboratory.

The morale of many of the researchers was low because their pay was generally low. This was particularly the case with Clay, who received his doctorate from a prestigious Ivy League university and consequently felt that he should be receiving a higher salary than the other researchers.

Many of the researchers at the laboratory were critical of Park because they felt that he was not sufficiently involved in the activities of their own research groups, was unaware of specific difficulties experienced by these research groups, and did not seem to appreciate that many of these difficulties had been overcome, and that a number of projects had come to successful completion. Park's view, however, was that he was much too busy to keep detailed track of such matters because he often had to be in Washington to gauge the interest of several federal agencies in various kinds of research in order to submit appropriate research proposals and to increase the funds from grants and contracts currently administered by the laboratory.

According to the inspection team, one of the problems of the laboratory was that Park made most of the decisions independently. Others had very little opportunity to register their views, and, in fact, Henson, Duff, and Barron almost never argued or raised issues with him. The majority of those associated with the laboratory felt that Park provided a setting within which they could carry on their work without having to go to Washington to find money to support their research. Thus, they were willing to put up with Park's pressures, but at the same time they resented them.

People did not seem to identify with GRDL. The majority of the researchers felt that it was a convenient setting for their research, but if they could work elsewhere they would just as soon do so.

The major current problem facing the laboratory is that the central administration of GRDL wants to take away half its space. Park has called everyone to his office to discuss what might be done to prevent this from happening. What recommendations would you have concerning attempts by the laboratory to change the attitude of the administration? What changes in working procedures may be instituted within the laboratory to improve its internal functioning and internal relationships.

5.4 CASE ANALYSIS

In thinking through this case try to consider who the best source of attitude change might be (e.g., Dr. Park, a friend of the top administrator, a committee?) What would be the best message (exactly what would it say so as to shift the level of adaptation, present the good news first, etc., as discussed earlier)? How should it be presented (face-to-face, in writing, etc.)?

There are a few additional points about attitude change that can be made. One technique that can work well is to have several sources. One of these might take an extreme position and thus change the audience's level of adaptation. Then the other source could make a "modest proposal" that would be immediately accepted.

Another approach that sometimes works is the "foot in the door" procedure. With this tactic one may be able to get the audience to accept a *very* modest proposal, and then in time, ask for more. There is also research on the way fear and threats of punishment can be mixed into the message. The general finding is that only modest levels of fear or threats can be effective. If one puts too much fear into the message the audience rejects the message.

This "foot in the door" analogy can be particularly relevant to research activities. For example, many research project outcomes are uncertain, while the resources required for completion of the entire research effort may be substantial. Consequently, asking for all the resources necessary for the research project at the outset may not be a prudent course of action. One approach that works quite well is to ask for sufficient research funding to do initial, or pilot programs to ascertain the feasibility of the research approach. This way one has a "foot in the door" and the sponsor is more likely to continue with the funding than if this initial step had never been taken.

Sources that are extremely credible and knowledgeable can have more of an effect on attitude change because they are likely to be listened to very carefully, and because they can get away with advocating more change. For example, to go back to our car buying case, if a credible source such as the editor of a national magazine on cars were to argue with our buyer that a $20,000 car was a better investment than any of the other cars he had in mind, there is a good chance the message would be effective, even though the gap between the buyer's upper limit and the advocated position is now very large.

Face-to-face communication is generally more effective than communication in writing, or through other media. However, in certain situations written communication can be more effective: for example, if the argument is very complex, and requires the audience to think about it step by step.

When an audience is highly involved with an issue it is difficult to change its attitude. In general, audiences that are intelligent, complex in their thinking, and self-confident are also very difficult to change. Such audiences usually attend and comprehend, but they do not yield. On the other hand, audiences that are less intelligent, and not confident or involved in the issue may not even pay attention to the message. In other words, the communicator has different problems with different audiences. As a result the relationship between variables such as involvement, intelligence, and self-confidence and attitude change is an inverted U. For very low or very high levels of these variables there is little attitude change; for moderate levels there is a fair amount of change.

5.5 COMMUNICATION ALTERNATIVES AND OUTCOMES

There are three kinds of communication that take place in organizations: interpersonal communication (e.g., among colleagues), group communication (e.g., a principal investigator talking to his team); and organizational communication (e.g., a top manager attempting to change attitudes of the rank and file). In interpersonal communication the major weak point is yielding; in organizational communication the major weak point is attention. So, for different kinds of communication the communicator has to develop different strategies in order to overcome different problems.

In reading the discussions of various communication alternatives presented here, one may feel that there is an attempt to manipulate others unfairly. This is not the purpose of this chapter. We are dealing with very intelligent people, consequently, any attempt to manipulate them is likely to backfire. In addition, one's ability to influence others regarding a project or an issue is fundamentally limited by the merits of the project or the issue. At times, managers, and even researchers, are frozen in a position or a mindset that does not allow them to review the project or an issue without preconceived ideas. In such cases, it is helpful to unfreeze a person so that he or she is able to see your viewpoint. Some of these communication alternatives might provide you with a winning edge.

Take Advantage of the Other's Cognitive Habits. It is possible to influence others by taking advantage of the cognitive habits they already have. For example, most people think that "expensive" is equivalent to "high quality" when it comes to purchasing goods. This can easily generalize to research, so that they may think that elaborate and expensive research is better than research done on a shoestring.

Another habit deeply ingrained in human thinking is reciprocity. We believe that we must return a favor, or if someone makes a concession, we feel obligated to make one in return. One can take advantage of this tendency. Conversely someone who is aware of the tendency can learn to resist manipulation. For example, suppose your boss wants you to do a job you really do not want to do. He or she might be able to influence you by asking you to do something that is even worse, thus shifting your level of adaptation in the negative direction, and then provide a concession by asking you to do the first job. Since the boss has made a concession, you have the tendency to make a concession also. This leads to the boss manipulating you and to your agreeing to do the job. If you can analyze the situation and identify the manipulation you can resist it better.

Use Information Optimally. When making judgments we use the information that is most readily available. Information that is used frequently is more available than information that is used rarely. It is the same principle as putting the things you use often in the front of your refrigerator near the door, and the things you do not use so frequently in the back. You can use this principle to influence others. For example, suppose you want to do research on X and your colleagues or supervisor are not interested in this kind of research. You mention the names of people doing research on X, you describe studies that have utilized that kind of research, and so on, thus shifting the cognitive availability of the information. When the time comes to decide on a new direction for research, the fact that information on this kind of research is more available in the cognitions of your colleagues can make a difference.

Use Analogies. We think by analogy. One way to convince your colleagues is to find good analogies when a particular kind of research you want to do has been successful. The analogy does not even have to be in the same area of research, as long as there is some congruence. The analogous research may be in another field, but has similar attributes, such as when and where it was done and the configuration of people who participated. Incidentally, the difficulty most people have in accepting a truly original idea can be traced to the same phenomenon. In that case they lack a ready-made analogy.

Use Repetition. Repetition can be helpful in influencing people. It has the tendency to make some ideas more available, and it also shifts the level of adaptation. For example, if your level of adaptation is at 10 units and you get exposed to three events at 11 units the new level of adaptation would be 10.74. So, while 11 units was "high" before the repetition, now it is almost "neutral."

Use Prior Imagination. Another well-known approach is to use prior imagination. "Imagine what would happen if we do this research." You describe exciting possible outcomes. That kind of line can prove quite convincing. Of course, there has to be some substance to the argument. When someone is using this approach, be on your toes!

Use Positive Experience. Finally, one tactic is to resurrect a positive prior experience. For example, you might describe to your colleagues a past event that was very positive to them, and link that event to your proposal.

Get People to Commit Themselves. Once your colleagues are committed to a course of action they are more likely to change their subjective probabilities of success. For example, until a proposal has been committed to paper and sent to a sponsor there may be a 0.5 subjective probability that it will succeed. Once work has started on it the subjective probability is likely to rise to 0.7 or 0.8. The general tendency is to make our feelings line up with our current behavior. Thus, this is something that one can take advantage of in influencing others.

Choose the Right Source of Influence. The choice of who is the source of influence is critical. A source who is physically attractive, similar on many dimensions (particularly values and general goals) to the audience, with whom the audience is quite familiar is a good one. Thus, if you are a biologist and you want to convince your supervisor, who is a physicist, arranging for a very attractive physicist to talk to your supervisor may be a better approach than talking to him directly. If such a person is also one of your supervisor's old cronies, that is even better. One might think that this approach sounds a bit naive. How can an intelligent manager be influenced by this? Since many judgments related to research funding are subjective and many research outcomes are unpredictable, some of the approaches presented here may make the crucial difference in getting a positive response. Try it and you may be pleasantly surprised.

Get Help from Others. Many judgments we make in life do not have objective bases. When we deal with ambiguous situations and we do not have a good way to test them objectively by using data, we rely on the opinions of others to validate our judgments. These others are usually chosen because they are similar to us, and have comparable levels of knowledge, prior experience, and the like. Thus, in many cases one might be able to convince another by first convincing that person's peers. The central person is usually more ego-involved with the issue than are his friends. So, while he may pay attention and understand the issue he may not yield as readily as his friends who, as third parties, are less ego-involved and thus more likely to yield when presented with a reasonable argument. Once the peer group has yielded and is convinced, it is easier to persuade the central person to yield and become convinced. Again, you can learn to resist such manipulation by becoming aware of how such a system works, and if you see your friends shifting in a given direction, identify the influences on them.

Stress Rare Events. Finally, events appear more desirable than they really are if they seem rare. For example, a scientific breakthrough can be seen as even more desirable if you can convince others that such breakthroughs seldom occur. Naturally, you may also be able to convince them about other issues if you convince them that the event is of great value.

Up and Down Communication. In most U.S. organizations there is a lot of downward communication and very little upward communication. There are many channels of upward communication, however, that are not immediately apparent. For example, suggestion systems, quality circles, and management by objectives are different ways to increase upward communication. It is important for managers to support such channels in order to correct the imbalance in the communication flow that is typical in most organizations.

Another channel of upward communication that is particularly effective is briefings given to visitors where management is present, or briefings given to management in order to seek its input. During such briefings it is not prudent to ask for more funds or more staff. These briefings should be designed to provide information succinctly and to seek comments from management. Critical comments should be encouraged and management concerns should be brought out. Management would, of course, understand that, to the degree possible, its concerns will be dealt with. Our experience indicates that this strategy for upward communication, though requiring some preparation and planning, works quite well. This also gives management a genuine feeling of participation in the project. A caution, however, is in order. In cases where management is likely to be autocratic and dictate a new direction for the project or place other poorly thought out restrictions or demands, such an approach will naturally not work.

Sideways Communication. There are studies of communication channels that show that people who are in central positions where communication flows through them are more satisfied than people who are on the periphery of the organization. Another problem is that the accuracy of the communication is not always high. Communications are often distorted as they move from person to person. "Telephone," a well-known party game, is unfortunately repeated in everyday life in some organizations. The distortions that usually occur are of three kinds: (1) some detail is dropped out, (2) some aspects become more salient than other aspects, and (3) the values of the communicators distort the message in the direction of wishful thinking. Of course, the more relay points there are between the originator and the target of a message the greater the distortion.

There are some differences in the kinds of communications that are most helpful to scientists, particularly those doing basic research, and to engineers, particularly those doing development work. The former get more of their information from journals; the latter get it mostly from face-to-face communications. An effective lab needs both kinds of communication, and management will do well to ensure that both types are widely available. Highly effective labs encourage publication, since that is the ticket that allows the scientist access to the prepublication work of other scientists. Participation at professional meetings is expensive, but managers would be foolish to save on travel to such meetings since their people are usually stimulated by such meetings.

Resistance to Change. Resistance to change is very common in most organizations and is one of the problems a communicator must overcome. It is often helpful to analyze a problem of resistance to change in terms of "forces opposed" and "forces supporting" the change. Such an analysis can often suggest where communications should be sent, and what the message should be in order to overcome the resistance. Research has shown that major change requires some people who can become "opinion leaders" and influence others. Such people are often secure in their positions, influential, and of high status. They have extra resources that allow them to take some risks. Once they adopt the innovation, it is likely that some others will follow, and the trickle becomes a flood.

Ingratiation and Impression Management. There is also quite a bit of research on the way people can influence others by using *ingratiation*, or *impression management*, by being vigilant about what aspects of themselves they present to others. Ingratiation, for instance, can be effective in getting a boss to like a subordinate more.

There are several tactics that can work in ingratiation. One is "other enhancement," which involves the subtle use of flattery. To be most effective this approach requires that you flatter the boss behind his/her back, with comments about qualities the boss would like to have, but about which he/she feels uncertain. "Opinion conformity" is agreeing with the boss, particularly about pet projects that others are not too enthusiastic about. "Rendering favor" is most effective if the donor is seen as really intending to do it, and at a cost. It is least effective if the donor is seen as enjoying rendering the favor.

There are problems with "other enhancement" with which one must be careful. For example, if the boss has a poor opinion of himself, praising him can backfire. Conversely, if the boss has too good an opinion of himself, praise can also backfire: "What? You did not expect me to do this well?" You can also make the boss anxious by praising him after a good performance that he is not sure he can pull off again.

"Opinion conformity" also has its tricky side. While agreeing with a rare and not commonly held belief can be effective, agreeing with a belief that most people hold can appear unoriginal and might seem to be an attempt to manipulate the boss. One approach is to disagree on trivial topics, thus lowering the boss's level of adaptation for your agreement, and then suddenly agreeing on something that matters to the boss. This appears to the boss as a "real coup," since you have created a reputation for being "difficult to sell."

Impression management involves making claims (e.g., I can do this difficult job) that the other might be able to accept. The boss will usually challenge the claim. A successful claim, therefore, is one that either is not challenged, or that can stand up to the challenge. If you can make the claim stick, you have won. But if the claim proves illegitimate, you lose, and not only are you likely to feel shame, guilt, or embarrassment, but you may even be fired. Thus, in making a claim you have to analyze in advance the possible consequences and their value. Basically what you have to do is to figure out the risks and the benefits from making a claim. If you can assess the probability and the value of each consequence and can come up with a positive outcome, it may be worth making the claim.

If you make a claim that is challenged and invalidated, you must do something to account for your behavior. You can, for instance, provide a *justification* (e.g., I wanted to test my limits, to see if I could develop this new system), you can claim to be *innocent* of the claim (e.g., I did not really mean the complete system, just develop a concept for the system), or you can make an *excuse* (e.g., my colleagues thought I could do this). The more severe the predicament that results from a successfully challenged claim, the more you will have to give an account of why you made that claim in the first place. All of this can be computed ahead of time, taking into account probable consequences and the value of these consequences, and trying to maximize outcomes.

If you really goof, you need to develop a good apology. There are a number of possibilities to choose from. For example, you might indicate that your previous action was an aberration, that was not at all typical of you. Ideally an apology has the following components: (1) admission of guilt ("The boss was right, I was wrong"), (2) a description of what should have been the correct behavior ("so the boss knows you know"), (3) a disparagement of self for misbehaving (e.g., "it was stupid of me"), (4) a promise of appropriate behavior in the future, and (5) an offer of compensation (if possible).

On the other hand, if a desirable event occurs, impressing management often involves making sure that others know about it, and requires an effort to increase the perceived desirability of the event (e.g., it resulted in a new contract). Boasting can be counterproductive, but there are tactics that can get the same effect (e.g., I know you expected 100 units and I produced 150. If I had been on the ball and done such and such I would have produced 200. Such an approach can be particularly effective in an R&D organization where researchers are expected to be high performers and are naturally optimistic about what they can accomplish). Some people are more skilled than others in presenting those aspects of themselves that will impress management. A scale exists to measure "self-monitoring" [Snyder, 1979]. Those high in self-monitoring present themselves better, because they stress those aspects of themselves that are likely to make a good impression. Those low in self-monitoring present themselves the way they are, and do not change their presentation tactics from audience to audience. High self-monitors are good actors, they remember the traits of other people better, they are guided by the situation, they define who they are according to the situation, and they know more about their audience than low self-monitors. The low self-monitors know more about themselves, and they do not try to impress others.

Discussion

Which of these various tactics is most likely to work under what conditions? The greater the difference in the status between two people the more indirect the ingratiation must be in order to be effective. If a first level manager meets the lab director, it would look foolish to compliment her about how good a job she is doing. However, an indirect compliment is another matter (e.g., "I heard about your new research project at the professional meeting I attended last week"). Similarly, the presentation of positive information about the self must be more indirect if there is a large status gap (e.g., I had such difficulties publishing three refereed papers this year), and doing a favor is best avoided unless the other explicitly asks for it. Opinion conformity is the most effective tactic for low status persons, while compliments and doing favors are the best tactics for high status persons. High status persons can improve their self-presentation by linking successful events with trivial mistakes (e.g., spilling coffee).

5.6 SUMMARY

In summary, there are a number of ways to influence others, and consideration of the various tactics outlined in this chapter can improve one's strategies and chances of successful influence.

In reading this chapter some may feel that the information may be used to manipulate the behavior of others. This is not the purpose of the material presented here. Opinions and views vary. At times people get attached to hopeless causes or to views based on erroneous information. The methods of influence presented here might provide tools to overcome some of these difficulties. Manipulative or unethical behavior is neither proposed nor condoned. Furthermore, we chose to include this material here because some people do use these methods to exert influence and their effectiveness can be reduced when these tactics are known to the public.

5.7 QUESTIONS FOR CLASS DISCUSSION

1   Which of the techniques of interpersonal influence is likely to backfire? Which of the techniques of interpersonal influence is likely to prove especially effective in R&D labs?

2   Now that you have had a chance to read more about influence, how would you change your plans about the Behavioral Science Division case? Go back, reread it, and think of Dr. Park's predicament. How can he approach the problem, taking advantage of some of the ideas you have just read?

5.8 FURTHER READINGS

Cialdini, R. B. (1985). *Influence*. Glenview, IL: Scott, Foresman.
Triandis, H. C. (1977). *Interpersonal Behavior*. Monterey, CA: Brooks/Cole.

_____6
MOTIVATION IN R&D ORGANIZATIONS

Goals determine a substantial amount of human behavior [Locke et al. 1981]. Motivation to achieve these goals is a major factor in researcher performance and in organizational effectiveness. For these reasons we devote a full chapter to this topic. Individuals have goals and organizations have goals. For maximal organizational effectiveness it is important to make these two sets of goals compatible. In fact, that is the major role of management. The R&D manager must have a clear understanding of both sets of goals and find ways to make them similar, overlapping, and at least noncontradictory.

Organizational effectiveness depends on (1) individual motivation for organizational effectiveness (i.e., individual goals that are compatible with the goals of the organization), (2) individual performance (just because one has the right goals does not automatically result in effective performance), and (3) adequate coordination of individual performances.

Performance depends on more than motivation. One must have adequate skills and abilities and proper training, and there must be a good match between the individual and the organization goals. Coordination depends on adequate communication, and can be improved when there is participation by employees in decisions that affect them, and when organizational goals overlap with personal ones.

In order to understand performance better, it is useful to focus on a model that links the probability of an act to particular determinants.

94

6.1   A MODEL OF HUMAN BEHAVIOR

For our purposes here an *act* is a short sequence of behaviors that eventually results in a desirable outcome, such as the publication of a paper or the development of a good research design. In other words, we are using the word "act" in a very specific way. Hundreds of these acts are necessary to produce a publication or to develop a product. What we are trying to understand is what makes these small acts more or less probable.

There are two variables that are important in this case: previous habits and self-instruction. For example, when a person says, "I should look up these references," that is a self-instruction or behavioral intention. Research has shown that behavioral intentions predict behaviors quite well [Triandis, 1977, 1980].

The model thus states that the probability of an act is dependent on two kinds of variables: habits and behavioral intentions. However, even when people have the proper habits and intentions to carry out a particular act, they may fail to do so because external conditions may not be favorable. We utilize the concept of *facilitating conditions* in order to explain the phenomenon that even though the individual may have all that is required, the act may not occur. Reasons beyond the intentions of the individual may not allow it. For example, there may be a lack of proper equipment of there may be distractions in the environment.

Consider a more specific example. If a person said, "I will look up this reference," but the book that contains the particular reference is not around, the probability that the act will occur decreases. Facilitating conditions modify the probability that habit and intention in themselves will result in the act. They reflect the situation within which behavior may occur.

For those who enjoy the precision that mathematical statements provide, the first equation of the model is

$$P_a = (W_H \cdot H + W_I \cdot I)F \tag{1}$$

where P_a is the probability of an act, W_H and W_I are weights that are positive numbers between 0 and 1.00, and sum to 1.00, H is a measure of habit, I is a measure of intention, and F is a measure of the facilitating conditions.

The weights depend on the novelty of the act for the individual. When the individual is faced with a new situation, the weight for intention is 1.00 and the weight for habit is zero. However, as the person performs the act over and over again the weight for habit keeps increasing until it becomes 1.00 and then the weight for intention is zero. For instance, when one learns a new skill (e.g., riding a bicycle) in the early phases one's behavior is under the control of intentions, but at the end it is entirely under the control of habits. Once behavior is under the control of habits, it is difficult to "explain" it to others without actually carrying out the act and observing one's own behavior.

Another variable that shifts behavior to habit control instead of intention control is stress. When people are under stress, as in an emergency, or under time pressure, their behavior is under habit control. That is why there is so much drilling of emergency procedures in the military or on ships. In an emergency one cannot depend on an intellectual analysis of the situation. One must have the right habits.

Determinants of Habits

What are some of the variables that determine the habit? Habits build up as a result of previous rewards. We call such rewards "reinforcements" because they reinforce the link between stimulus conditions and behavior. Behavior is a function of its consequences. As people engage in a particular behavior in the presence of a certain configuration of stimuli, and when desirable events follow the behavior, the probability increases that the configuration of stimuli will in the future produce the same behavior. The behavior eventually becomes automatic, without thinking. When this happens, we say that the act has become "overlearned" and occurs under the control of habits. In that case, behavioral intentions are not relevant as explanations of the behavior.

Determinants of Intentions

Let us now examine what determines behavioral intentions. There are three classes of variables that are relevant for the determination of behavioral intentions. They are social factors, act satisfaction, and perceived consequences.

Social Factors

Social factors include roles, norms, self–concept of the person, and interpersonal agreements.

1. *Roles*. These are evident when a person says to himself, "I am supposed to be doing this because it is my job." In short, the role has become embedded in the person's thinking and has certain activities associated with it. The probability of these activities (acts) increases when the person thinks that he is doing the job. If the researcher feels it is his job to keep the supervisor informed, he is more likely to do it.
2. *Norms*. These are messages that reflect the expectations others have regarding your job. In some cases, these expectations are quantitative,

such as "producing three papers a year." In other cases, they are qualitative, for example, the expectation of an important scientific contribution, or the development of a new product that will benefit the company.

3. *Self–Concept of the Person.* This includes the ideas a person has about the types of activities that are appropriate for him or her. If a researcher feels it is appropriate for him to present his views, even though they differ from others, he is likely to participate actively in discussions and meetings.

4. *Interpersonal Agreements.* These are similar to management by objectives. The supervisor and subordinate agree that the subordinate will try to reach a particular goal. Interpersonal agreements increase the probability that the goal will be reached through behavioral intention (self-instruction). Some research projects use milestones that are really interpersonal agreements as conceptualized here.

Act Satisfaction

The second class of variables that determines behavioral intentions is satisfaction associated with the act itself. Many acts are enjoyable in themselves, such as eating certain types of foods, playing the piano, or working on computer problems. Often such acts associated with pleasure have been formed through classical conditioning. In other words, the activity itself is associated with pleasant events in the past and is pleasant to think about, so this factor involves affect (emotion) toward the behavior itself. This affect motivates the person to self-instruct to do the act, and this in turn becomes the behavioral intention that causes the behavior. Working on a challenging research project or working with a noted scientist could fall in this category.

Perceived Consequences

Finally, the *perceived consequences* of the act are also important. When we do something, such as publish a paper, we perceive certain consequences. For example, when we publish a paper, we might have the perception that this could lead to a promotion, to recognition, or to a particular reward. It is obvious that each of these consequences is probabilistically associated with the act since there is no certainly that the behavior will have the particular consequence. For example, if the scientist publishes a paper, the probability of promotion may be 0.60; the probability that there will be some recognition associated with the paper may be 0.90. Thus, each act has associated with it a probability between zero and one. So the person says to himself, "If I do such and such, then there is a high probability (or a low probability) that x will happen." In this case, x is a consequence. Each consequence also has some value to the person. For example, some people would see a promotion as very desirable, but others might not. Obviously, if the consequence has a positive value attached to it, it will increase the probability of the behavioral intention. If the consequence is perceived as negative it will decrease the probability that the corresponding behavioral intention will be activated. For each of the acts that the person may consider, there is a whole string of consequences, each of which has some probability and some value attached to it. To obtain the total effect of these perceived consequences, each person must multiply the probability and the values for every consequence and then sum these products. Intelligent people will make better estimates of these probabilities and values than unintelligent people.

Thus, we can say that behavioral intentions are a function of: (1) social factors such as roles, norms, the self-concept, and interpersonal agreements; (2) the affect toward the act itself; and (3) the total value of the perceived consequences. Because there are some people who are susceptible to social factors, and others who are susceptible to the perceived consequences of the act, each of the three factors can now be given a weight. For example, people who have been socialized to be very sensitive to the views of others, and who have received a lot of rewards and punishments in their interactions with others, develop great sensitivity to social norms. Their behavioral intentions are much more influenced by the social factor than by the other two sets of factors. On the other hand, people who have been socialized to be quite independent of others often give attention to how much pleasure they can get out of a particular situation. Thus, they are likely to pay a great deal of attention to the affect that is attached to the act. Still others are quite interested in the future and to the way the act is going to bring "good outcomes." Such people look at the consequences of the act and are likely to give weight to those consequences.

The consequences of the act can include job autonomy, vacations, fringe benefits, and the opportunity to use time flexibly. For example, to work at home when you otherwise are expected to be at the office can be highly rewarding. Setting difficult but reachable goals with feedback is one of the ways in which a supervisor can motivate a subordinate. In addition, it has been found that interesting work that provides both challenge and variety can be rewarding. Deadlines are like an interpersonal agreement and can also function as a goal. Recognition, promotions, the opportunity to grow, to receive more pay, or to have a more secure job can all be motivators.

It is also useful to consider situations that are demotivating. One such situation occurs when the employee feels that the organization discriminates against him or her. Other causes for demotivation are poor interpersonal relationships with a supervisor or with peers, low pay, indifference by the organization, lack of promotion or recognition, and having to work for an incompetent supervisor.

Again, for the sake of those who like mathematical formulations, what we have said above can be summarized by the following equations:

$$I = W_S \cdot S + W_A \cdot A + W_C \cdot C \tag{2}$$

$$S = R + N + S_c + I_A \tag{3}$$

$$C = \sum_{c=1}^{n} P_c V_c \tag{4}$$

where I is a measure of intentions
   A is a measure of affect toward the behavior itself
   C is a measure of the value of the consequences
   S is the social factor, that reflects roles (R), norms (N), the self-concept (S_c), and interpersonal agreements (I_A)
   P_c is the probability of a consequence
   V_c is the value of the consequence
   W_S are weights that are positive numbers between zero and one, that sum to 1.00.

If a supervisor wants to change the behavior of a subordinate, every one of these variables may be influenced, and of course combinations of these variables may be optimal. For example, the supervisor can associate pleasant events with the desired behavior, so that even a minimal quantity of the desired behavior may elicit the pleasant event (a nod, a smile, a pat on the back, etc.). A discussion of roles, norms, and the resultant interpersonal agreements can influence the S-factor. A discussion of the probable consequences of particular behavior can influence the P_c. The association of important values of the subordinate with the desired behaviors can lead to higher C. Goals are most effective if they are specific, difficult, and attainable. Such goals can become interpersonal agreements.

Facilitating Conditions

There are a number of factors that facilitate the performance of a behavior. Most of them are situational, such as helpful conditions, the right setting, or access to the resources needed to carry out the behavior. However, there are also internal conditions over which the individual does not have much control, such as the person's physiological state (e.g., hormonal balance), beliefs that the behavior is possible and likely to lead to the successful reaching of goals (sense of self-efficacy), and level of difficulty of the task relative to the persons's ability. For instance, no matter how intensive a researcher's intention to invent a new product, and how brilliant the past record of inventions (habits), there are situations in which no invention will be possible because the person is feeling depressed, or believes that he is not able to have a new idea, or the task is much too difficult relative to the available talent. Some of these conditions can be measured objectively, and others may be estimated by objective observers of the total situation. The point about the F component of Equation 1 is that when it is zero, it can bring the probability of the act to zero, no matter how high the levels of habits or intentions.

Links between desirable behavior and challenges, variety on the job, recognition, promotions, growth, extra pay, extra security, and so on are too obvious to mention in detail. One can also motivate people by providing deadlines.

Of special importance in R&D labs is whether the organization rewards reasonable risk-taking, innovation, and creativity. Does the organization provide feedback and rewards for good work? What kind of facilitating conditions and environment is the organization providing for motivation of this unique group of talented individuals—the researchers?

Common sense suggests that job satisfaction results in high productivity. However, the empirical evidence is not supportive of this expectation. This happens in part because one can get high production without satisfaction (e.g., in coercive situations, such as among slaves and in prisons, where people may not be able to eat if they do not produce enough) and one might also be able to have high satisfaction without much production (as in situations in which the management lets workers do whatever they like). The evidence suggests that those who receive high pay and have supportive supervisors are high in "extrinsic" satisfaction, which in turn leads to high performance. On the other hand, high performance leads to intrinsic satisfaction, that is, to people enjoying the work itself. If we perceive the work situation as equitable, that is, if our effort is rewarded about equally as that of others, we are more likely to be satisfied than if we feel that others are getting more for their effort.

Scientists crave visibility. Managers should provide opportunities for visibility (e.g., invitations to give a lecture or to make presentations to important customers) as a reward. There are many studies of compensation, and this is a topic we will not discuss in detail, except to point out the desirability of linking the scientist's behavior to the goals of the laboratory by offering personal rewards, prizes, or recognition for actions that promote such goals.

At different stages in their careers people need a different mixture of rewards. Young scientists and engineers need to increase their skills, to learn more. So training, growth, and transferring to different jobs can be seen as rewards. In middle career (age 35–50), recognition, esteem, and visibility are the most important rewards. In late career (50–70 years), security, health and pension benefits, as well as recognition and visibility are the important rewards.

Support for the Model

There are numerous studies that support this formulation [see Triandis, 1980 for a review]. We will mention only two as examples. In one study foremen were instructed by the experimenters to behave as s.o.b.s. In a control group foremen were instructed to behave normally. Half the workers were doing a new job; the other half did a job that they had been doing for a long time. The instructions to the foremen influenced the productivity of the workers *only* when the workers were doing a new job. In other words, when the job was under habit control, the supervisor's behavior was irrelevant, but when it was under intention control a supervisor who treated the subordinate badly depressed the subordinate's performance. In other studies [Fiedler, 1986a] the effect of a leader's intelligence (which is relevant to the utilization of intentions, as we will see below) and years of experience (which is relevant to the extent the leader's behavior is under the control of habits) were related to the effectiveness of the team under the supervision of the particular leader. Under conditions of time pressure, stress, or in an emergency (when habits are likely to control the behavior) the experience of the leader correlated with group effectiveness. Under those conditions the leader's IQ was unrelated to effectiveness. However, under conditions of low stress the opposite pattern of correlations was obtained. In short, when people are under stress they use their habits more than their intentions, and so they do not utilize their intelligence as much.

The example with the foremen who were s.o.b.s for experimental purposes makes another important point: it is possible for people to be very dissatisfied and yet to be highly productive. For example, an employee who sees high productivity as a means to a promotion out of a boring job may be very low in job satisfaction, but extremely high in productivity.

In fact, the factors that determine productivity are *not* the same as the factors that determine job satisfaction. Productivity depends on how many high effort–high quality behaviors are attempted by the person. The model we just described indicates the factors that will lead to high productivity: beliefs that others expect high productivity, the person's beliefs that high productivity is appropriate and that she/he is the type of person who is highly productive, instructions from supervisors that point to high but attainable goals, specific goals, the availability of clear procedures for reaching goals, feedback from supervisors concerning goal attainment, enjoyment of high effort–high quality behaviors, beliefs that such behaviors will have desirable consequences (e.g., promotions), and the conversion of the intention to produce much of high quality into habits, that is, automatic behaviors that the person carries out without thinking.

Job satisfaction, on the other hand, depends on how much one gets (resources such as status, training, money, goods, services) relative to what one expects. If one gets slightly more than one expects this will boost productivity, but the effect is likely to be short-lived. One soon rationalizes that the extra resources obtained are "well deserved." If one gets less than expected one is dissatisfied. Expectations depend on our *perception* of what we bring to the job, relative to what others bring, and what we get out of the job, relative to what others get. So, a researcher who believes that her international reputation is much greater than that of her colleagues, is likely to be dissatisfied with the same pay as her colleagues. Note that we are discussing *perceptions*, not reality, It is perceptions that determine expectations.

In other words, the manager of an R&D laboratory who wants subordinates to be productive must ensure that the norms of the laboratory (perceptions of what people are expected to do, what is "proper" behavior) call for high effort and high quality, and must present difficult but attainable, specific goals to subordinates. Furthermore, the environment should be structured in such a way that there are clear procedures for reaching such goals and the feedback is provided when the goals are reached. Rewards should be given liberally, for both minor accomplishments (a nod, a pat on the back), and major accomplishments (special prizes and awards). This will link the high productivity behaviors to enjoyable situations and to beliefs that such behaviors result in benefits.

A manager who wants subordinates to be satisfied should provide as many rewards as feasible (see below for varieties of rewards) and also realistic expectations concerning such rewards. Publishing wage surveys that indicate that the laboratory pays better than average, for instance, would be helpful. The fact that a famous scientist at another laboratory is underpaid is worth mentioning to one's subordinates. Discussing how much value is placed on various factors that one brings to the laboratory—advanced degrees, years of experience, publication record, editorships, listings on the masthead of specific journals, honorary degrees, elections to high status positions in scientific societies, and so on can be helpful. This is true because a subordinate may think that one of these factors is worth much more than does a supervisor, thus creating a discrepancy between what the subordinate expects and what she is likely to get. For example, does the laboratory *really* care if a scientist gets an honorary degree? Usually such events promote the individual but not the lab and may not improve the lab's productivity. Or is a book summarizing a program of research worth as much as *N* refereed publications? Again, a major discrepancy between subordinate and supervisor *perceptions* can occur, and clear discussion of such issues can be most beneficial.

6.2 CHANGING THE REWARD SYSTEM TO SUPPORT TECHNICAL CAREERS

Thompson and Dalton [1976] suggest that there are a number of things organizations can do to improve the motivation of technical personnel. For example, they can pay for performance and not position. In other words, people who are doing first-rate work that is important to the organization should receive the same pay, regardless of their title or position level. But there are objections to this idea. The implication of such a change is that a person whose performance deteriorates gets less pay, and this is something that many employees find very difficult to accept.

Another approach is to increase the visibility of those who are extremely effective. Most organizations do this by promotion, but usually that means promotion to management and many employees want to continue their technical activities rather than become members of management. Organizations have to find ways to provide recognition that do not require promoting the employee. There are a number of ways to do this. One is to structure the organization with a triple hierarchy. Other activities that provide recognition may be as simple as having the successful performers make presentations for the top management, inviting them to meet important customers, or giving them nonmonetary honors and awards. These honors and awards, of course, have to be meaningful and reflect genuine recognition to be effective.

At one research lab a researcher is annually selected by a vigorous peer review process to be the "Researcher of the Year." The Researcher of the Year is given a reserved parking space for the year and he or she is invited to all senior management conferences. The Researcher of the Year serves on the peer review panel for the selection of next year's Researcher of the Year.

Another way is to equalize the status symbols that are used in managerial positions for those professionals who are exceptionally effective. For example, there is no reason why the size of the office of a researcher should be smaller than the size of the office of a manager. Another possibility is to increase office privacy or to provide attractive furniture for the researcher.

As mentioned earlier, different mechanisms should be used to reward individuals during the various periods of their career (see Hall and Mansfield, 1975). For the young engineer or scientist, during the first period of their career, the most important reward is self-fulfillment and growth. Satisfaction and the sense of accomplishment that go with it are maximized when such a person feels that the job provides opportunities for growth and self-fulfillment. So the organization should make sure that the job provides such opportunities. For the person in mid-career, organizational recognition and esteem derived from the organization are the most important elements of motivation. For the person in late career, security and a good system of health and pension benefits, as well as organizational recognition, are important rewards. Such persons should have the sense that they have contributed to the organization and that the organization is grateful for the contributions they have made.

6.3 STRUCTURING THE ORGANIZATION FOR OPTIMAL COMMUNICATION

People are more motivated if they have clear goals, and know how their job fits the goals of the organization than if they do not have this information.

Thus, structuring the organization for optimal communication can help individual motivation.

There has been a good deal of literature on the question of how to expose members of research and development laboratories to the information they need to have to do their jobs well. One concern has been the accessibility of technical literature to the members of the laboratory [Fisher, 1980]. To ensure that people will become acquainted with other activities of the laboratory and with new technical developments, there has been a greater focus on increasing interdependence among projects within a laboratory.

It has been argued that people should become aware of activities in other parts of the laboratory because they can often pick up ideas from seeing what others are doing [Allen, 1970; Fisher, 1980]. One idea has been to increase the sharing of such facilities as coffee pots, restrooms, and computer equipment in order to increase interaction and the likelihood that people in the laboratory will get to know one another well.

It is obvious that members of a laboratory should be encouraged to participate in national meetings and professional societies, to hold offices in professional associations, and to serve on the editorial boards of journals, since all these activities increase communication and are likely to bring new information to the laboratory. Establishing contacts with academic scientists who are working in the same general area as the laboratory can also be very helpful [Fisher, 1980]. Finally, the architecture of the laboratory can have some very beneficial effects for the flow of information.

Allen [1970] has described the effects of a so-called nonterritorial office that was built by the research and development section of a small chemical firm. In this case, all of the office walls were removed and an individual could choose to work anywhere that suited him in the area, depending on what was convenient. The effect of this change appeared to increase communication, both in the number of communications per person and the number of individuals with whom the average engineer communicated. This, of course, would not work well in situations where projects are of longer durations and considerable uninterrupted time is required for research activities.

6.4 TYPES OF REWARDS

A variety of factors can be used to motivate an individual. Foa and Foa [1974] have analyzed the motivation that is provided by different resources. They have identified six resources, with money, of course, as an obvious one. However, a person can be motivated by the services the organization provides such as legal advice or an opportunity to find a good house. There are a number of other activities (some of which may sound paternalistic) that could be included under "services."

Still another factor is status. People often make very fine distinctions about status. For example, in a study of a restaurant [Whyte, 1948], it was found that different kinds of cooks had radically different statuses! Foa and Foa [1974] also mentioned love as a motivator. An individual can be motivated by having a very good relationship with a supervisor who provides emotional support and help in solving personal problems. This kind of motivator is used much more in Japan than in the United States and is consistent with other aspects of Japanese culture. Still another reward is information. For instance, training or opportunity to grow can be a very important reward. Goods are important motivators in some organizations. For instance, special discounts for particular products that are produced by the organization or gifts given on certain occasions can be motivating, at least for some people.

The variety of rewards is not exhausted by the ones just mentioned. For example, giving time to an employee can also be a reward. The superior can accomplish this by paying attention to an employee's problems or by granting time off when there is a family crisis or when the employee needs to get away from it all. Allowing the employee to work at home is yet another form of reward.

An analysis of the way these various rewards function suggests that there are hierarchies of such rewards. Maslow [1970], for example, has argued that there are some basic, physiological needs, for example, for food, water, and sleep that have to be fulfilled before the next higher needs can be activated. After these basic needs are met relatively well, the next higher level needs—protection from danger, threat, and deprivation—become important. These are followed by social needs that include the need to belong, the need to be associated with others, and the need for love and for acceptance. The next level includes ego needs, which, according to Maslow, involve the need for self-confidence, for achievement, for competence, and for knowledge. Finally, the highest need, self-actualization, can be activated. This is the need to develop one's own potential and to maximize self-development.

Maslow has conceived of these needs as hierarchically structured. Although the evidence for a multilevel hierarchy of needs is very weak, physiological needs are the basis for all others. If physiological needs are not satisfied, then other needs do not become activated. The evidence for this point comes from studies of hunger that were done during the Second World War [Guetzkow and Bowman, 1946]. In these studies, volunteers agreed to live on 900 calories a day. This starvation diet resulted in an extremely disturbing experience for the participants. They stopped functioning as normal adults; they no longer had an interest in development, in sex, or in interpersonal relationships. Their only concern was obtaining food. Food dominated their thoughts, their dreams, their everyday life. This example supports Maslow's thesis and suggests that at least a two-level hierarchy is valid. Some other theorists, such as Alderfer [1972], have argued that a three–level hierarchy can be identified. He called them existence, related-ness, and growth needs (the ERG theory). Existence includes physiological and safety needs, relatedness includes membership and self-esteem needs, and growth includes self-actualization needs.

The presence of a goal can create a need. As indicated above, there is evidence that individuals who have been given specific, difficult, but attain-able goals are much more motivated to work hard to obtain them than those individuals who have not been given any goals or who have been given goals that are too easy or too difficult [Locke, 1968]. Thus, management by objectives, where specific, difficult, but attainable goals are established for a research project, and where the manager and researchers discuss and agree on specific goals, and later review the extent to which these goals have been reached, is an approach to motivation.

Another factor that is very helpful in motivating people is receiving feedback. Feedback takes many forms. It can include evaluation by the supervisor, formal recognition by the organization, receiving data of various kinds about how well one is doing, and comparisons with others or compari-sons with the self at different points in time. Here information regarding scheduled vs. actual specific goals' completion rate can be used as one mechanism for such feedback.

The research shows that at least in some organizational settings, certain kinds of feedback are more effective than others. For example, Herold and Parsons [1985] have found that positive formal recognition is the most powerful form of feedback. Other forms of effective feedback are positive supervisory behavior, positive comparisons with the self at another point in time, and positive comparisons with internalized standards.

Some feedback can be ineffective because it makes people defensive. For example, negative comparisons with others, and negative evaluations by co-workers may do more harm than good.

The evidence generally indicates that managers need to provide both goals and feedback. One without the other is unlikely to be effective [Bec-ker, 1978]. To be most effective, feedback should be given by the person who is most important to the employee, with the least delay possible. It should be positive and relevant to the job, referring specifically to the goals, and be frequent enough to be noticed [Brickman et al., 1976; Ilgen et al., 1979]. If individuals are allowed to set their own goals when the assigned goals are easy, they are likely to set difficult ones; and when the assigned goals are difficult individuals are likely to set easier ones [Locke et al. 1984; Murphy et al., 1985]. Goal setting is more effective than instructions such as "do the best you can." It becomes even more effective when the person is aware that he/she will be evaluated, and when the person receives positive cues (e.g., when somebody says: "this is a fun job, it is a challenging job"). The combination of these variables is most effective [White et al., 1977]. Providing a challenge can be particularly effective with a researcher.

6.5 REWARD SYSTEM DISCUSSION

We asked earlier: What acts does the organization reward? For example, does the organization reward innovation? Does the organization reward having original ideas that are not very popular? One can analyze the way the organization gives rewards for specific kinds of behaviors and come up with a profile that suggests why an organization is not very creative or not very successful. The reason usually is found in the nature and frequency of the rewards that are being distributed. You can have rewards that are given every month, such as a salary, but this is not nearly as motivating as rewards that occur with a variable schedule. There is evidence that a variable schedule of rewards is much more motivating than one that occurs on a regular basis [Saari and Latham, 1982]. Receiving recognition after each publication is less effective than getting a major recognition following a series of publications.

While motivation is an important aspect of individual performance we must not neglect to mention that the availability of proper skills and adequate training is also crucial to good performance. Furthermore, the rewards that the person receives from the organization should be tied to organizational performance. Otherwise, the person may function extremely effectively, but his or her performance may have no impact on the organization. Consider, for example, the case of an employee who is inspired on the job to invent something that could make a million dollars. However, the organization has neither the need for such a product nor the resources to take advantage of the invention. Such a person is performing very well at the individual level, but not at the organizational level!

The most important principles of compensation are (1) equity, (2) competitiveness, and (3) link to performance. Equity is achieved by making sure that employees are rewarded according to their education and merit. Competitiveness requires salary surveys. Links to performance are difficult to establish but are important. Specifically, if salary is the major means of compensation, it does not correlate sufficiently to performance. Bonuses do so much more. Systems of compensation that review the employee's achievements every few months and that provide a raise according to the outcome of these reviews link compensation and performance even more effectively.

In such evaluations an important issue is what attributions the evaluator uses to account for the behavior of the subordinate. In other words, is the behavior attributed to ability, task difficulty, effort, or luck? After a failure it is important for the effort attribution to be made, both by the employee and the supervisor. An attribution to ability is likely to result in giving up. Effort is by far the best attribution for supervisors to make, and that is particularly so in the case of failure. In short, they should say: "try a bit harder and you will succeed."

Which exact mixture of rewards, such as profit sharing, salary, fringe benefits, vacations, working at home, and so on, is likely to be most effective will vary depending on the attributes of the employee, as well as on the organization and its environment. Based on data from 33 high–tech and 72 non-high–tech firms with research and development units, Balkin and Gomez-Mejia [1984] concluded that high-tech firms place greater emphasis on profit sharing than traditional firms. Firms that are just getting established usually cannot afford to pay high salaries, but are able to offer a share of the profits. Of course, exactly what share depends on many factors, including profitability, sales valume, the stage of the product's life cycle, and attrition rates. However, profit sharing seems to be desirable in the case of commercial R&D organizations because such firms depend so much on innovation, and new products introduced by their scientific personnel can easily be associated with particular improvements in profit. Furthermore, those scientists who receive large shares of the profits do not have to try to become managers. They already have an excellent income doing technical work. Thus, some of the problems discussed in the previous chapters, concerning the need for dual and triple hierarchies as a means of motivating professionals to stay in technical work, can be solved if profit sharing is used widely.

Atchison and French [1967] examined which of three systems of pay for scientists and engineers is perceived to be most equitable. One system was based on job evaluation, one was based on years of professional experience and judged quality of performance, and one was based on Jaques' [1961] notion of time span discretion. According to Jaques' idea, the more important the job the longer it takes to obtain feedback on how well one is doing. Also, the more important the job the longer it takes for higher authority to review one's performance. Hence, the time span of discretion (how long it takes before one's work is reviewed) can be used as a measure of the importance of the job. Atchison and French [1967] found that the traditional job evaluation method of determining pay and the time span of discretion method were considered more equitable than the method of using years of professional experience and quality of performance. However, the results may be due to the fact that people object to having others evaluate their performance. There are studies of performance appraisal that show that more than 80% of those appraised think that they perform above average (which, of course, is a statistical impossibility).

Since a large number of researchers work for not-for-profit organizations, governmental agencies, and universities, pay can hardly be tied to the profits of the employing organization. No one really knows for sure how pay for researchers in such organizations is determined or should be determined.

Individual researchers are at a distinct disadvantage in negotiating an equitable salary. Bargaining units where union representatives negotiate wages exist in few universities and research organizations. The leverage for obtaining equitable salaries through individual negotiations comes primarily from the threat of loosing the researcher. However, the individual faces considerable uncertainty when starting a new position and financial and social costs for relocating can be high for both the individual and the family. This, therefore, works to the advantage of the organization. Good starting salaries, with low potential for salary increases as the researcher gains experience, become normal management practices. This, in turn, creates dissatisfaction among experienced researchers.

Comparability salary surveys provide one of the best leverages. When such surveys continually show that salaries in certain research organizations, universities, or governmental labs are markedly lower than in comparable organizations, recruitment for new employees, especially for inducing quality researchers, suffers.

Take the case of a U.S. government research organization in which one of the managers stated that "due to a salary lag of 20 to 25 percent, he has not been able to recruit a single researcher holding a Ph.D. in engineering from one of the premier research universities during the last five years." Such pay policies may not affect work quality immediately because researchers hired prior to the period when the pay disparity developed are not likely to leave at once. But the long-term consequences of such policies on the quality of the research staff are predictable and inevitable.

Some may argue that market mechanisms properly determine salaries. However, President Derek Bok, in his commencement address to the Harvard Class of '88, provided comprehensive and compelling arguments to disprove this myth. There are few salaries that are determined by such mechanisms. For instance, salaries of chief executive officers of corporations are not really determined by a free market mechanism. If that were the case, why would the president of Chrysler get $16 million a year more than the president of Toyota?

Organization policies that attempt to provide competitive and equitable salary compensation to the researchers, in the long run, are likely to attract and retain highly talented research staff. In an R&D organization, nothing is more crucial than the quality of the research staff.

6.6 SENSE OF CONTROL AND COMMUNITY

Organizational effectiveness does depend on individual motivation and individual effectiveness. It obviously depends on individual performance, but it also depends on communication and coordination among individuals, and between the individual and the organization. Certain techniques, such as gain sharing and profit sharing, are techniques for bringing the goals of the individual and the organization into line with each other and are also methods for motivating the individual. One of the most successful plans to motivate employees has been developed by Lincoln [1951] and involves profit sharing.

In addition, openness of information is necessary so that the individual knows what the organization expects and hopes to get from him. Job rotation can help the individual get a better feel for what the organization is trying to achieve, and intrinsic rewards (getting a kick out of doing the job) that are tied to individual performance can help the individual line up his own rewards and goals with the goals of the organization.

Finally, designing jobs in such a way that individuals have a sense of control over their activities is very important. Individuals must feel that a lot of what they do is consistent with their goals. Thus, the individual should have a certain amount of choice. Individuals who see themselves as having some alternatives are much more satisfied and have a greater sense of control than individuals who are told "this is it." Having only one alternative is demotivating.

Furthermore, self-esteem is linked to a sense of control. In other words, people who see themselves "*in control*" have higher self-esteem; conversely, having high self-esteem often means that the individual is in control. There are also studies showing that people who do not feel that they are in control feel depressed [Langer, 1983]. The need for control is so strong in humans that in certain experiments [Thomson, 1983] people have been found to prefer receiving a punishment in the form of a loud noise that they could control, rather than a reward in the form of chips that they could later use to buy something, but over which they had no control. In other words, something as fundamental as reward and punishment can change meaning when matched with control and no control.

Thomson [1983] has also suggested that job design is relevant to developing a sense of control because there are jobs in which the individual experiences so much role conflict and role ambiguity that the individual does not feel in control. Such jobs have been associated with dissatisfaction and high turnover.

To achieve a high level of satisfaction, good morale, and productive R&D activity requires that scientists and engineers be given as much of a sense of control over their job environment as is feasible. It is also important to give employees a sense that they are being appreciated by the organization. Good management should coordinate the goals of the individual and the organization by providing rewards that shape the goals of the individual. Specific activities that increase the sense of community within the laboratory can also be helpful in linking the individual to the organization. For instance, allowing the individual to be "in-the-know" can be very helpful and very motivating; however, too much information can confuse. A good principle is that a person should be given as much information as is desired without being overloaded with facts by management.

A true story, from our file, that occurred in a government R&D laboratory, with the names changed, of course, illustrates the way a supervisor can demotivate a subordinate. Section 6.7 describes the case, as developed by Harry Triandis and David Day.

6.7   A FEDERAL R&D LABORATORY CASE

Some people believe that there is considerable inconsistency in the way vacation time, flextime, being allowed to work at home, and other personnel matters are handled by the various department managers. Some managers are very liberal, while others are not at all. Some employees see their friends in other sections of the organizatioin behave in ways in which they are not allowed to behave.

While the personnel department allows considerable flexibility in such matters, it interferes when performance evaluations are done. A case in point is Dr. Blank, who is a researcher and has provided the following account. He was asked by his supervisor, Dr. Ablex, to do some work that was rather unskilled, simply because this work had high priority. Dr. Ablex assured Dr. Blank, at the time the work was assigned, that this would not affect his income, but when the personnel department did an evaluation of Dr. Blank they found he was doing less-skilled work and demoted him. Dr. Ablex claimed that he could do nothing about the personnel department's action. Contributing to Dr. Blank's demotion were, however, several other factors. First, it appears that the high-priority work that Dr. Ablex wanted done precluded publication of papers. Yet, the personnel department considered publication as one of the criteria for performance evaluation. Second, the job assigned to Dr. Blank required his undivided attention, and was such that one person could perform it without subordinates. So, there were no technicians, graduate students, research assistants, or associates under Dr. Blank. The personnel department, on the other hand, considered the extent a person supervised others as a criterion for evaluation. Finally, Dr. Blank had been encouraged by the directors of the R&D laboratory to participate in national and international associations and committees of his discipline. However, Dr. Ablex did not want Dr. Blank to spend his time in such activities instead of doing the high-priority study, and provided no funds for travel. Rather than paying for such travel out of his pocket, Dr. Blank simply did not participate in committees, but the personnel department considered participation in national and international committees as a factor in the evaluation of Dr. Blank's performance. The result is that Dr. Ablex's job assignments and behavior created conditions that made Dr. Blank's job look unimportant and made Dr. Blank look professionally isolated and without influence; hence the recommendation that he be demoted. Dr. Albex's behavior has been a problem in other ways and to other people as well.

In this example Dr. Ablex is getting his high-priority job done, but the results, in terms of motivation, are devastating to Dr. Blank. The situation is demotivating in a number of ways: there is little overlap between the goals of the organization and the goals of Dr. Blank; the consequences of pursuing organizational goals have been disastrous for Dr. Blank; it is unlikely that Dr. Blank is enjoying this high-priority job; and while such jobs may have to be done, occasionally, to have them become so central to a person's career is undesirable.

The case also indicates that the situation in Dr. Ablex's division is unsatisfactory since some people get privileges that others do not. Such inequities are bound to be demotivating. One can defend the principle that some inequities are unavoidable, but when they have to happen it is good to evoke Rawls' principle that equality is desirable, except when inequality is to the advantage of the least powerful. In other words, if the young scientists are given some extra privileges, so they can finish their dissertations, that is fine; but if those with power are given the privileges, that is undesirable. In any case, Ablex should have discussed the rules he uses in granting such privileges, and his subordinates should have had an opportunity to argue and to participate in the formulation of the rules, and once these rules are set they should have been followed.

6.8 QUESTIONS FOR CLASS DISCUSSION

1   Go over the model presented in the chapter and analyze it from the point of view of how to develop specific procedures in an R&D lab that will favor increased productivity.

2   Go over the model again, and analyze it from the point of view of how to develop specific procedures in an R&D lab that will favor job satisfaction.

6.9 FURTHER READINGS

Dowling, W. F., and L. R. Sayles (1978). *How Managers Motivate*. 2nd Edition, New York; McGraw–Hill.

Drews, T. R. (1977). Motivational factors relevant to R&D employees. *Industrial Management*, July–Aug.

Foa, U., and E. Foa (1974). *Societal Structures of the Mind*. Springfield, IL: Thomas.

Lawler, E. E., III. (1986). *High Involvement Management*. San Francisco, CA: Bass.

Locke, E. A. (1968). Toward a theory of task motivation and incentives. *Organizational Behavior and Human Performance*, **3**, 157–189.

Locke, E. A., K. N. Shaw, L. M. Saari and G. P. Latham (1981). Goal setting and task performance: 1969–1980. *Psychological Bulletin*, **90**, 125–152.

Shapira, R., and S. Globerson (1983). An incentive plan for R&D workers. *Research Management*, **26** (5), 17–20 (Sept–Oct).

Triandis, H. C. (1980). Values, attitudes and interpersonal behavior. *Nebraska Symposium on motivation, 1979*. Lincoln, NE: University of Nebraska Press.

___7

LEADERSHIP IN RESEARCH AND DEVELOPMENT ORGANIZATIONS

During the past 30 years the study of leadership has utilized a variety of approaches. Some researchers have spent a good deal of time observing the behavior of groups and the emergence of leaders. As a result, they have seen that the activites of leaders fall into two general categories. The first involves maintaining the group by paying attention to the needs of the members and making sure that conflicts do not become serious. The second involves that actual task that the group must perform, the definition of the task, how and when it is to be done, and so on. We can label these two types of activities *consideration* and *structure*.

"Consideration" involves paying attention to people, being considerate of their needs and goals, being employee-oriented, and paying attention to the human factor. "Structure" refers to what is to be done and to where the group is going. What is to be accomplished? How is it to be accomplished? How can the activities of the members be controlled?

People who observe groups note that leaders may specialize in one of these activities, they may sometimes engage in both, or in the case of "*great leaders*" they will perform the two activities with high frequency.

First providing general theory, and then focusing on R&D organizations, this chapter covers:

- Theories of leadership and leadership styles;
- Leadership in R&D organizations;
- R&D leadership—a process of mutual influence;
- A leadership style case (where the problem of abdication style of leadership is presented);
- Leadership in a creative research environment.

113

7.1 IDENTIFYING YOUR LEADERSHIP STYLE

In characterizing the behavior of their supervisors, subordinates used similar ideas, e.g. bossy or structured vs. considerate or people–oriented. Similarly, when leaders are questioned, some claim they pay attention to people and others say they focus on the task.

As it turns out, however, the distinctions are not so clearly drawn. Extensive research by Fiedler [1967, 1986a] found that some people are task-motivated when they are relaxed but person-motivated when they are under stress, while others show the opposite pattern, they are person-motivate when relaxed and task-motivated when under stress. It might be useful to find out for yourself what kind of leader you are. To do that, look at page 115. Follow Fiedler's instructions in *"Identifying Your Leadership Style"* (Fiedler, 1977).

You can score your own Least Preferred Co-Worker test. If your score was 64 or more on that test, Fiedler's evidence is that you are person-oriented under stress and task-oriented when relaxed. A score of 53 or less is evidence that you are task-oriented under stress and person-oriented when relaxed. If you got more than 64 you are a high LPC (least preferred co-worker) and if you got less than 53 you are a low LPC. If you scored between those two numbers, Fiedler's data do not have anything to tell you about your leadership style.

Fiedler argues that people are difficult to change, and that it is easier to change the situation in which people find themselves than to change the people. At least for routine, everyday behaviors that are normally under habit control, people act in ways over which they do not have much control. So, rather than change themselves they should try to change their leadership situation. Fiedler has provided us with ways to measure the situation. On pp. 118–121 you will find the Leader–Member Relations Scale, the Task Structure Rating Scale, and the Position Power Rating Scale. You can answer these scales, and score them, following the instructions on the forms. Next comes the Situation Control Scale (p. 122). Follow the instructions and get your score. If your score is 51–70 you have high control; if it is 10–30 you have low control. Fiedler and others have done literally hundreds of studies linking LPC and the Situational Control Scale on the one hand, and group effectiveness (profits, high productivity, speed in getting the job done, accuracy) on the other hand. The findings from these studies fall into a pattern. It turns out that low LPCs do well in situations in which they have either high or low situational control, but do not do as well in situations where they have intermediate control. On the other hand, high LPCs do well in situations where they have intermediate control. So, first find out how much control you have in your particular job situation.

Now you know your LPC score and your situational control score (based on your particular leadership situation, your team, group, department, or division). Do they match? That is, if you are a high LPC are your situational

(text continues on p. 123)

Identifying Your Leadership Style*

Your performance as a leader depends primarily on the proper match between your leadership style and the control you have over your work situation. This section will help you identify your leadership style and the conditions in which you will be most effective. *Carefully read the following instructions and complete the Least Preferred Co-worker (LPC) Scale (page 117).*

INSTRUCTIONS

Throughout your life you have worked in many groups with a wide variety of different people—on your job, in social groups, in church organizations, in volunteer groups, on athletic teams, and in many other situations. Some of your co-workers may have been very easy to work with. Working with others may have been all but impossible.

Of all the people with whom you have ever worked, think of the one person now or at any time in the past with whom you could work *least well*. This individual is not necessarily the person you *liked* least well. Rather, think of the one person with whom you had the most difficulty getting a job done, the *one* individual with whom you could work *least well*. This person is called your *Least Preferred Co-worker* (LPC).

On the scale below, describe this person by placing an "X" in the appropriate space. The scale consists of pairs of words which are opposite in meaning, such as *Very Neat* and *Very Untidy*. Between each pair of words are eight spaces which form the following scale:

Very Neat ___ ___ ___ ___ ___ ___ ___ ___ Very Untidy
            8   7   6   5   4   3   2   1

Think of those eight spaces as steps which range from one extreme to the other. Thus, if you ordinarily think this least preferred co-worker is *quite neat*, write an "X" in the space marked 7, like this:

Very	___	X	___	___	___	___	___	___	Very
Neat	8	7	6	5	4	3	2	1	Untidy
	Very Neat	Quite Neat	Somewhat Neat	Slightly Neat	Slightly Untidy	Somewhat Untidy	Quite Untidy	Very Untidy	

---

* Material on pp. 115–122 is from Fiedler, F. E., M. Chemers, and L. Mahar, *Improving Leadership Effectiveness: The Leader-Match Concept.* Copyright 1977 John Wiley & Sons. Reprinted by permission of the author and publisher.

However, if you ordinarily think of this person as being only *slightly neat*, you would put your "X" in space 5. If you think of this person as being *very untidy* (not neat), you would put your "X" in space 1.

Sometimes the scale will run in the other direction, as shown below:

Frustrating   ___   ___   ___   ___   ___   ___   ___   ___   Helpful
          1   2   3   4   5   6   7   8

Before you mark your "X," look at the words at both ends of the line. *There are no right or wrong answers.* Work rapidly; your first answer is likely to be the best. Do not omit any items, and mark each item only once. Ignore the scoring column for now.

Now go to the next page and describe the person with whom you can work least well. Then go on to page 118.

LEAST PREFERRED CO-WORKER (LPC) SCALE

										Scoring
Pleasant	—	—	—	—	—	—	—	—	Unpleasant	—
	8	7	6	5	4	3	2	1		
Friendly	—	—	—	—	—	—	—	—	Unfriendly	—
	8	7	6	5	4	3	2	1		
Rejecting	—	—	—	—	—	—	—	—	Accepting	—
	1	2	3	4	5	6	7	8		
Tense	—	—	—	—	—	—	—	—	Relaxed	—
	1	2	3	4	5	6	7	8		
Distant	—	—	—	—	—	—	—	—	Close	—
	1	2	3	4	5	6	7	8		
Cold	—	—	—	—	—	—	—	—	Warm	—
	1	2	3	4	5	6	7	8		
Supportive	—	—	—	—	—	—	—	—	Hostile	—
	8	7	6	5	4	3	2	1		
Boring	—	—	—	—	—	—	—	—	Interesting	—
	1	2	3	4	5	6	7	8		
Quarrelsome	—	—	—	—	—	—	—	—	Harmonious	—
	1	2	3	4	5	6	7	8		
Gloomy	—	—	—	—	—	—	—	—	Cheerful	—
	1	2	3	4	5	6	7	8		
Open	—	—	—	—	—	—	—	—	Guarded	—
	8	7	6	5	4	3	2	1		
Backbiting	—	—	—	—	—	—	—	—	Loyal	—
	1	2	3	4	5	6	7	8		
Untrustworthy	—	—	—	—	—	—	—	—	Trustworthy	—
	1	2	3	4	5	6	7	8		
Considerate	—	—	—	—	—	—	—	—	Inconsiderate	—
	8	7	6	5	4	3	2	1		
Nasty	—	—	—	—	—	—	—	—	Nice	—
	1	2	3	4	5	6	7	8		
Agreeable	—	—	—	—	—	—	—	—	Disagreeable	—
	8	7	6	5	4	3	2	1		
Insincere	—	—	—	—	—	—	—	—	Sincere	—
	1	2	3	4	5	6	7	8		
Kind	—	—	—	—	—	—	—	—	Unkind	—
	8	7	6	5	4	3	2	1		

Total _____

LEADER–MEMBER RELATIONS SCALE

Circle the number which best represents your response to each item.

	strongly agree	agree	neither agree nor disagree	disagree	strongly disagree
1. The people I supervise have trouble getting along with each other.	1	2	3	4	5
2. My subordinates are reliable and trustworthy.	5	4	3	2	1
3. There seems to be a friendly atmosphere among the people I supervise.	5	4	3	2	1
4. My subordinates always cooperate with me in getting the job done.	5	4	3	2	1
5. There is friction between my subordinates and myself.	1	2	3	4	5
6. My subordinates give me a good deal of help and support in getting the job done.	5	4	3	2	1
7. The people I supervise work well together in getting the job done.	5	4	3	2	1
8. I have good relations with the people I supervise.	5	4	3	2	1

Total Score ☐

TASK STRUCTURE RATING SCALE—PART I

Circle the number in the appropriate column.	Usually True	Sometimes True	Seldom True
Is the Goal Clearly State or Known?			
1. Is there a blueprint, picture, model or detailed description available of the finished product or service?	2	1	0
2. Is there a person available to advise and give a description of the finished product or service, or how the job should be done?	2	1	0
Is There Only One Way to Accomplish the Task?			
3. Is there a step-by-step procedure, or a standard operating procedure which indicates in detail the process which is to be followed?	2	1	0
4. Is there a specific way to subdivide the task into separate parts or steps?	2	1	0
5. Are there some ways which are clearly recognized as better than others for performing this task?	2	1	0
Is There Only One Correct Answer or Solution?			
6. Is it obvious when the task is finished and the correct solution has been found?	2	1	0
7. Is there a book, manual, or job description which indicates the best solution or the best outcome for the task?	2	1	0
Is It Easy to Check Whether the Job Was Done Right?			
8. Is there a generally agreed understanding about the standards the particular product or service has to meet to be considered acceptable?	2	1	0
9. Is the evaluation of this task generally made on some quantitative basis?	2	1	0
10. Can the leader and the group find out how well the task has been accomplished in enough time to improve future performance?	2	1	0

Subtotal ☐

TASK STRUCTURE RATING SCALE—PART 2

Training and Experience Adjustment

NOTE: Do not adjust jobs with task structure scores of 6 or below.

(a) Compared to others in this or similar positions, how much *training* has the leader had?

3	2	1	0
No training at all	Very little training	A moderate amount of training	A great deal of training

(b) Compared to others in this or similar positions, how much *experience* has the leader had?

6	4	2	0
No experience at all	Very little experience	A moderate amount of experience	A gread deal of experience

Add lines (a) and (b) of the training and experience adjustment, then *subtract* this from the subtotal given in Part 1.

Subtotal from Part 1.

Subtract training and experience adjustment

Total Task Structure Score

POSITION POWER RATING SCALE

Circle the number which best represents your answer.

1. Can the leader directly or by recommendation administer rewards and punishments to his subordinates?

2	1	0
Can act directly or can recommend with high effectiveness	Can recommend but with mixed results	No

2. Can the leader directly or by recommendation affect the promotion, demotion, hiring or firing of his subordinates?

2	1	0
Can act directly or can recommend with high effectiveness	Can recommend but with mixed results	No

3. Does the leader have the knowledge necessary to assign tasks to subordinates and instruct them in task completion?

2	1	0
Yes	Sometimes or in some aspects	No

4. Is it the leader's job to evaluate the performance of his subordinates?

2	1	0
Yes	Sometimes or in some aspects	No

5. Has the leader been given some official title of authority by the organization (e.g., foreman, department head, platoon leader)?

2	0
Yes	No

Total [   ]

SITUATIONAL CONTROL SCALE

Enter the total scores for the Leader–Member Relations dimension, the Task Structure scale, and the Position Power scale in the spaces below. Add the three scores
together and compare your total with the ranges given in the table below to
determine your overall situational control.

1. *Leader–Member Relations Total*

2. *Task Structure Total*

3. *Position Power Total*

Grand Total

Total Score	51–70	31–50	10–30
Amount of Situational Control	High Control	Moderate Control	Low Control

control scores in the 31–50 range or if you are a low LPC are they in either the 51–70 or the 10–30 range? If they match, you need not do anything. But if they do not match, Fiedler suggests making some changes. For example, if you want to increase your Leader–Member Relations you may make a special effort to communicate with your subordinates, to decrease the level of conflict among them, and to be accessible to them. If you want to increase your task structure you may make a special effort to develop procedures for doing the job. If you want to increase the power you might ask for more power from your supervisor. Similarly there are things to do to decrease structure (design the task so that subordinates can decide how to do the job) and power (let subordinates make more of the important decisions). You can train subordinates, rotate them into other jobs, and so on. The point is to do things to change your environment so it will match your leadership style.

The emphasis on Fiedler's leadership theory is based on the fact that Fiedler, more than any other researcher, has tested his theory with a variety of methods, in a wide range of realistic settings. For example, Fiedler et al, [1984, 1987] reported on a study of several mines, where a particular management training program based on theory [Fiedler et al., 1977] was compared with a widely used program to develop supervisory skills that used organizational development approaches that require consultant expenses on the order of $80,000 to $150,000. The management training program, which was estimated to cost between $4,000 and $10,000 at most sites, was more effective than the other methods in improving both productivity and the mine's safety record.

While Fiedler's is by far the best-researched theory of leadership, there are a number of other theories that should be noted.

7.2 THEORIES OF LEADERSHIP AND LEADERSHIP STYLES

No leader can afford to ignore either "consideration" or "structure." How much one emphasizes one or the other is a matter of degree; it is always necessary to pay some attention to each of these activities.

Another way of looking at leadership is to say that the leader is supposed to supply what is necessary for the followers to reach their goals. This is called the *path–goal theory of leadership*. Basically, this theory argues that the way a leader acts should be determined by what the followers need. For example, if the followers do not know how to do the job, then it is necessary for the leader to be very structuring. If the followers have several needs that are not met, then it is important for the leader to be especially considerate.

Consider another example. If the job is very monotonous, then the leader must provide some excitement, some change. Obviously, this is not necessary if the job already has variety. In one study, it was found that when the job had a lot of structure and people knew what they were supposed to do, considerate leaders were particularly effective.

There are a number of other factors that interact with the ones just mentioned. For example, if the task is very complex or requires creativity, then it is better to let the employees decide for themselves what to do, and, therefore, consideration is more important. If the abilities of the subordinates are very highly developed, then it is desirable to leave them alone. On the other hand, if they do not have much ability, then a certain amount of structure is appropriate. Several other factors, such as the needs for independence of the subordinates, their readiness to assume responsibility for decisions, their tolerance for ambiguity, their interest in the problem, and their feeling that the problem is important, make the less bossy supervisor more effective. When there is identity between the goals of the subordinates and the organization, when the subordinates have the skills and knowledge, and when their expectations are that they should participate in decisions it is again important for the leader to emphasize consideration rather than structure.

It also depends on the age of the relationship between a leader and subordinates whether one or another leadership pattern may prove more effective. Hersey and Blanchard [1982] have argued that in the beginning of the relationship the leader is supposed to tell, later to sell, still later to use participation, and finally to use delegation.

If the leader must make a very important decision, his behavior will be under intentional control. He will have the time to think about what to do. This contrasts with the situation when the leader behaves under habit control. In the case where time is available, the leader can change his behavior according to a scheme developed by Vroom and Yetton [1973].

Consider the following different kinds of leadership styles:

1. *The directive style*, in which the leader simply makes the decision and tells the subordinates what to do;

2. *The negotiator style*, in which the subordinates give the information that the leader needs in order to make the decision, but then the leader makes the decision;

3. *The consultation style*, in which the leader asks for information and suggestions on what to do and makes the decision on the basis of these suggestions;

4. *The participative style*, in which the subordinates provide information and suggest solutions, the leader negotiates with them, and together they reach a mutually satisfying agreement and the best decision;

5. *The delegation style*, in which the leader provides information to the subordinates about the problem and suggests possible solutions. The responsibility for the decision is ultimately given to the subordinates. In this case, the leader does not even ask the subordinates to report what solutions were adopted.

Vroom and Yetton [1973, pp. 13, 194] provide a decision tree that indicates when each of these five leadership styles is appropriate. It consists of a number of questions, and, depending on the answers to these questions, it recommends a particular leadership style.

There are seven questions that are arranged in a particular order. The first question is: "Are there quality requirements that one solution is likely to be more rational than another?" Depending on the answer (yes or no), one goes on the second question: "Do I have sufficient information to make a quality decision?" Depending on the answer, one asks a third question: "Is the problem structured?" This process continues until the leader has been directed to the best leadership style.

It is useful to say a word about the difference between the approach of Fiedler and the approach of Vroom and Yetton. The Fiedler approach assumes that leaders have fixed personalities. If they discover that the conditions within which they operate are not consistent with their style, they "engineer the environment" to make it consistent with their style. By contrast, in the Vroom and Yetton approach, the individual uses different leadership style, depending on the situation. He or she may decide to delegate in one case or be directive in another case. The leader's style is decided through an analysis of the situation and on the basis of the answers to specific questions.

Both approaches assume that there is no "best" leadership style. Leadership effectiveness depends on the situation. The Fiedler approach, in fact, is called the "contingency model," since it states that effective leadership behavior is contingent on the situation. Vroom's approach also is a contingency theory, but while Fiedler's is based on personality, Vroom's relies on logical analysis of the situation.

In some ways both the Fiedler and Vroom and Yetton viewpoints are correct. In Chapter 6 on motivation we discussed the importance of habits and behavioral intentions as determinants of behavior. We also indicated that when the job is new, and there is plenty of time to decide what to do, behavioral intentions are likely to be the major determinants of behavior. When the job is well-learned, if there is an emergency, or time pressure is high, habits are likely to be the major determinants of behavior. In situations when habits are all-important, Fiedler is likely to have the correct theory because he assumes that the behavior of the leader is fixed, that is, under the control of habits or a deeply ingrained personality. When behavioral intentions are the important determinants of behavior, then Vroom and Yetton are likely to give the best guidance. That is the time to use the decision-tree and to teach oneself to use the correct decision-making style.

It seems likely that for everyday decisions and the sort of routine day-in–day-out behavior that is typical of leaders, Fiedler's point of view is more likely to be descriptive of the realities of leadership behavior. On the other hand, when the leader is just starting on a job, or when the decision is very important and there is the time to think carefully about it, the Vroom and Yetton analysis can be helpful.

As we stated earlier, if habits are important, then the leader's experience is all-important too; when behavioral intentions are important, the leader's intelligence is all-important. Research shows that the leader's intelligence is not correlated with group effectiveness, or, to put it more accurately, the correlation is so low that it is not of practical significance. However, there is one condition when the correlation of leader intelligence and group effectiveness is high: when the leader is very dominant *and* the subordinates respect and admire him. Fiedler [1986a] reported correlations around 0.70 in that condition and around 0.10 in all other conditions. This finding is particularly relevant in R&D organizations, since the subordinates are likely to be very intelligent. If they have IQs around 130 the leader would have to have an IQ around 140 (something quite rare, since it occurs only among three people in a thousand) *and* have a record and personality that inspires respect and admiration to get away with being dominant. On the other hand, if the leader is participative, he/she can use the intelligence of the followers to increase the quality of the group's output.

In summary, while the dominant, structured behavior of the leader can be effective, this is only so under relatively rare conditions. On the other hand, consideration behavior is effective under a relatively wide range of conditions. This is even more likely to be true in R&D labs than in industrial settings, because the subordinates are highly intelligent, want to be autonomous, and often can do very good work when left alone.

Yet there are important additional jobs for the leader. As Bennis [1984] has suggested, the manager's four competencies are *attention* (making people attend to goals that serve the organization), *providing meaning* (using metaphors to communicate these goals), *creating trust* (being predictable, reliable, consistent), and *managing the self concept of subordinates* (making them feel significant, enjoy work, feel like a community or team). Even better is the leader who can inspire (is a model for subordinates), who provides individualized consideration (gives personal attention to members who seem neglected), rewards frequently, and provides intellectual stimulation (enables subordinates to think of old problems in new ways) [Bass, 1985].

Some special problems that have occupied researchers in R&D labs will now be examined.

7.3 LEADERSHIP IN R&D ORGANIZATIONS

It is clear that when the subordinates are professionals, it is more appropriate to show consideration than to initiate structure. However, subordinates still require a certain amount of guidance from the manager, otherwise their activities will become unrelated to the needs of the organization. Pelz and Andrews [1966a,b] have shown that when there is either excessive or insufficient autonomy, the contributions of the professional to the research organization are minimal. An intermediate amount of autonomy provides optimal conditions for the professional. Only then can the contributions of the scientist to the organization be maximized.

Some R&D managers feel that administration is just paper-pushing and that the "real" work is technical. Thus, they miss the point that consideration is needed to develop the right kind of environment for subordinates. Also, some of these managers feel that "holding hands" (an aspect of *consideration*) is not consistent with their self-image; it is too soft or feminine an activity. Perhaps it would help such managers to know that research on psychological adjustment suggests that better adjusted people have both traits that traditionally were considered masculine *and* feminine ones. That is, they are independent, and self-reliant, but also warm, supportive, and nurturing. A person who has trouble relating to others will be better off restructuring the environment to make it compatible with his leadership style, as suggested by Fiedler, or he may find it is better to limit himself to technical work.

One way to paraphrase this is to say that good managerial policy requires "*controlled freedom.*" This view is also consistent with the writings of Andrews and Farris [1967], Fisher [1980], and Smith [1970]. Some examples relevant to R&D organizations follow.

Research by Pelz and Andrews [1966b] also suggests that the most effective scientists in R&D laboratories are those who are allowed to do some basic research in addition to their applied research. It is frustrating for a scientist to come up with an idea that requires basic research and then not be allowed to pursue it because it is not obviously linked to the needs of the organization. A manager who protects his subordinates from this kind of frustration is a good manager.

A good manager also makes sure that his subordinates do not become overspecialized. One of the problems in many laboratories is that some people become so specialized that when their specialization becomes obsolete, so do they. Further research by Pelz and Andrews [1966b] suggests that the effectiveness of a scientist increases with the number of demonstrated areas of specialization.

According to Pelz and Andrews, the scientist who spends about 50% of his or her time in research and 50% doing other things often is more effective than the one who spends 100% of the time on research. The manager who is sensitive to these issues and makes his assignments so that they take into account this fact is likely to be more effective.

A large dose of delegation is essential in the case of research scientists. Praise, recognition, and feedback are also extremely important. The manager who rewards, praises, and recognizes good work is more effective than the supervisor who simply grins when he sees good work, but says very little. On the other hand, the good manager should be able to identify incompetent work and to make sure that it is not rewarded. A good manager encourages subordinates to take sabbaticals, to develop and apply new skills, and to set difficult but achievable goals. Goal achievements are reexamined every 6 months or so and rewards are given.

Another problem that is unique to many research and development organizations is that people often have two bosses. Usually, there is both a functional supervisor (who is a specialist in the particular field that the scientist has been trained in) and a project supervisor (who focuses on a particular problem that has to be solved). Classic organization theory warns against arrangements in which there are two supervisors, but this arrangement can be made to work.

In such cases, the effectiveness of the scientists often depends on the balance between the influence of the two supervisors [Katz and Allen, 1985]. The best performance in the studies by Katz and Allen occurred when the project manager was mostly concerned with relating the project to the outside world (i.e., the suppliers, the customers, the organization), while the functional manager did most of the inside work. These authors say "project performance appears to be higher when project managers are seen as having greater organizational influence." This is an outward orientation and, as a result, they should be concerned with gaining resources and recognition for the project, linking it to other parts of the business, and ensuring that the project's direction fits the overall business plan of the organization. According to Katz and Allen, functional managers, on the other hand, should be concerned with technical excellence and integrity, that is, seeing that the project is scientifically sound and includes state-of-the-art technology. Their orientation is inward and focuses on the technical content of the project. The technical decisions should be made by those who are closest to the science and technology.

The location of technical decision-making in functional departments, however, implies important integrating roles for project managers, who are responsible for ensuring that the technical directions overseen by several different functional managers all fit together to yield the best possible end result. Clearly, the greater the influence of project managers on the organization, the easier it is to integrate and negotiate with the various functional managers, whose technical goals are often in conflict.

From this study one might conclude that project managers should have more organizational experience and more status than functional managers. A good tactic might be to deliberately place highly competent young professionals in the role of functional manager to supervise the technical aspects of the work, while having the older ones act as project managers.

7.4   R&D LEADERSHIP: A PROCESS OF MUTUAL INFLUENCE

Based upon a study of R&D organizations, Farris [1982, p. 344] states:

> In the high innovation groups the supervisors were more active participants in the informal organization. They were especially helpful to group members for critical evaluation, administrative aid, and help in thinking about technical

problems. In addition, group members were more helpful to these supervisors for providing technical information, aid in thinking about technical problems, critical evaluation, and original ideas.

Leadership in an R&D organization is essentially a process of mutual influence between the supervisor and the employees. Based on this approach, Farris suggests four styles of leadership or supervision [1982, p. 344]:

Collaboration: Both the supervisor and the employees have a great deal of influence in making decisions.

Delegation: The employees are given considerable responsibility for the decisions and the supervisor has little influence.

Domination: The supervisor has a great deal of influence and employees have very little input.

Abdication: The supervisor neglects to assign a particular task to the employees and neglects to work on it himself. In this case, neither the supervisor nor the employees have much influence on a particular decision.

Studies clearly indicate that the collaborative style, both in terms of setting schedules and in terms of informal organization, is most conducive to higher performance in innovation. There are, however, situations in which other styles of leadership and supervision have to be used. For example, when there are time constraints in making a decision there may not be sufficient time to seek extensive input from the employees. Consequently, the collaborative style is not possible. Depending on the situation, domination or delegation would be preferred alternatives. There are also situations in which an R&D manager lacks the competence or ability to provide the necessary leadership. In the cases, it is very common to use extensive delegation or abdication.

Abdication takes place more often than most organizations would like to admit. It is likely to happen when supervisors who are either technically incompetent or lacking in intellectual abilities find themselves "surrounded" by more competent people, above (higher level managers) and below (lower level researchers) them. In hierarchical bureaucratic settings, situations can easily arise in which individuals who are technically incompetent and unable to provide effective leadership can still occupy important managerial positions in R&D organizations. This may also occur as a result of organizational growth or change.

In summary, studies by Farris [1982, pp. 345–346] show that collaboration, not delegation, is likely to produce the most successful innovations. The supervisors of low-performing innovation teams frequently think they are delegating, when in fact they are abdicating.

7.5   A LEADERSHIP STYLE CASE

In governmental and large nongovernmental (industrial or academic) research organizations that are hierarchical in nature, lack of effective leadership characterized by abdication exists quite frequently. How does the organization cope with this?

Let us take the actual case of a research laboratory,* where a research division director, Mr. Lewis, manages seven departments with a total research staff of 150. Mr. Lewis, has no research training, that is, his educational background is limited to an undergraduate engineering degree, has made no attempt to continue his technical training, has never taken any graduate level courses, has never published, and has never been active in scientific and professional organizations. The personnel records show that he is considered one of the high performers and any time there is organization growth or change, he acquires some new functions. And when there is organization contraction, he maintains his position while technically more competent division directors are sent back to the bench. Analyzing this case, let us review these questions:

- What is the leadership style and behavior pattern of the division director?
- How is the organization performing?
- What clues does one have that there is a substantial leadership problem?
- How does the organization cope with it?

Leadership Style. The leadership style is a combination of abdication and delegation. All technical responsibility is delegated to the department heads, integration at the division level is minimal, and responsibility for decisions normally made at the division level is abdicated and passed on to a higher level—the laboratory director, Ms. Himler. Her views are sought and essentially all decisions normally made by the division director are in fact made by the laboratory director. The behavior pattern of the division Director is characterized by his readily admitting lack of technical competence, building strong aliances with selected research divisions, degrading division directors who may have distinguished scientific records, doing what the laboratory director, Ms. Himler, wants him to do, getting marching orders on all division operations from Ms. Himler, and taking zero risk.

Organization Performance. The organization performance is quite adequate. Increasingly, emphasis is on technical assistance instead of research. Innovative research programs never reach fruition; they are downgraded to technical assistance activities.

---

* The situation is real but all the names and facts in this case are fictional.

Leadership Problems. Clues to the existence of the problem manifest themselves via the leadership style and the behavior pattern of Mr. Lewis (the division director) and via lack of substantial innovation by the division over the years.

Organization Response. An organization can cope with such problems in a number of ways. Before discussing that, it might be useful to see how such a situation arose.

Mr. Lewis started managing a group of three to five technicians providing laboratory analysis of building materials. As the parent organization grew, the research needs of the organization grew substantially. Initially, a small research and technical assistance group was formed under Mr. Lewis. Later, a separate research laboratory with three divisions was created. A new geographic location was selected for the laboratory and a proper research facility was built for the purpose. Because of Mr. Lewis's pleasant and nonthreatening personality, he continually assumed increasingly more important managerial responsibility. During organization contraction, Mr. Lewis maintained his higher managerial position because of his inability to make a meaningful contribution at the lower or research performance levels.

Now, how best to cope with the situation?

Discharging or demoting Mr. Lewis may seem like one of the choices. Often, in hierarchical bureaucratic organizations that would cause more trouble than it is worth. The Personnel process in often cumbersome and time-consuming, and even if management is successful, Mr. Lewis could end up at a lower, research-execution level, where he is clearly unable to perform. Mr. Lewis never claimed to be technically competent and never falsified or exaggerated his record of accomplishments. He is a dedicated, hardworking employee whose performance, considering his lack of technical and intellectual background, has been adequate. It would seem the problem lies less with Mr. Lewis than "the system." Consequently, any adverse action against him would seem unfair.

Other choices might be assigning a high-level, technically competent assistant to Mr. Lewis to affect the necessary integration of effort; assigning technical assistance activities to Mr. Lewis's division instead of innovative research programs; or assigning Mr. Lewis to another part of the organization where his pay level is preserved and where his long association with research could benefit the organization in terms of technology transfer and research liaison activities.

7.6 LEADERSHIP IN A CREATIVE RESEARCH ENVIRONMENT

In an R&D organization, a person holding an important leadership position would normally have a significant research program. In many U.S. government departments and in industry, some individuals have oversight responsibility for research organizations, although they are not involved in research program execution. It is therefore useful to focus on those leadership and managerial aspects that are directly involved in managing and executing an important research program involving a significant number (say 50 or more) of scientists and engineers.

Mintzberg [1975, p. 61] suggests a number of leadership or managerial skills that are important. These are: developing peer relationships, conducting negotiations, motivating employees, resolving conflicts, obtaining and disseminating information, making decisions in conditions of extreme ambiguity, and allocating resources. In an R&D organization, some additional activities are important, such as establishing information networks in order to relate to the wider scientific community and to attract and recruit highly qualified personnel.

When one reaches the position of managing a significant research program, time constraints preclude thinking deeply or broadly about anything. In most R&D managerial positions, managers are not able to do any serious, original, or conceptual work. Most people in these positions work long hours and are very busy. They must deal with a number of constituencies, which include such typical individuals or groups as the director of the research organization, research sponsors (who normally provide funding for the research effort), the user community (who might use the research effort and have some effect on research funding), researchers within the group, peers in the scientific community, and, last but not least, the nonscientific bureaucracy (this may include the comptroller, personnel office, and contracting office). Any experienced R&D manager knows that difficulties are likely to arise if any one of these constituencies is ignored. Effectively executing the research program and meeting demands placed by individuals in these constituencies can keep an R&D manager quite busy indeed. A quotation attributed to Thoreau states: "It is not enough to be busy...the question is, what are we busy about?"

The question, then, is what is a manager to do? It is important to realize that a manager in an important leadership position must continue to meet the day-to-day responsibilities placed on him or her by the job. In addition, he or she must focus on the long-term requirements of the organization and must consider strategic and policy implications for the research group. In terms of individual performance and organization effectiveness discussed earlier, the manager has to look at issues not just in terms of process and result indicators, but must also take strategic indicators into account. Focusing on strategic issues requires creative thinking and serious reflection: it has the added problem of inherent uncertainties, risks, and delayed gratification (if any). This focus, perhaps more than anything else, provides for the long-term productivity of an R&D organization and for the excellence for which a leader may want to strive. Being busy doing day-to-day things simply is not enough. An effective R&D manager has to integrate the efforts of others, provide foresight for strategic issues, and, at the same time, make technical contributions in the area of his/her speciality.

7.7 SUMMARY

For everyday decisions and actions, your personality is likely to determine how you act. To make sure that your actions will be effective you may
want to change your work environment so that it matches your personality
[Fiedler, 1977].

If you are a high LPC (see Section 7.1), avoid environments that are too
easy (you have much control) or too difficult (you have little control) for
you as a leader. In other words, foster an environment in which you have
moderate control and influence, which is common in R&D organizations.
Then, your leadership style should be participative or relationship-oriented.

If you are a low LPC, your ideal, then, is to be liked, to have no conflict
among your subordinates, to have a clear task, and a lot of power. If, on the
other hand, you have no power and your subordinates hate you, and you
do not know what they are supposed to be doing, do not panic. To get high
performance, you will have to rely on task orientation and a directive form
of leadership.

Since you are dealing with rather bright and autonomous people, task
structure is going to be low; since you want to minimize stress, you want the
group to like you; since your power and influence in an effective R&D
organization are going to be moderate, you really need to work toward a
relationship-oriented management style.

For important decisions, when you have a lot of time, ask the questions
Vroom and Yetton have recommended, go through the decision-tree they
have developed, and use the leadership style that is recommended.

If other factors are critical, the above recommendations need to be taken
with a grain of salt. You should emphasize participation if the following hold
true:

- You have egalitarian values
- You respect your subordinates' skills
- You know too little about their jobs
- You can live with uncertainty
- You feel it is very important that your subordinates like you and your
  subordinates get along with each other and know much about the job
- The job is interesting and requires many solutions and high quality
- There is no crisis, the job does not involve conflicts of interest and
  permits interpersonal interactions, and you work in an environment
  where things are changing fast.

If these factors do not hold, you might shift toward more directive
management styles.

When you have a new employee, you can get away with a style that
involves telling people what to do; with a more mature subordinate, selling
is better; with a still more mature subordinate, participation is highly desir-

able; with a subordinate who knows a lot and has been around a long time, delegation may be ideal [Hersey and Blanchard, 1982].

Look at your subordinates' job situation. What is missing from the ideal work environment? Suppose they do not know what they are to do; then tell them. Suppose they are bored; then entertain them. In other words, your job is to help them reach their goals, to supply the missing resources (path–goal theory).

There are other factors that moderate what was just said: you can be more bossy if you have deadlines or limited resources, or if you are expected to be bossy (expectation can come from the culture, the organization, your supervisor, your subordinates, your peers), or if your followers are incompetent or inexperienced.

Finally, there are some unique situations related to R&D organizations. Thus, leadership concepts and styles need to be explored in the context of R&D organizations.

7.8 QUESTIONS FOR CLASS DISCUSSION

1. Under what conditions is Fiedler's theory of leadership likely to predict high effectiveness in an R&D lab?

2. Under what conditions should Vroom's theory be used in an R&D lab?

7.9 FURTHER READING

Bass, B. (1985). *Leadership and Performance Beyond Expectation*. New York: Macmillan.

Dowling, W. F., and L. R. Sayles (1978). *How Managers Motivate*. 2nd ed.. chapter 10, "Leadership," New York, McGraw-Hill.

Fiedler, F. E. (1967). *A Theory of Leadership Effectiveness*. New York: McGraw-Hill.

Fiedler, F. E. (1986a). The contributions of cognitive resources and leader behavior to organizational performance. *Journal of Applied Social Psychology*, **16**, 532–548.

Hersey, P, and K. H. Blanchard (1982). *Management of Organizational Behavior*, 4th ed. Englewood Cliffs, NJ: Prentice-Hall.

Vroom, V., and P. W. Yetton (1973). *Leadership and Decision Making*. Pittsburgh: University of Pittsburgh Press.

___8
MANAGING CONFLICT IN R&D ORGANIZATIONS

There are three kinds of conflict that we need to discuss in this chapter: intrapersonal conflict, interpersonal conflict; and intergroup conflict. The first occurs within the individual, the second between individuals, and the third between groups.

8.1 CONFLICT WITHIN INDIVIDUALS

There are many kinds of conflict that occur within individuals. The first one that will be discussed is *role conflict*. Roles are ideas about correct behavior for a person holding a position in a social system. For example, the position of chief engineer specifies particular activities that are appropriate for the position. When analyzing roles, it is important to talk about *prescribed*, *subjective*, and *enacted* roles. A prescribed role is a role that is prescribed by other people. In other words, the chief engineer usually receives definitions of what he is supposed to do from his boss, from his subordinates, and from his peers, and each has specific ideas about the engineer's role, which are integrated into a concept of what he is supposed to be doing. In other words, when the chief engineer says, "I am doing this because I am the chief engineer," that is an element of the *subjective role*. Finally, we have the *enacted role*, which is the actual role behavior of the chief engineer.

It is useful to look at the enacted role and see if it corresponds to the subjective role or to the prescribed role. According to research, the three kinds of roles, the prescribed, the subjective, and the enacted, frequently do not match very well. In other words, what is prescribed may actually not be similar either to the subjective role or to the enacted role.

In one of the situations of role conflict, the various prescribed roles are usually quite different. That is, the person receives prescribed roles from a variety of others, and these role senders disagree among themselves about what the role of the particular individual should be. As a result, the *subjective role* the person develops is confused or contains elements that are in conflict because the boss says one thing, one subordinate says a different thing, and a second subordinate says yet another. Other situations of role conflict occur when a person does not develop a subjective role that resembles the prescribed role or when the person developing an enacted role fails to match the prescribed one.

Research done by Kahn, and summarized in Katz and Kahn [1980], indicates that about 50% of the people studied in various organizations have experienced a great deal of role conflict, much of it due to conflict with the hierarchy. That is, the person's definition of what he is supposed to be doing is different from the definition that his boss is sending or that the top manager is sending to the boss.

A second kind of role conflict is related to *workload*, in other words, how much is one supposed to do. Given a particular role, there are different definitions of how much one should do.

A third conflict has to do with *creativity*. Who is supposed to initiate what or who is supposed to do new things does vary according to role senders.

Finally, there are conflicts that have to do with *organizational boundaries*, in other words, who has responsibility for what activity (e.g., who must decide whether a laboratory member is to go to a conference).

The research by Kahn shows that the greater the role conflict: (1) the greater the dissatisfaction of the individual, (2) the more frequent the physical symptoms of the individual, (3) the greater the number of hospital visits the individual undertakes, and (4) the less confidence the individual has in the organization.

A good example of role conflict in research and development organizations is the conflict that occurs when the person is part of a team that is developing a new product that involves both research people and marketing people. Depending on the structure of such teams, a person may experience varying degrees of conflict. In the chapter on the design of jobs, we discussed a very interesting project by Souder and Chakrabarti [1980] in which they identified three kinds of relationships between a research and development team and a marketing team. They were the state-dominant, the process-dominant, and the task-dominant structures within the organization. We identified the conditions under which the various forms of organization might be more or less effective. The greatest role conflict is apt to occur in the task–dominant form of organization, since it is in that particular structure that the individual is *both* a marketing person and a scientist. In the state-dominant structure, there will be a minimum amount of conflict, since in that form of organization there is a very clear separation between the scientist and the marketing team. In the process-dominant form there will be an intermediate amount of conflict.

Technicians vs. Researchers

Other kinds of intrapersonal conflict occur when certain technical employees have problems with the way they are perceived by members of the organization. A good example is provided by Fineman [1980], who discusses the problem of technicians in large R&D organizations. They are often in a supportive role; in other words, they are supposed to be helping the researcher do the work. This frequently makes them feel like second-class citizens who are being "used" by the researchers as servants rather than as co-workers. Furthermore, their job appears to lack creativity, since it is the researcher who does all the original work and they are only providing the technical support. Naturally, such people often feel that their technical skills and qualifications are underutilized and that their superiors do not take their personal needs into account. In R&D organizations, quite often, support personnel experience helplesseness and lack of power and influence. Managers must find ways to integrate support staff by providing common goals for them and for the researchers.

Furthermore, in research organizations people are likely to get promoted primarily on the basis of technical excellence rather than managerial skills. As a result, the managers tend to be technically competent but rather poor administrators. Managers who focus on technical problems often do not take the personal needs of their subordinates very seriously, and, as a result, their subordinates are upset, unhappy, and experience a good deal of conflict about staying in the organization.

Fineman [1980] provides a number of suggestions that may reduce some of these problems. For example, organizations might give higher-sounding titles to the support personnel and develop promotion policies that allow them to feel better integrated into the organization. In addition, they can enrich their jobs by doing a greater variety of activities. Organizations may also find it useful to pay more attention to the training of their R&D management personnel. Finally, selecting technicians and support personnel who are "thick-skinned" enough to put up with poor managers might be a good strategy for this kind of situation.

Supervisor–Subordinate Expectations

A frequent problem in most organizations is that the expectations of one's supervisor and of one's subordinates may be quite different. This problem becomes especially difficult to solve when the training backgrounds of the supervisor and the subordinates are very different. For example, in some commercial organizations the top management has M.B.A. training or degrees in law or in accounting. Managers of the R&D functions may report to an M.B.A. while their subordinates might be physicists or engineers. The expectations of people with such varied kinds of training can be very different. As a result the managers find that their supervisor expects a particular set of behaviors while their subordinates expect a different set with a minimal overlap between them. Such "role conflicts" have been found to result in health problems (e.g., ulcers), job dissatisfaction, and even depression.

It is important for people who find themselves in role conflict situations to first identify that they are facing a role conflict, and second to bring the relevant parties to a conference table to "negotiate" the kind of role that they should have. Generally, when such a problem is identified and discussed, solutions can be found. One technique that is especially helpful is to discuss with co-workers what they expect the manager to do "more of" and "less of." For example, subordinates may indicate that they want to be evaluated more frequently, but be given explicit directions about how to do their jobs less often. It is through such discussions that roles can be clarified, negotiated, and agreed on. Role conflict can, in principle, be eliminated if reasonable people are allowed to discuss the problem and to seek constructive solutions.

Engineers' Status and Organizational Conflicts

An analysis of the kinds of stresses that professional engineers face is provided by Keenan [1980]. Keenan also identifies, as a problem, the fact that professional engineers have a relatively low status in society (mostly the case in the United States, not so in Japan and Germany) despite their academic level of qualifications and their level of contributions to society. He has reviewed studies that found that a substantial percentage of engineers feel they are not sufficiently high in status and are dissatisfied and frustrated by this. A number of scholars have pointed out that scientists and engineers who work in industrial organizations are likely to experience strains due to the conflict between their professional values and the goals of the organization for which they work. Conflicts between the technologist and the organization over issues such as which projects to focus on and how and in what way to do them can drain the engineer's energies.

An important basis for these conflicts is the fact that technologists generally desire to be involved in projects based on their technical and scientific merit, whereas the primary consideration of the organization is product marketability. Keenan further summarizes a number of studies that show that there is a good deal of stress among technologists and scientists in various organizations. Among the complaints of engineers and scientists is that they do not have enough job autonomy and that they lack the opportunity to use their research skills. This dissatisfaction is particularly high among the younger engineers and scientists. There is also some evidence that those organizations that provide freedom to do research, promote personnel on the basis of technical competence, and allow individuals to attend scientific meetings to improve their professional knowledge and skills generally have scientists and engineers who are less dissatisfied than those in organizations that do not have such policies.

Role Ambiguity

In addition to role conflicts, some of the scientists and engineers experience *role ambiguity*, that is, uncertainly about the meaning of communications received from a variety of important "others" in the organization. About 60% of the engineers and scientists in one study experienced role ambiguity. In other words, they did not really know what the boss wanted.

Role Overload and Underload

In some cases, there is *role overload*, i.e., the work that needs to be done is too difficult and exceeds the individual's abilities, skills, or experience. In a study summarized in Keenan's [1980] paper, French and Caplan [1973] found that engineers and scientists more frequently experienced situations in which the job was too difficult than did administrators. Another problem is role *underload*; the demands made by the job are insufficient to make full use of the skills and abilities of the scientist. The Keenan paper suggests that this is a frequent problem among engineers. Engineers receive sophisticated training (e.g., in mathematics) that results in skills often not required by their job. In one study, more than half of the engineers complained that many aspects of their jobs could be handled by someone with less training.

Boundary Role

Another source of stress or interpersonal conflict comes from occupying a *boundary role*, one that connects the organization with the external environment. There is some evidence that engineers who are in such roles experience more stress and strain than other engineers. Individuals in boundary roles frequently complain that they experience greater deadline pressure, fewer opportunities to do the work they prefer, and less opportunity for advancement. They also claim that they are not attaining the maximum utilization of their professional skills.

Coping with Conflict and Stress

The ways engineers cope with work-related stress is discussed by Newton and Keenan [1985], who point out that there are different ways in which one can cope. For example, one can talk with others, take direct action, withdraw from the situation, or simply resent it. Exactly what is done depends on (1) individual differences (for example, people who are characterized as having a Type A personality are more likely to be resentful), and (2) situational variables (for example, withdrawal or doing as little as possible occurs more frequently among those who work in organizations that lack a supportive climate). Withdrawal appears to be more common in some fields of engineering than in others. Also, the way the person looks at the stressful situation determines whether the person will talk to others or take action, such as quitting. One cannot generalize and say that there is an effective coping technique that should be taught to everyone, because coping differs from person to person and from organization to organization. It also depends on the way the person perceives the conflict situation. Nevertheless, in training engineers and scientists, we can sensitize them to intraperson conflict, and teach them stress–reduction techniques (such as biofeedback). Often, being able to understand that role conflict and role ambiguity are "normal" in organizations makes dealing with such conflict more manageable. Facing the conflict squarely by "negotiating" one's role is most helpful.

It is important to realize that one of the best ways to reduce role ambiguity and role conflict is to use participative management. In participative management situations employees determine what they are going to do, when they are going to do it, and how they are going to do it. When such factors are decided either by the supervisor or by the job itself, i.e., by "external" determinants, there is more role conflict and role ambiguity [Jackson and Schuler, 1985]. In this study, which analyzed 29 correlates of role ambiguity and conflict, it was found that across a large number of empirical investigations the best correlates of low conflict were participation and feedback. In other words, when the employee sets the task cooperatively with the supervisor and the supervisor (or the task) provides feedback to the employee there is minimal role conflict. Incidentally, the same study showed that when there is conflict there is tension, dissatisfaction, and low self-ratings of performance.

8.2 CONFLICT BETWEEN INDIVIDUALS

Evan [1965a,b] has developed a typology of interpersonal conflict in organizations. Three types of conflict in two distinct areas can be defined. There can be conflict (1) with peers, (2) with supervisors, or (3) with subordinates, and this conflict can occur in the technical area and in the interpersonal area. Conflict with peers, supervisors, or subordinates in the technical area involves technical goals, milestones, the means of reaching a particular goal, and interpretation of data. Conflict with peers or subordinates at the interpersonal level involves personal likes and dislikes, trust, and fear that the other person misperceives what one is doing. The conflict with the supervisor usually deals with project administration or with power relationships. This includes conflict over who is supposed to decide what to do or what rules or procedures are in effect.

Research shows that conflict is more likely to occur in those situations in which two individuals have different attitudes and values. In one such situation, for instance, one person believes it is very important to keep a distance between the supervisor and subordinate, while the other person does not think that a large distance is appropriate. Similarly, one person may require an exact clarification of rules or specifications of what is to be done, while the other person does not feel that such clear statements are necessary. Conflict can also arise if one person believes that people should be independent, while the other person thinks that there should be greater interdependence and coordination in activities, and that the most important thing is to have good interpersonal relationships.

Such conflict is more acute when one or both of the individuals are cognitively simple, and tend to see things in black and white, in stereotypes, or in a very simple manner. Generally, the conflict is less important when the people are cognitively complex. Some conflict can be traced to incompatible personalities. It is beyond the scope of this book to discuss this type of conflict, but when it occurs, counseling or the use of a clinical psychologist ought to be investigated by management.

Conflict in general is more difficult to reduce when there are major discrepancies of power. If one person can totally dominate the other, it is possible for the lower status person to take the view that he has nothing to lose if he makes a tremendous mess of the relationship. When the relationship has a reasonable balance of power (in other words, the subordinate has some power) the relationship is likely to allow reductions of conflict. It is obvious, also, that when two people have a history of bad relationships with others and with each other, it is much more difficult to improve these relationships in the future. One of the ways to get around poor relationships is to put the two people into a situation in which they have what is known as a *superordinate goal*, that is a goal that both of them want to attain and that neither can reach without the help of the other. Creating opportunities for communication, getting help from professional counselors, and organizational restructuring should all be considered as alternative options to reduce this type of conflict.

8.3 CONFLICT BETWEEN GROUPS

Conflict between groups is very common in organizations. In what follows, we will summarize some of the major finding in social psychology concerning the study of intergroup relationships [Worchel and Austin, 1985].

In-Groups, Out-Groups

The first point is that it is very easy to create confrontations between *in-groups* and *out-groups*. An in-group is one with which the individual is ready to cooperate and whose members consist of individuals who trust each other. An out-group consists of people one distrusts.

It is very easy to create in-group/out-group distinctions. For example, in a laboratory experiment, one can take teenagers and say to them "You belong to the yellow group" and the others constitute "the red group." With no other visible distinction, one says: "All right, you yellows, here is a pile of money. Divide the money between your group and the other group." This simple manipulation is sufficient to make the individuals who do the dividing favor their in-group. For instance, they may give 60% of the money to the in-group and 40% to the out-group. It is as if there were a natural way of thinking that "since I belong to this group and the other group is my 'enemy,' it is natural for me to give more to my group and to be a little distrustful of the other group." The research also shows that out-groups are perceived as more homogeneous than in-groups. In other words, the "other" people are "all the same." By contrast, in-groups are perceived as relatively heterogeneous. The members of one's in-group are perceived as "all different" from one another. These tendencies imply that we stereotype members of out-groups and may perceive them more inaccurately than we perceive the in-groups.

It is useful to distinguish relationships that are *intergroup* from those that are *interpersonal*. In an interpersonal relationship, the individual is very much aware of who the other is. In the intergroup relationship, the individual is not aware of the other's personal characteristics. For example, if you shoot at the enemy you do not care who the particular individual is. It is just a global reaction or judgment about the other person as a representative of a group. Intergroup relationships are more likely to develop than interpersonal relationships under the following five conditions: (1) when there is intense conflict, (2) when there is a history of conflicts, (3) when there is a strong attachment to the in-group, (4) when there is anonymity of membership in the out-group, and (5) when there is no possibility of moving from the in-group to the out-group.

Let us examine these conditions with an example from the relationship between researchers and marketing specialists. If the marketing specialists look at the world in a different way from the way the researchers look at the world, then there is much more likelihood that the researchers will say that the marketing people are "all the same". On the other hand, if there is less conflict they may see differences between one member of the marketing group and other members of this group. Second, if there is a history of conflict between the two groups then they are much more likely to look at each other in terms of their group rather than as individuals. Also, if the researchers feel very strongly about being researchers or the marketing types feel very strongly about being marketing types, they will perceive the people in the other group as undifferentiated. Anonymity means that you do not really know who the other people are. A marketing committee will make a decision and say "No!," or send a letter to the research people that says "we have decided not to support your proposal." There is no indication of who the people are that made the decision and this increases the tendency to perceive them as all alike, as a group, and not as individuals. Finally, perception also tends to be intergroup when there is no possibility of moving from one group to another, as happens when the organizational structure is such that engineers and scientists never work in marketing or market department members do not work in research.

The interesting thing is that in-group favoritism occurs even when these five conditions do *not* operate! In other words, intergroup favoritism is such a common and fundamental idea (given that you are in my group I *must* favor you) that people are not critical of their own actions. In order to show favoritism, people do not need tension or conflict, a history of conflict, strong attachment to their group, anonymity of the out-group, or the inability to move to the other group.

The fact that the out-group is seen as a homogeneous entity means that stereotypes increase. Stereotypes are overdetermined because they occur for at least two reasons: (1) it is easier (requires less cognitive work) to *see* others as being more or less alike; and (2) it is so much simpler to *deal* with others as if they were alike. Studies have shown that people are more likely to generalize in the negative direction (toward criticism) from the behavior of one individual who is a member of an out-group to the whole out-group than to do so in the case of the in-group. In our example, our researchers are much more likely to stereotype and evaluate unfavorably the whole marketing department on the basis of the behavior of one member of the marketing department than they are likely to change their view of the research department on the basis of the behavior of one researcher.

Biased Information-Processing

An interesting example of biased information-processing is that people attribute positive actions by the in-group to internal aspects (e.g., they are honest), but positive actions by out-group members are considered due to external aspects (e.g., they were forced to act that way). In other words suppose the marketing people unexpectedly did something very nice for the researchers. The researchers would claim that the marketing department members were forced to act in this way by outside circumstances. On the other hand, if they did something nasty, it would be explained as being "their nature," that is, people make dispositional attributions (they were nasty people) when negative behavior of out-groups is perceived. Conversely, if the researchers (the in-group) did something nice, it would be ex-

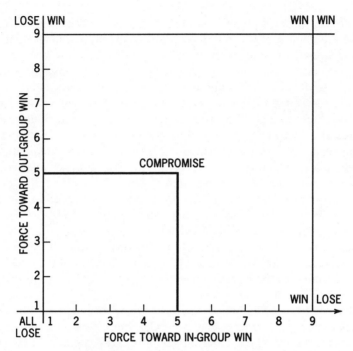

Figure 8.1. Intergroup win–lose orientation.

plained as "their nature," but if they did something nasty, they would be perceived to have acted that way as a result of external circumstances.

Coping with Conflict between Groups

What we said in the case of interpersonal conflict also applies in the case of intergroup conflict: if superordinate goals (goals of *both* groups that neither group can reach without the help of the other) can be found, the relationship can be improved.

There are two orientations that one can adopt in an intergroup situation: one is called a *win–lose* orientation and the other a *win–win* orientation. In the win–lose orientation, one tries to win for one's in-group something that the out-group loses, while in the win–win orientation, one tries to win something for both groups. Another way to look at conflict is to examine the Conflict Resolution Grid of Blake and Mouton [1986, p. 76]. The win–win orientation corresponds to position 9.9. The win–lose orientations are 1.9 and 9.1. Two other orientations—compromise and all lose—both less satisfactory than the win–win, are also shown on the diagram of Figure 8.1.

For example, suppose the researchers have a design that satisfies many technical and production criteria, but which the marketing people find almost impossible to market. In a win–lose orientation the technical people manage to impose the design or the marketing people manage to eliminate the design from further consideration. In a win–win orientation a new design is developed that has the advantages visualized by the research group, but also the advantages of the ideal marketable design. Other positions shown on the diagram would be the lose–lose position in which no design is adopted, and the compromise position in which a design is adopted that has some, but not all, of the desirable elements of the designs of each of the groups in conflict. It is obvious that the win–win orientation is the most desirable. However, it should also be obvious that in order to reach that design one has to be very creative, and come up with a very new concept. Such a concept may have none of the elements of the original design of the technical people, or the elements of the original ideas of the marketing people. It is a fact that the win–win solution requires "insights" not available before the confrontation took place that leads to successful conflict resolution. So, in this case we can talk about "productive" or "constructive" conflict, as opposed to talking about "destructive" conflict.

Research shows that the win–lose orientation is associated with cognitive distortions, that make the outcome of the conflict undesirable for both sides. The "product" that is an outcome of this conflict (e.g., a negotiated agreement) is likely to the poor. In such cases the position of the in-group is perceived as very much more desirable than the position of the out-group. While the in-group knows its position well, it does not know or fully understand the position of the out-group. The position of the in-group appears to be much more desirable than it is. The "common ground" between the two positions is seen as belonging to the in-group's solution, and the in-group perceives only its own position as acceptable, using a "narrow cognitive field" to understand the positions of the various parties. In other words, in the win–lose orientation, the groups look at the conflict in a distorted, overly simple way.

In the case of a win–win orientation the product of the conflict (e.g., the negotiated agreement) often shows much creativity. It is more insightfully conceived and therefore more valuable. The in-group does not distort its view of the desirability of its own solution, and understands much better the position of the out-group than is the case in win–lose orientation. The full complexity of the issues is perceived. In other words, in the win–win orientation there is little distortion and the perception of the positions and values of the proposals of each party in the conflict is realistic.

On the other hand, when a win–win orientation is used, there usually is acceptance of the other side. There is trust, confidence, and communication between the two groups. Usually there are no threats and there is less cognitive distortion. In other words, people do understand that there is common ground between their position and the other side's position. Also, they look for and are likely to adopt a creative orientation. In other words, they say, "Let's solve this problem together and let's solve it creatively. Let us find a solution that we have not thought about before, that will be satisfactory to both sides."

The distortions of information processing are particularly strong when there is no objective way to evaluate the information each side presents to the other. Distortions are minimized when the behavior of the other group is predictable. Predictability also has an impact on the trust that each group feels toward the other. We trust people whose behavior we can anticipate.

One of the issues that comes up quite often when there is intergroup conflict concerns the question of who should go to a negotiation session? There is research showing that a satisfactory agreement is less likely to be reached when the negotiation session is attended by representatives of the group and not by the whole group. In other words, the representatives feel constrained by the fact that they are representing a group and so have little flexibility to move. They freeze in a particular position and the two sides become deadlocked. On the other hand, when the whole group participates in the discussions there is usually some movement. If there is a choice, it is, therefore, much better to have a session in which both groups are present in the negotiations.

When a representative is given full power to represent the group and reach an agreement as he/she sees fit (in other words, when he does not need to go back to the group to convince its members that a particular decision is the best one obtainable), deadlock can be avoided. Such representatives represent their group, and also represent themselves. When they see that there is a possibility of an agreement they agree. It is a desirable (low conflict) condition when the meeting becomes an interpersonal meeting involving two representatives of the two groups honestly seeking to reach the best agreement that they, as individuals, can reach. The chances of creative solutions increase in such situations. The disadvantage of this solution however is that the group often feels the representative did not get a "good enough" agreement.

There are certain conditions that increase the probability that the intergroup conflict will become productive rather than destructive. First, when there is a perception that cooperation is highly desirable. Second, when the out-group is seen as being heterogeneous rather than homogeneous (in other words, when we teach members of the in-group that there are people with different views in the out-group). Third, when the in-group and the out-group have common goals. Fourth, when there is mobility and some members of the in-group were members of the out-group in the past.

This is one of the rationales for job rotation in an R&D organization. By having people in organizations change their jobs and moving them from one department to another, they become able to deal with members of these other departments in conflict situations. Finally, it is helpful to have a condition in which the in–group is not using the conflict with the out-group as a means of consolidating the leadership position of the in-group's leader. In some situations the in-group is not sufficiently cohesive and its leader tries to create unity by leading the in-group into battle. This, however, is highly undesirable since it makes conflict difficult to resolve.

Conflict can become destructive when one or both sides see only a single issue as important. Usually when several issues are involved, it is possible for each side to concede on some issues, but when only one issue is critical, it is difficult for one or the other of the two sides to yield.

Blake and Mouton [1986] have described in detail their approach to conflict resolution. They utilized groups of 20–30 executives from industry who came together for 2 weeks to discuss interpersonal and intergroup relations. They were first exposed to controlled laboratory experiments, and then to the results of the experiments.

In Phase 1, in-groups were formed and in-group cohesiveness developed. Usually each in-group was concerned that another group might "do better," and these feelings were expressed kiddingly during coffee breaks. At that point, each group was provided with an identical human relations problem. The solutions were then compared by the researchers who explicitly stated which solution was better and why, thus creating competition and a win–lose orientation. In some cases a group of outside judges was used or each group was invited to do the judging. When a group evaluated its own solution in relation to the others, it typically focused on the differences between solutions and the good points of its own solution, ignoring the strengths of the other group's solution.

Blake and Mouton discuss the barriers to cooperation that arise from the win–lose orientation. Of special interest to R&D managers who may be in conflict with accountants, finance experts, or marketing specialists, is that these, and other [e.g., Davis and Triandis, 1971] studies show that one can resolve conflict better if the entire groups meet together rather than when each group elects a representative to negotiate with the other side. In short, have all the people in your department who are affected meet with all the accountants or the marketing people who are relevant.

Conflict is usually resolved better when the solution is arrived at by the two parties in conflict than when the solution is imposed by outsiders. It is very helpful to identify distortions in perception, which occur when one's perspectives become narrow, as usually happens when one is tense, or when one thinks the in-group products are much more desirable and of higher quality than they really are, or if the common ground between the solutions of the two sides seems to be part of the in-group's solution exclusively. This job can often be helped by having a third party listen to the positions of the two sides.

Superordinate goals have been found to be helpful in reducing conflict. As already mentioned, such goals are common goals that one side cannot reach without the help of the other. Experiments, field studies, and consultant experiences suggest that such goals are highly desirable. Managers will do well to search for and foster such goals for groups that might be in conflict.

8.4 INTERCULTURAL CONFLICT

Intercultural conflict is a special case of intergroup conflict. "Culture" here is defined as unstated assumptions, beliefs, norms, roles, and values found in a group that speaks a particular language and lives in a specific time period and place. Potentially, there can be cultural conflict whenever people speak a different language including dialects (e.g., black English), live in a different place (e.g., Australia versus Canada), or have been socialized in different time periods (e.g., old versus young). Other contrasts, such as differences in religion, social class, and race can also create intercultural conflict.

Socialization in a particular culture results in a specific "world view." Unstated assumptions (e.g., one must not start a new venture without consulting an astrologer), customs, and ways of thinking (e.g., starting with facts and abstracting a generalization versus starting with a generalization or an ideological position and finding facts that fit it) can create more trouble in interpersonal or intergroup relationships than even having something valuable to divide. This is because unstated assumptions appear so natural to the thinker. Intercultural disagreement can be more damaging to interpersonal relationships than disagreement within culture situations because rational arguments are not particularly helpful.

One often finds a cultural mixture of people working together in R&D laboratories since selection is usually on the basis of competence. For example, in the U.S. observatory in Chile, the staff is largely Chilean, but many of the scientists are from North America. Thus, it is important to consider what to do to improve intergroup relationships in situations of intercultural conflict.

There are numerous techniques, most of which involve training, that are designed to improve intercultural relationships. Triandis [1977] describes them in some detail and Landis and Brislin [1983] do so in even greater detail. These publications are designed for social scientists who will train others. Managers of R&D laboratories will want to know only that these techniques exist and what they do.

There are basically four approaches to intercultural training: the cognitive approach, the affective approach, the behavioral approach, and self-insight.

The Cognitive Approach. The cognitive approach teaches people the world view of the other culture. This is done with a series of "critical incidents" in which interpersonal behaviors between members of cultures A and B are described. After each incident, there are four explanations of the behavior of the people in the incident. If one is training a person from culture A to understand the point of view of persons from culture B, three of the four explanations are commonly given by people in culture A and one by people from culture B. The incident and the explanations, presented in multiple choice format, are shown to the trainee, who chooses one explanation, turns to the appropriate page, and receives feedback on the choice. If the trainee has chosen the correct explanation, about a page of feedback is given that explains the particular cultural point of view and the probable reasons for its emergence in that culture (i.e., it is usually functional to have that point of view in that culture). When the trainee chooses an "incorrect" explanation, the feedback simply instructs him or her to read the episode one more time and choose another explanation. Thus, the trainee is gradually exposed to the point of view of the other culture. The construction of these training materials has been streamlined, and the determination of what answers are to be included is done empirically. Albert [1983] provides a detailed explanation of how to construct such training materials. Evaluation studies have shown that people trained with such materials feel better about their relationships with members of other cultures.

The Affective Approach. The affective approach involves exposing trainees to situations in which their emotions are aroused when in interaction with members of the other culture. This can be done by having them interact with members of the other culture in specific situations. When negative emotions develop, they are exposed to a positive experience that competes with the negative emotions. In some cases, simply breathing deeply or doing some exercise that reduces stress in the presence of the negative emotion is helpful. In other cases, arranging for pleasant experiences, such as the sharing of tasty food, listening to enjoyable music, or being exposed to agreeable perfumes can create the right mood.

The Behavioral Approach. The behavioral approach involves shaping the behavior of the trainee to make sure that behaviors that are objectionable in the other culture do not occur. For example, crossing your legs and showing the bottom of your shoes is absolutely insulting in some cultures, but many Americans do this and are not even aware of it. Simply telling them that they must not do it (the cognitive approach) is not effective. They have to experience rewards and punishments that will change their habits. The best way to accomplish this is to reward a competing behavior, such as keeping one's shoes on the ground.

Self-Insight. Self-insight is an approach designed to make the trainee understand how much culture influences behavior. The aim, in this case, is to give the trainee a chance to analyze his or her own culture. Understanding how much of one's own behavior is under the influence of norms, customs, and values unique to one's culture can be very instructive. The technique used in this kind of training is to have the trainee interact with a person who is a trained actor and acts in the *opposite* way from the way people in the trainee's culture usually act. The experience of interaction with such a person and discussion of the experience with the trainer makes very clear that one's behavior and feelings are shaped by culture. When people know how culture influences their behavior, they are able to be more sensitive to culture as a variable affecting social behavior and interaction.

These four ways of training are not incompatible. On the contrary, they are complementary. A good program of training will use all of them in some mixture. It is beyond the scope of this book to discuss how to develop such training. The important point is for the manager to know that such training does exist, that it can be provided by social scientists specialized in interpersonal and intercultural behavior, and that is does help develop better relations and reduce intergroup conflict.

8.5 PERSONAL STYLES OF CONFLICT RESOLUTION

Each person has a particular style for resolving conflict. Do you want to know what your style is? If you do, respond to the statements in Table 8.1 by strongly agreeing (score it a 5), agreeing (4), disagreeing (2), or strongly disagreeing (score it 1) with each item. If you are not sure, use a score of 3. In the blanks imagine the words *boss*, *subordinates*, or *peers*. You can do this three times, to get an idea of your style when you are dealing with these three types of people. It is likely that your style will be a bit different when you deal with your boss than when you deal with your subordinates or peers. *Please do this before you read the next paragraph.*

Now take another look at Figure 8.1. The win–win style of that figure corresponds to the *integrative* style of conflict resolution, i.e., when you try to get all the information and jointly come up with a creative solution that satisfies all parties in a dispute. Sum your scores to items 1, 4, 6, 15, 28, 29, and 35 and divide by 7 to get your score on the integrative style.

The lose–win corner of Figure 8.1 corresponds to the *obliging style*, when you try to give in to the other. To measure that style, sum your scores to items 2, 12, 13, 17, 25, and 30 and divide by 6.

The win–lose corner of Figure 8.1 corresponds to the *dominating style*, when you try to impose your views on others. To measure this style sum the scores to items 10, 11, 18, 24, 27, and 31 and divide by 6.

The lower left corner of Figure 8.1 corresponds to the *avoiding style*, where you avoid conflict. To get a measure of that style, sum your scores to items 3, 7, 22, 23, 32, 33, and 34 and divide by 7. Finally, the compromise position of Figure 8.1 corresponds to the *compromising style*, and can be measured by summing items 9, 20, 21, and 26 and dividing by 4.

The Rahim Conflict Resolution Style Inventory (Table 8.1) was developed by Rahim [1983], who validated the items, and reported how various groups

TABLE 8.1   The Rahim Conflict Resolution Style Inventory*

1. I try to investigate an issue with my _____ to find a solution acceptable to us.
2. I generally try to satisfy the needs of my _____.
3. I attempt to avoid being "put on the spot" and try to keep my conflict with my _____ to myself.
4. I try to integrate my ideas with those of my _____ to come up with a decision jointly.
5. I give some to get some.
6. I try to work with my _____ to find solutions to a problem that satisfy our expectations.
7. I usually avoid open discussion of my differences with my _____.
8. I usually hold on to my solution to a problem.
9. I try to find a middle course to resolve an impasse.
10. I use my influence to get my ideas accepted.
11. I use my authority to make a decision in my favor.
12. I usually accommodate the wishes of my _____.
13. I give in to the wishes of my _____.
14. I win some and lose some.
15. I exchange accurate information with my _____ to solve a problem together.
16. I sometimes help my _____ to make a decision in his favor.
17. I usually allow concessions to my _____.
18. I argue my case with my _____ to show the merits of my position.
19. I try to play down our differences to reach a compromise.
20. I usually propose a middle ground for breaking deadlocks.
21. I negotiate with my _____ so that a compromise can be reached.
22. I try to stay away from disagreement with my _____.
23. I avoid an encounter with my _____.
24. I use my expertise to make a decision in my favor.
25. I often go along with the suggestions of my _____.
26. I use "give and take" so that a compromise can be made.
27. I am generally firm in pursuing my side of the issue.
28. I try to bring all our concerns out in the open so that the issue can be resolved in the best possible way.
29. I collaborate with my _____ to come up with decisions acceptable to us.
30. I try to satisfy the expectation of my _____.
31. I sometimes use my power to win a competitive situation.
32. I try to keep my disagreement with my _____ to myself in order to avoid hard feelings.
33. I try to avoid unpleasant exchanges with my _____.
34. I generally avoid an argument with my _____.
35. I try to work with my _____ for a proper understanding of a problem.

* From M. A. Rahim, "A measurement of style of handling interpersonal conflict," copyright 1983, *Academy of Management Journal*, 371–372, Reprinted by permission.

respond to it. For example, females were found to use more integrating, avoiding, and compromising and less obliging styles than males.

8.6 UNIQUE ISSUES OF CONFLICT IN R&D ORGANIZATIONS

For a research organization, there are some ethical issues that either create special cases of conflict or provide a rather different framework for resolving conflicts. The following discussion of conflict within individuals, interpersonal conflict, and intergroup conflict focuses specifically on R&D organizations.

Conflict within Individuals. The need to find an intellectually challenging research environment, necessary research facilities, and, indeed, the simple need for employment forces many scientists to work in an organized environment. In addition, the needs of the organization and of society as they relate to a research project can be at variance with the moral beliefs or convictions of individual scientists. Some recent cases have involved scientists who are opposed to R&D related to the defense industry. However, when one looks at investment by defense organizations in R&D worldwide, it should come as no surprise that the majority of scientists are involved in activities related to the defense industry. However, managers should be aware that many scientists feel differently about the direction and nature of research programs in the defense industry. When some prominent scientists at major research universities in the United States question programs such as the Strategic Defense Initiative, the so-called "Star Wars" they are perhaps responding to a conflict between their desire to make a contribution to science and their disapproval of the expenditure of resources for research programs that, from their perspective, may be serving no meaningful human needs. In an open democratic society such differences should be expected.

Interpersonal Conflict. One scientist may be competing with another scientist within a research group for promotion, status (for example, principal investigator versus associate investigator), or other rewards (attending conferences, office space, etc.). Since many of these things are perceived by the individual as a zero sum game, the ethos of a scientific community, which emphasizes cooperation, universalism, and sharing of ideas as its underpinning, is often lacking. This, in turn, creates conflicts within the organization and also adversely affects the productivity of the organization.

Intergroup Conflicts. It is not unusual for one group in a research organization to compete with another for projects or resources. This inevitably creates conflicts. Again, the total resources and other amenities (such as laboratory space) that are available are finite. If one group gets a certain portion of these resources, then the other group may feel that they did not get their fair share. This inevitably leads to some conflicts and also may lead to a lack of cooperation between the groups. Some organizations have competing divisions undertake the same research project. This type of competition can, for some situations, speed up the innovation process by making participants work very hard and perhaps work very cooperatively within the division. Competition among different research groups in an R&D organization is inevitable and so is some of the resultant conflict. Some of this competition and conflict may in fact be beneficial. This may provide motivation to excel and thus positively affect performance. Benefits may exceed any adverse effect that may result from conflict and a lower level of cooperation among different groups.

Perhaps one should look at the fundamental issues involved with problems created when there is no sharing of knowledge or cooperation and conflict is viewed as a zero-sum game in which one group loses proportionately what the other one gains.

Zero-sum conflict needs to be avoided, and alternatives must be sought. One must take the position that most, if not all, conflicts can be translated into win–win situations provided people have sufficient imagination and creativity. If the contestants see their confrontation as the result of a lack of creativity (rather than due to conflict), this lack of creativity becomes "our problem." One no longer sees the other side as the "enemy," but as a collaborator in the search for creative solutions that will be mutually satisfactory.

One of the problems one often faces in organizations is well described by the concept of the "tragedy of the commons." If every individual acts in a selfish way, the individual will obtain short-term benefits but the community will suffer. How can we persuade individuals to act less selfishly? Group discussions, in which norms of proper behavior in the laboratory are examined and shaped, can be beneficial. The individual can then be told: "You are not behaving the way we all agreed to behave." Some retaliation or "fines" for incorrect or norm-violating behavior may be needed in the case of certain individuals, but most people are sufficiently concerned about their good name to adapt their behavior to the norms.

Supervisors can also help by discussing with their subordinates the need for cooperation rather than competition. In doing this, they might use the results of a study that may or may not apply to all researchers, but that certainly seem convincing. In that study the researchers sampled all the social psychologists who were members of an elite organization. Membership in the organization required several refereed publications that were judged as significant by its membership committee. At the time of the study, the organization had a membership of 200. A random sample of 200 "ordinary" social psychologists was also obtained. These 400 individuals received a personality test in the mail. About 60% of each sample completed the test. One of the attributes measured by the test was "competitiveness." The data show that those who belonged to the elite organization were significantly *less* competitive than those who belonged to the random sample of social psychologists. One interpretation of these results is that the more competitive social psychologists were so concerned with whether or not they were doing well that they did less significant research than the elite social psychologists. In other words, some good advice to give to subordinates is: "Do your best, work hard, and do not worry about what other people are doing."

An important benefit of noncompetition with other scientists is the increased likelihood of joint publications. When researchers discuss their work with others, and are not protective and secretive, it is more likely that joint publications will occur. Some of these publications may be of higher quality because they are joint. In short, noncompetitiveness, openness, and cooperation may have great advantages. Finally, the emphasis on joint publications is desirable because such publications constitute a superordinate goal (see above).

8.7 ETHICS

Two principles of ethics should be stressed in the laboratory: *reciprocity* and *benefiting the least powerful*.

Reciprocity is an old principle found in the ethical systems of both East and West. The dictum "Whatsoever ye would that men should do to you, do ye even so to them: for this is the law and the prophets" (*Matthew*, 7, 12) can be translated into "Do not do unto others what you do not want others to do unto you."

The principle of benefiting the least powerful is less well-known, and is based on the idea that in every social system some have more power than others. In a lab, the supervisors have more power than the subordinates and directors and principal investigators more than nondirectors and nonprincipal investigators; those with large research budgets have more power than those with small budgets, and so on. When a conflict develops between two people with unequal power, the more powerful has the duty to act generously (*noblesse oblige*.) If there is any doubt, bend backward to benefit the less powerful. So, if there is doubt, about who should be a co-author on a paper, the principal investigator should make sure that those without power are listed as co-authors.

8.8 SUMMARY

Conflict within individuals, in the form of role conflict or role ambiguity is widespread. Individuals who understand this can do something to manage it better. Conflict between individuals is also common, and developing superordinate goals is very helpful in reducing it. Conflict between groups is commonplace. There are a number of ways of reducing conflict, including taking a win–win orientation, emphasizing problem-solving and creativity, finding superordinate goals, and developing a system of norms and laboratory ethics that will reduce it.

8.9 QUESTIONS FOR CLASS DISCUSSION

1 What forms of role conflict are likely to develop in R&D organizations?

2 What are some of the major ways to reduce intergroup conflict?

3 What are some of the major ways to avoid intercultural conflict?

8.10 FURTHER READINGS

Albert, R. (1983). The cultural sensitizer or culture assimilator. In D. Landis and R. Brislin (Eds.), *Handbook of Intercultural Training*, Vol. 2. New York: Pergamon.

Kanfer, F. H. and B. K. Schefft (1987). Self-management therapy in clinical practice. In N. S. Jacobson (Ed.). *Psychotherapists in Clinical Practice*. New York: Guilford.

9

PERFORMANCE APPRAISAL—EMPLOYEE CONTRIBUTION—IN R&D ORGANIZATIONS

In this chapter we will examine what researchers and managers in R&D organizations do, and the way we can tell how well they do it. We will also discuss the need for focusing less on "appraisal" (evaluation, judgment) and more on employee contribution to the organization.

Accepted wisdom would suggest that for an organization to function efficiently and effectively, the employees must work well toward meeting organizational goals and objectives. From a manager's point of view, it would seem prudent to reward those employees whose performance contributes to organizational success. Logically, performance appraisal systems need to be designed to motivate employees to improve performance and thus contribute to organizational productivity, effectiveness, and excellence.

In practice, there are many problems. Few management activities have challenged and intrigued executives as much as performance appraisal has. To some, appraisal suggests supervisors sitting in judgment as "Roman Emperors." To others, performance appraisal is thought of as a method of manipulating employees and intruding into their lives.

9.1 SOME NEGATIVE CONNOTATIONS OF PERFORMANCE APPRAISAL

The problem may lie in the negative connotations of the words "performance appraisal." Appraisal implies evaluation and making judgments as to the quality and quantity of an individual's productivity. To make such an evaluation or a judgment, a certain yardstick has to be available to ascertain whether the individual has measured up to the performance level envisioned by the evaluator. How is one to compare the performance of one individual who has clearly exceeded the low standards he set for himself versus another individual who failed to meet the rather difficult standards he set for himself? Dimensions associated with the yardstick are variable and procedures available to evaluate many of these dimensions are subjective and often not well understood by the employee or the supervisor.

Would changing the focus from "performance appraisal" to employee "contribution" to the organization make a difference? Would this allow the supervisor to move away from evaluation in a negative sense and move to the concept of employee contribution to the organization? Would this allow the supervisor to say that, "Your contribution to the organization has been..."? The discussion can then move on to how the organization could provide the right environment, support, and resources for this contribution to be increased, and perhaps allow for achieving goal congruence between the employee and the organization objectives.

We often talk about the "success" of an individual and, in turn, the success of the organization in which the individual works. We find that we define success in terms of organization profitability, productivity, or effectiveness. Is it really possible to define "success" without defining "failure"? Has an organization failed if it is not profitable for one year? Has the employee failed if the organization does not stay profitable every quarter, every year? Temporal aspects of success and failure are often overemphasized in organizations. The performance review process is tied too closely to time periods, with the focus on achievements during 6 months or a year, while R&D organizations need to look at achievements over the long-term, say, 3–5 years.

Let us take the case of Employee "A," who attempts ten activities, succeeds in eight, but fails in two, vs. Employee "B," who attempts five activities and succeeds in all. Experience clearly shows that the weight given to failure is greater than the weight given to successes. Consequently, the probability is very high that Employee "B" would be rated higher than Employee "A" by the supervisor. This could be partly due to the emphasis on making judgments and evaluations rather than focusing on employee contribution to the organization. Employee "A" may in fact have made a considerably higher contribution to the organization than Employee "B." In an R&D organization, where the nature of work would naturally include some failures, this example case would point to a fundamental problem in the employee appraisal system. Employees who are risk averse and low performers are likely to get better appraisals than innovative researchers who take initiative and make mistakes.

Recognizing that some of these issues are crucial to enhancing employee contribution to the organization, the first discussion that follows focuses on *difficulties with employee appraisal*. It is often stated that performance appraisal needs to be linked to the managerial activities and the management system, and that performance appraisal should be tied to the stage of development of the organization. These items, along with performance appraisal and organizational productivity, are discussed. Most technology-based R&D organizations are staffed by engineers and scientists. Since there are differences in the goals and aspirations of engineers and scientists, as discussed in this chapter, the concept of employee contribution needs to be differentiated for engineers and scientists.

In an acquisitive and consumption-oriented modern society, monetary rewards could be thought of as the litmus test for the level of contribution an employee makes to the organization. As seen in the discussions that follow, *monetary rewards* do not work out as well as one would initially assume. After discussing performance appraisal in practice and the university department case, we propose a *performance appraisal implementation strategy* that focuses on employee contribution to the organization.

9.2 DIFFICULTIES WITH EMPLOYEE APPRAISAL

When a supervisor appraises a subordinate the process of appraisal can be analyzed as follows: First, the supervisor must have observed some performances. However, such observations in the case of R&D personnel are unlikely to be sufficiently coherent to be valid. If the supervisor were to observe a simple operation, he might be able to judge it. But R&D work is complex, and doing any one thing well is unlikely to provide a clue to the total performance. Thus, rather than observe an individual's specific performance the supervisor is much more likely to observe large chunks of performance, such as the presentation of a research plan, or the completion of a project. Usually these are products of groups rather than individuals. It then becomes difficult to know how much the particular scientist has contributed to the group product.

Second, the observations must be integrated into some sort of "schema." Unfortunately, there are several biases in the formation of such schemata. For example, research has shown that first impressions are extremely important. If the scientist has a good reputation many acts that are ambiguous will be evaluated positively. Also, recent events tend to be given more weight in the formation of such schemata than events that occurred during the middle of the period of observation.

The fact that negative events are given more weight in such judgments than positive events creates a further bias. If the supervisor has observed ten events, and eight are positive and two are negative, the negative ones will be given more weight because they "stand out" as "figures" against the "background" of the eight positive events. This is because in our own lives we generally encounter few negative events, but when we do they are major negatives (e.g., loss of loved ones). On the other hand, although we encounter mostly positive events, they are seldom *major* positive events (e.g., getting married, winning a million dollars), and so we become especially vigilant about the negatives. Furthermore, a manager who overlooks the negative may be far sorrier than a manager who overlooks the positive. After all, if the manager does nothing about a major mistake, top management will blame the manager; but the manager is not likely to be blamed for failing to praise good performance.

Once the "schema" has been formed, regardless of the observations on which it is based, and it has been distorted by various biases, there is the problem of remembering it long enough to register it on paper. Here we have additional biases influencing what happens. Humans tend to remember positive events better than the negative ones. Also, we are helped in our memories by previous schemata, such as stereotypes. That means we tend to distort what we remember in order to make it consistent with our stereotypes.

When making such judgments we often make major mistakes. For example, we generally do not give proper weight to the "base rates" of events. Suppose a department has a 15% failure rate for the projects that are carried out. When judging a particular failure we usually do not take this into account.

Employee appraisal used in salary administration is affected by numerous other problems such as the "halo effect" (because an employee is good at one thing he is seen as good at a lot of other things) and the "leniency effect" (everybody is first rate). Appraisal ratings tend to correlate with job difficulty, age, pay, and seniority, and tend to increase each year. Such correlations suggest that they are contaminated by other factors.

In order to overcome these difficulties psychologists have developed a number of strategies. These include forcing comparisons among subordinates [in a paired comparison format of N employees the supervisor makes $N(N-1)/2$ comparisons]. This may not really solve the problem because if all of them are excellent they should all get a high rating. Another approach is to ask supervisors to check specific statements using behaviorally anchored scales, or ask them to make forced choices between two statements describing the employee that are of equal social desirability but only one of which correlates highly with performance. In this way, only the selection of the "valid" alternative will ensure that the employee gets a high rating. These matters are beyond the scope of this book and are mentioned here only to sensitize the manager to some of the methods that the personnel department can use that are slight improvements over the simpler rating scales.

There is a good deal of research that shows that observers attribute the other's behavior to internal factors (ability, attitude, personality, effort), while actors attribute their behavior to external factors (the situation, pressure from others, perceived consequences in the particular environment). Such biases are due, in part, to what observers and actors are looking at. The observer looks at the actor, and naturally attributes the actor's behavior to internal causes. The actor looks at the environment and also knows that on other occasions he has acted differently. So, it is the particular environment on *this* occasion that is seen as determining the action.

The attributions we make give meaning to the behavior. If a failure is due to the difficulty of the task it can be excused; if it is due to laziness it cannot. People also tend to use their own behavior as a measure of how "typical" some action of the actor is. They underuse base rates (see above) and they see the actor as more responsible for acts leading to rewards than for acts that prevented failures. Furthermore, if they like the actor, they will attribute good actions to the person and bad actions to the environment; but if they dislike the actor good actions are attributed to the environment and bad actions to the person.

If you keep these biases in attribution in mind, you might be able to improve your judgments. But in any case, a discussion with your subordinates of the way you look at their actions can increase the convergence between your attributions and the attributions made by your subordinates. If you two agree on these attributions, the subordinates will feel that the evaluation has been fair.

9.3 PERFORMANCE APPRAISAL AND THE MANAGEMENT SYSTEM

Performance appraisal needs to be linked to the managerial activities and the management system. Cunningham [1979, p. 657] has categorized the management system into two distinct areas: the *process* of management and the *function* of management. The process of management includes activities such as planning, organizing, controlling, budgeting, and staffing, and the key orientation of these processes focuses on integrating (work activities), making decisions, recording information, motivating, and negotiating. The function of management includes procurement, production, adaptation, and so on. The orientations of these functions are adaptability, productivity, efficiency, and bargaining.

The managerial processes are concerned with the administration of inputs, while the managerial function deals with the way inputs produce outputs (production) that are important and relevant to the organization. Managerial processes respond to day-to-day problems, and primarily involve problem-solving. The managerial functions, on the other hand, are concerned with prescribing specific operations, procedures, and standards for achieving a certain level of production or output.

Four major activities have been identified under managerial function: adaptability, productivity, efficiency, and bargaining. Twenty-one elements were listed under the managerial process. They included items such as integration, information recording, decision-making, and motivation. In evaluating managerial performance, the manager's effectiveness in accomplishing the specific process and function elements just mentioned can be considered.

9.4 PERFORMANCE APPRAISAL AND ORGANIZATIONAL STAGES

Some of the purposes of performance appraisal relate to management control and to achieving the congruence of organizational and individual goals and objectives. Management control and strategies for goal congruence also depend on the stage of development of the organization, and several other factors such as the technology of the organization.

Salter [1971, p. 41] has defined four stages of corporate development in terms of "the structure of operating units" (dependent variable) and "product–market relationships" (independent variable). In a general sense, at Stage 1, the organization has a single operating unit, producing a single line of products on a small scale. At Stage 2, operating units increase and production becomes large scale, but the focus is still on a single line of product. At Stage 3, operating units may be at different locations and decentralized, each producing different or related products using multiple channels of distribution. At Stage 4, the number of autonomous units producing different products increases. Basically, as organizations move from Stage 1 to 4, the number of autonomous operating units increases, they become geographically decentralized, and the operating units produce technologically different product lines or research outputs for diverse markets using multiple channels of distribution. As this development progresses, the number of variables related to organizational products, operational centers, and market relationships increases. This would also point to the organization increasing in size (number of employees and volume of sales or the size of the research budget); it may, in some cases, lead to an increase in assets and profits.

Management control at each of these four development stages is different. At the earlier stages, the organization is small, and one owner or director can oversee most of the activities. At later stages the organization grows in size and in number of products, and may also by geographically dispersed. As authority becomes decentralized, performance elements need to be designed differently, depending on the development stage of the organization. For example, performance elements could be less formal during the early stages of development and more structured and quantitative later. This approach was successfully used by Salter for four high tech electronic firms. It should be used also by managers whenever they are setting up an appraisal system. Start by analyzing your situation. In what stage is your laboratory? Then design a system that fits your stage.

9.5 PERFORMANCE APPRAISAL AND ORGANIZATION PRODUCTIVITY

Organizational productivity can be defined as the ratio of outputs to inputs. Inputs can be determined by the level of resources invested. Outputs can be conceived as income minus costs. For a profit-making organization, profitability can provide a good measure of the organization's productivity. Since many R&D organizations are nonprofit enterprises, output measures are more complex. Nonetheless, it would seem highly desirable to link performance appraisal to output measures and, thus, provide a link between performance appraisal and organization productivity. We must keep in mind that behavior is shaped by its consequences. If we want specific behaviors to occur we need to use an appraisal system that rewards them when they occur.

Output measures for a research organization can be subjective or objective, quantitative or nonquantitative, discrete or scalar, and can include some measure of quality [Anthony and Herzlinger, 1975, p. 139]. While the measurement of quality requires extra effort and, at times, human judgment, this dimension of output should not be ignored.

Since R&D organizations have multiple objectives and their outputs are often incommensurate, the output measures are usually nonquantitative and subjective. Quantitative measures for the output elements are usually in different units, thus defying precise comparison between different quantitative outputs. Anthony and Herzlinger [1975, p. 145] suggest that it might be feasible to combine a multidimensional array of indicators into aggregate units, which could then provide trends, indicators, and patterns of the individual (and organizational) output measures.

One suggested categorization of output measures includes the following:

- Process measures (related to activities carried out in an organization; useful for the measurement of the current, short-run performance)
- Result measures (stated in measurable terms; end-oriented)
- Social indicators (stated in broad terms, related to overall objectives of the organization rather than specific activities; useful for strategic planning) [Anthony and Herzlinger, 1975 p. 141].

Thus, based on these output measures one could construct requisite performance appraisal elements.

9.6 GOALS OF ENGINEERS VERSUS SCIENTISTS

Most technology-based research and development organizations are staffed by engineers and scientists. In developing performance appraisal systems, differences in the goals and aspirations of engineers and scientists need to be recognized.

In general, influence in an engineering-oriented organization is largely a function of position on the management ladder, while in a science-oriented organization, it is based on the scientist's reputation in the external scientific community. Terms such as "local" and "cosmopolitan" have been used to differentiate between an engineer and a scientist. "Locals," or engineers, are more interested in working on technology that is applicable to the business aims of the company; they pattern their behavior and measure their success against internal company standards. "Cosmopolitans," or scientists, are more interested in new concepts and basic research (the focus here still can be on the business aims of the organization); they interact more freely with the wider scientific community and pattern their behavior and measure their success against its standards [Ritti, 1982, p. 372].

These differences are not so rigid as to exclude one behavior pattern from the other; rather, they are described as typical examples of relative emphases by the two groups. Both groups still desire career development and advancement in their organizations. It is important to note that some scientists in research laboratories have had extensive engineering practice experience and are able to span the boundaries between these two categories.

Scientists and engineers working in technology-based research organizations make contributions to science. This contribution in turn is reflected in the progress science makes. Commenting on scientific progress Brooks, [1973, p. 125] states:

> There are no simple objective measures of scientific progress external to the social processes of the scientific community which produces it. Thus, to evaluate scientific progress we are compelled to rely on a consensus of the scientific communities in each field...the highly structured system of mutual criticism; refereed publications; peer group evaluation of research projects; and personal recognition through prizes, fellowships, and academic appointments constitutes a kind of intellectual marketplace in which scientific contributions are valued in a more or less impersonal way.

Thus, in assessing the performance of many scientists and engineers, their contribution to science as reflected by refereed publications, personal recognition through awards and prizes, and contribution to scientific and professional society activities is quite proper. Since these contributions are external to the firm, "local" types will not do so well. In establishing performance standards, depending on the goals and objectives of the organization, appropriate emphasis can be given to these external contributions. And performance requirements can be established that accommodate the organizational goals and individual capabilities—whether "local" or "cosmopolitan."

Since most R&D organizations have both research and development activities in addition to contribution to science (reflected by publications, etc.), development of marketable products and technical assistance for product improvement should be used as important aspects of performance. In practice, there are conflicts. Researchers who work on successful development projects often feel that their contribution is not as well recognized as researchers conducting mostly basic research. Since most research projects require a team effort, one way to overcome this conflict is to have a team share in the development and research activities based on individual capabilities and interests. Rewards and recognition can then be provided to the whole team. This approach would, in turn, suggest that the best way to structure teams in an R&D organization is to have a mix of locals and cosmopolitans.

9.7 PERFORMANCE APPRAISAL AND MONETARY REWARDS

Giving monetary rewards to those who perform well seems logical enough. In an acquisitive and consumption-oriented modern society, higher pay satisfies basic human needs and more. For an individual, receiving monetary remuneration above what is required for basic human needs can also provide security, autonomy, recognition, and esteem.

The motivation model, generally referred to as the expectancy model, suggests that high performance is likely to occur if the individual feels capable of achieving it, if pay is closely tied to performance level, and if the individual finds pay to be important (this would of course vary across individuals).

In a research and development organization, indeed in most complex professional organizations, a number of reasons make tying pay inexorably to performance appraisal an imprudent approach:

- Significant accomplishments in an R&D organization often require input by many individuals. Singling out one person for a monetary reward creates the problem of inequity for others.
- The purpose of performance appraisal shifts, on the part of the supervisor, to justifying the pay decision already made, and, on the part of the employee, to comparing himself or herself to others and shaping his or her performance data to outdo others.
- Cooperation among peers is reduced because of competition for pay for performance, where total monetary rewards are viewed as a zero-sum game.
- During performance appraisal the employee is likely to exaggerate (some might suggest falsify) his or her performance to gain higher monetary rewards. This would not create the proper environment for counselling and feedback—two of the important purposes of performance appraisal.

It is therefore desirable to hold performance appraisal discussions at one time, and then, later, at a different time, discuss pay increases or monetary rewards, if any. Frequency of discussions can depend on factors such as duration of projects, the employee's tenure, and organization policies. If projects are of long duration these discussions could be as far apart as 6 months or a year; for shorter duration projects discussions could be tied to completion of projects. New employees are most anxious to find out how well they are doing. Feedback after the first 30 days, however brief, is most reassuring to a new employee. Tenured employees are quite satisfied to have these discussions held roughly at a time when some pay decisions are going to be made.

Some of the pay decisions are rather subjective. While no system can provide complete equity in pay, it should be recognized that "relative deprivation" in terms of pay, or any other rewards, acts as a strong demotivator and, thus, adversely affects performance. External equity (by reviewing data from a professional society and other wage surveys) and internal equity (by reviewing the contribution of the individual vis-à-vis others in the organization) are essential. Any mechanism one can use to minimize inequities in pay is worth the effort. Academic institutions often use committees to review performance of faculty members. This tends to minimize individual biases. This practice is not so common in industry and government. Most managers find this committee approach an intrusion into their domain. Periodically seeking input from an independent board or committee about researcher performance can be worthwhile. A manager can always choose to use the outside review to justify a salary decision.

9.8 PERFORMANCE APPRAISAL IN PRACTICE

It is generally felt that a person should know where he or she stands and, consequently, the supervisor should periodically discuss his or her performance with the employee. In practice, however, experience shows that neither the employee nor the supervisor is anxious to participate in the performance appraisal process.

To illustrate this problem, McGregor [1972, p. 134] cites an example. In one company with a well-planned and carefully administered appraisal program, an opinion poll included two questions regarding the performance appraisal system. More than 90% of those answering the questionnaire approved the idea of an appraisal system. Nearly 40% of the respondents indicated they never had performance appraisals done at this company. The record, however, showed that over 80% of them had signed a performance appraisal form and that they had had more than one appraisal interview with their supervisors since they had been with the company. This is an interesting dichotomy. The respondents had no reason to lie, nor was there any reason to believe that the supervisors had falsified the performance appraisal signatures of the employees. The most likely reason is that the supervisors were basically reluctant to undertake performance appraisal activities and, thus, had conducted the interviews in such a perfunctory manner than many subordinates did not realize or did not remember what had happened.

Could this be due to the fact that, in practice, the focus is on "evaluation" and "judgment" rather than on employee "contribution" to the organization?

In additon to the problem described above, it is very difficult to decide exactly what all the elements for performance appraisal ought to be so that measures used include all the behaviors expected, activities to be performed, and results to be achieved by the employee. When strictly quantifiable measures are used, this can introduce an intolerable rigidity into the system to the detriment of overall organizational goals. Subjective performance elements, though necessary, can be criticized because they have a built-in bias. Also, one could argue that in most organizations, the proper environment for mutual (the employee and the supervisor) goal setting and complete trust does not exist. Consequently, the ambivalence about performance appraisal and evaluation continues to be shared by both the supervisor and the employee. In practice, therefore, there are many underlying difficulties with the performance appraisal process. Yet, it is an important activity for organizational effectiveness and employee and organization goal congruence.

9.9 A UNIVERSITY DEPARTMENT CASE

In one university department, each faculty member writes an annual report that includes two pages on each of the following topics: teaching, research, impact, and service. Under teaching, there is information about the quantity and the quality (student comments, syllabi, textbooks written) of the professor's work. Under research, there is information about the particular problem the professor is attacking and the success so far; two reprints of papers from the current year are appended. The impact section indicates what reviewers had to say about the work, who is working on the same topic, how often the professor has been quoted in the refereed literature and by whom, and the number of invitations for major lectures or participation at major conferences or colloquia. The service shows membership on the editorial boards of journals, on national and international committees, and on university committees. The information that is relevant to two categories is entered twice. For example, the invitation to become an editor of a journal is an index of impact, but doing that job is also recorded under service.

The reports for the whole faculty, based on these four categories, are read by a committee of nine elected from among the faculty. Having at least that many members on the committee ensures that the biases of a single judge will be avoided. Getting a substantial panel means balancing different perspectives and provides a range of expert opinion.

The ratings on each of the four criteria are converted into z-scores $[z=(X-\bar{X})/\sigma]$, which have a mean of zero and a standard deviation of σ. The sum of these four z-scores constitutes the professor's evaluation. However, one can use any number of criteria (see Chapter 3 for a discussion of criteria of effectiveness; and especially the following section on Implementation Strategy). If in a given year the department of the particular university receives, let us say, a 5% raise, then those with a sum of z-scores of 0.000 get 5%. Those with z-scores around 1.0 get 10%, and those with -1.0 get nothing. Of course, the formula that translates z-scores to percentages should be arrived at participatively by the laboratory. The point of this example is that this model can be adapted in a number of ways for the use of a particular lab. Members of the lab should be encouraged to take part in the discussions. For example, one might introduce job evaluation as a factor by computing the z-scores only within the same range of job evaluation scores. One might introduce gainsharing by paying some bonus to all on the basis of the success of the whole lab. The 5% figure in the example might be adjusted to take lab performance into account.

One might also provide flexible benefits since different employees have different needs for money, security, status, and so on at different points of their careers. People should also be given some choise of fringe benefits, since not everyone wants the maximum of cash as opposed to vacation time, insurance policies, and so on.

9.10 IMPLEMENTATION STRATEGY WITH EMPHASIS ON EMPLOYEE CONTRIBUTION

The preceding discussion identified some of the underlying issues associated with the performance appraisal system. Commenting on performance appraisal, Dalton [1971, p. 1] states that "few things have been more baffling to managers than the results of their attempts to develop workable performance measures and controls, thus channeling the energies of their employees towards the firm's objectives."

Recognizing all the complex issues involved in implementing a meaningful performance appraisal system, an attempt is made here to focus on three items:

- What does an individual's performance depend on?
- Why performance appraisal is needed.
- A suggested strategy.

Performance Dependency

One of the fundamental question in an R&D organization that needs to be addressed is: What does the performance of an individual really depend on? For a technology-based R&D organization, Roberts [1978, p. 7] points out

"Theory Y is lovely, and McGregor and Maslow are fine. But if you look for explicit measures of what affects a technical person's productivity, then all of the boss's [human] relations skills turn out not to matter very much at all. What matters for more, at the first-line technical organization level, where you're really talking about employing the scientist and engineer more productively, is the technical competence of this first-line supervision."

This is not to say that the supervisor should be insensitive to people and not have the ability to motivate and stimulate the researcher; rather it stresses the crucial role the *supervisor's technical competency plays in productivity* and *excellence*.

Studies indicate that in an R&D organization, the diversity in professional activities and the diversity in skills of American scientists both relate to enhanced levels of performance. Scientists who work on diverse R&D functions (such as basic research, applied research, and consultation) make greater scientific contributions and are more useful to their organizations than those who do not work in diverse areas. In addition, scientists who spend part of their time in teaching or doing administrative work outperform those whose sole activity is research. Diversity in terms of knowledge of several areas of specialization (rather than just one) and involvement in more than just a single research project are also related to higher levels of performance [Andrews, 1979, p. 269].

Lawler [1973, p. 9] suggests that an individual's performance depends not only on motivation but also on ability. This can be described as follows:

$$\text{Performance} = f\,(\text{Ability} \times \text{Motivation})$$

where $\text{Ability} = f\,(\text{Aptitude} \times [\text{Training} + \text{Experience}])$
    $\text{Motivation} = f\,(\text{Extrinsic Rewards} + \text{Intrinsic Rewards})$

The performance of a researcher then would depend on factors such as aptitude, training (academic and on-the-job training), experience (e.g., working with colleagues who impart knowledge through discussions and examples), extrinsic rewards (rewards given by the organizations, e.g., pay, promotion, job assignments, fringe benefits, and conference travel), and intrinsic rewards (rewards giving internal satisfaction, belonging to the essential nature or constitution of an individual). For intrinsic rewards, all the organization can do is to create conditions (for example, a proper work environment) that make it possible for the individual to experience these rewards internally.

As we have seen in Chapter 6 on motivation, motivation can be broken down into social factors, the affect toward the behavior, and the perceived consequences of the behavior times the value of these consequences. The affect toward the behavior can be considered an intrinsic reward; the other two factors can be considered extrinsic rewards.

The performance of an individual thus depends on many factors. Organizations and their managerment can influence some factors—but not all. A person's aptitude, academic training, and previous experiences are givens, and only some aspects of these can be modified with time. Even when poor performance is caused by low motivation, management can work on extrinsic rewards and create conditions for the individual to experience the intrinsic rewards. In the final analysis, it is the individual who, by building on his or her abilities (aptitude, training, and experience) and by looking at the extrinsic rewards and the satisfactions provided by the work environment, puts in the necessary effort to perform effectively.

Regarding intrinsic rewards, it is important to note that if researchers are to be committed to their work, they must feel that their research efforts are inherently worthwhile and serve some useful social purpose. It would seem that the researchers' interaction with the user community and their participation in technology transfer would provide the necessary feedback concerning the utility of their research effort and would further reinforce the intrinsic reward structure. If researchers are fundamentally opposed to the overall goals and objectives of an R&D organization, the real commitment may be diffficult to achieve. In such a case, it would be best for the individual to seek employment in a different organization.

Performance Appraisal Purposes

As suggested by McGregor [1972, p. 133], performance appraisal could have the following purposes:

Evaluation. To provide a systematic means of evaluating an employee's performance to back up salary increases, promotions, transfers, and sometimes demotions or other adverse personnel actions.

Feedback. The appraisal can serve as a means of telling the employee how he or she is doing and suggesting needed changes in employee behavior and attitude. In turn, the employee should be encouraged to bring out any concerns he has about the supervisor's behavior. That may not be easy for the employee to do. The supervisor could, however, ask the employee if he has any concerns about their mutual working relationship. This way, the employee does not have to attribute the problem only to the supervisor. The employee can also be asked to provide suggestions for making his work professionally more rewarding and for improving the organization's effectiveness.

Counseling. The performance appraisal system can also be used as a basis for counseling the employee, and identifying training and other developmental needs.

Added to these are the following suggested purposes:

- Increasing the motivation of the employee
- Instituting organization control and goal congruence
- Enhancing organizational effectiveness and excellence

Suggested Strategy

No specific list of performance elements and no rigid step-by-step strategy would properly encompass the many complexities inherent in R&D or other professional organizations. The following categories of performance elements, along with suggestions that follow, might provide a framework or a general guide for developing a performance appraisal system at different levels of the organization. It is important to keep in mind the manifold problems and issues related to implementing effectively a performance appraisal system, and understanding on what the performance of a researcher or a manager really depends.

Emphasizing employee contribution to the organization, the three categories of elements suggested are

Process Measures: Routine activities, short-run outputs

Result Measures: Ends-oriented activities, tangible, significant outputs

Strategic Indicators: Indicators focusing on recognition, awards and reputation internal and external to the organization

It is important to note that these category titles are identical to the ones used in Chapter 3 on Creating a Productive and Effective R&D Organization. The items included under these categories, however, have different emphases; the emphasis is on employee contribution to organizational goals and objectives. Organizational effectiveness is ultimately based on the performance of the individuals that comprise it. In other words, in order to achieve a one-to-one correspondence of individual performance and organizational effectiveness there should be goal congruence between individuals and their organization.

Specific elements in the appraisal would also depend on the position the individual occupies in an R&D organization. For example, a first line supervisor or a principal investigator may have "quality of leadership in project planning" as an important element of her appraisal while an associate investigator or a research assistant may have "completion of assigned project tasks within allotted time and budget" as an important element of his appraisal. To focus effectively on this, employee position descriptions can be used.

Because research activities are a collaborative effort of many participants, considerable similarity in the performance elements of many participants, albeit at different levels of the organization, is quite understandable. Performance appraisal can be used to further strengthen this collaborative effort by giving some employees primary responsibility for certain elements and others supportive or secondary responsibility. For example, while "project planning" may be the primary responsibility of the principal investigator, associate investigators may also have project planning as a secondary responsibility. Since effective project planning is important to the ultimate success of the project, this would encourage associate investigators to provide input to project planning and facilitate the collaborative process.

The level of detail and actual appraisal elements would further depend on the organization itself. For a commercial, profit-making organization, ultimate profitability from research outputs may be given appropriate emphasis. Even for not-for-profit organizations return on investment studies conducted by a third party can provide important information for individual employee performance and for organization effectiveness.

As an example, at the end of this chapter (Appendix 9, 14), three documents used by the Argonne National Laboratory for performance review purposes are included. One document describes the main steps for effective performance review and the second document is a typical position description. Measure of effectiveness included in the position description can form a basis for developing appraisal elements. The third document is the actual form used to document performance assessment.

Some other suggestions that might assist in the performance appraisal process follow:

- The employee and the supervisor should attempt to look at the performance appraisal process beyond "judging" or evaluating the employee. The focus ideally ought to be on employee contribution to the organization. In addition, focusing on other important aspects (such as feedback, counselling, motivation, and goal congruence) discussed earlier in this chapter would, to a great degree, overcome the problem of reluctance on the part of the employee and the supervisor to participate in the appraisal process.

- Generally, supervisors are very reluctant to rank order employees or even give them overall ratings such as exceptional, excellent, good, fair, and unsatisfactory. Before deciding to rank order employees, or giving them an overall rating, one should consider the purpose this would serve and what benefits or problems would result. Among the benefits might be an explicit message to the employee as to his performance vis-à-vis other employees. To do this, in practice, each performance element would have to be rated quantitatively. In addition, performance elements themselves would have to be rank ordered or given relative weights, and all subjective elements would require some implicit quantification. In a typical performance appraisal case, one is dealing with more than 20 such elements. Reducing the number of elements is a good idea, but experience shows that the number of element actually grows over the years. Even if the number is small, this quantification is subjective and using this approach creates some problems.

A supervisor soon finds out that the employee who is ranked number 6 in a group of 15 feels his ranking should have been better than one who is ranked number 5 and certainly equal to the one who is ranked number 3. Number 3 does not understand why he was not ranked number 1, and number 1 has a hard time understanding how number 3 could have received that high a ranking and so on. Giving overall ratings (such as exceptional, good, unsatisfactory) creates similar problems.

In organizations where performance elements can be explicitly stated and where reviews are conducted by a panel or a committee to minimize biases, such ratings or rankings may work well, as shown in our example case for a university department. Normally, where possible, rank ordering or overall personnel ratings should be avoided. They do not serve as an effective means of communication between the employee and the supervisor. They also tend to affect adversely a mutually supportive environment so necessary within an R&D group. Assigning ratings to individual performance elements without assigning an overall rating to the individual, is preferable.

Many R&D organizations, however, require managers to assign an overall rating to the employee. So, what is a manager to do? One approach might be to downplay the overall rating and focus more on individual performance elements than an overall rating or rank ordering when discussing performance appraisal with an employee. From our experience, this works quite well. The employee is more relaxed and there is more feedback and counseling than would otherwise be the case.

- While the appraisal system can interact with the reward system, linking the appraisal system *tightly* to monetary awards is not desirable. This suggestion seems contrary to the accepted wisdom—higher pay for higher performance. So, let us examine the situation.

A higher performing employee can indeed get a higher salary. The point here is that during performance appraisal reviews, discussion of pay and monetary rewards, as indicated earlier, would reduce the probability of any feedback or counselling. Organizational policies should encourage the utilization of a repertoire of items for rewards beyond the monetary aspects. If the premise is that pay will motivate an employee, one finds very quickly that pay has only a limited ability to do that. The suggestion here is simply that is it not very useful to tie pay tightly to performance determined during the appraisal process. Of course, in situations where performance requirement can be specified explicitly and individual biases are minimized by using a committee or a panel, it may work quite well.

- In developing performance measures and goals, the supervisor needs to work with the employee so that the employee's needs can be positively related to the organizational goals. This can assist in establishing goal congruence. In fact, this means that the employee first establishes performance goals for himself/herself based on his/her knowledge of the goals objectives of the organization. The supervisor then reviews performance elements and helps the employee relate career goals to the needs, and indeed, the realities of the organization.

- To the degree possible, performance appraisal elements should comprehensively cover all activities an employee is expected to perform and all results an employee is expected to achieve, as well as the total contribution an employee is likely to make to the organization beyond the performance appraisal period.

- Working with the employees, managers should set goals that are specific, difficult, but realistic. They should emphasize a code of ethics, such as the one we discussed in Chapter 8 on conflict. They should schedule special events to celebrate reaching goals, and give recognition to those who have been unusually successful. They should not hoard information. They should provide and communicate a *vision* of an organization that focuses on *excellence* and *productivity*.

- A vexing problem of dealing with poor performers or problem individuals is not easily handled. The problem could result from employee ability, organization environment, or conflict between the employee personality and the supervisor and/or the organization culture. At times, separating such an employee from the organization is best for all concerned. When that is not easily done, for example in the case of a tenured employee, a different strategy is needed.

    In one case, a new laboratory director found that the research organization environment had ben confrontational rather than collaborative. Serious turf problems were endemic. Researchers had to compete for research program funding, special purpose equipment, and laboratory and office space in such a way that all problems were viewed as zero-sum games. Poor performance and low organization effectiveness were the direct cause of this organization culture.

    In another case, a new laboratory director found that one research division director who had been viewed as a "star performer" actually mainly focused on process indicators. He did what the previous laboratory director asked him to do and never took any initiative or provided any technical or management leadership. Division productivity over the years was mediocre.

Such organizational culture and individual behavior problems cannot be changed precipitously or rashly. Methodical change while reinforcing the positive behavior would indeed take some time. During the performance review session, the supervisor may focus on the following:

a. Positive aspects of the employee contribution.

b. The behavior and its adverse effects on the organization effectiveness and the employee contribution to the organization.

c. Seek employee input as to the source of the problem and ways to overcome the problem.

d. Use peer pressure and rewards rather than "sticks" or exhortation as instruments of change. For example, demonstrating to the employee how his peers are able to do what he has not been able to or is reluctant to pursue can be quite effective.

e. Finally, the supervisor should be firm and reach a mutually agreed on strategy and a timetable for change. If the change is handled methodically and incrementally, this mutual agreement should not be too difficult to achieve.

9.11 SUMMARY

In summary, regardless of the many problems associated with implementing a meaningful performance appraisal system in an R&D organization, a system for performance appraisal that focuses on employee "contribution" to the organization is indeed needed to enchance organizatinal productivity and effectiveness. A performance appraisal system can be used to achieve organizational and individual goal congruence and organizational excellence. The vexing problem of dealing with poor performers or problem individuals, sometimes caused by a lack of employee ability or by the organization structure, is not easily handled.

Discussions here have focused on providing a basic understanding of problems and issues related to performance appraisal in R&D organizations; where possible ideas to overcome these problems were presented. The chapter culminated with a discussion of individual researcher performance dependency, performance appraisal purpose, and performance appraisal strategy that focuses on researcher contribution to the organization.

9.12 QUESTIONS FOR CLASS DISCUSSION

1 What is a good stystem for rewarding creativity in a R&D lab?

2 What principles should we keep in mind when we design performance appraisal systems?

3 Take the case of an R&D lab. Take position descriptions of a principal investigator and his supervisor. Develop main elements of the performance appraisal for both positions.

9.13 FURTHER READINGS

Performance Appraisal, Harvard Business Review (1988). Special Collection of Papers, No. 90070.

9.14 APPENDIX: ARGONNE NATIONAL LABORATORY PERFORMANCE REVIEW INFORMATION*

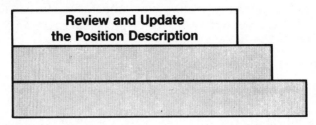

Review and Update the Position Description

POSITION DESCRIPTIONS, WITH THEIR AGREED-UPON MEASURES OF EFFECTIVENESS, FORM THE ESSENTIAL FOUNDATION FOR PERFORMANCE REVIEWS.

Each employee should have a current position description. These descriptions should be prepared using a single-page standard format and should include the following sections:

BASIC PURPOSE — A brief explanation of the essential function of the job.

TYPICAL ACTIVITIES — A listing of six to eight key activities of the job. Each activity written in the format: what the employee does, how the employee does it, and why the employee does it. Usually, these statements cover 85% of the workday and tend to be recurring, typical, or very important facets of the job.

WORK ENVIRONMENT — The working conditions under which the job is performed. This might include such elements as extended hours, deadlines, health hazards, and travel.

KNOWLEDGE, SKILLS, AND EXPERIENCE — A summary of the knowledge, skills, and experience necessary to perform the job.

MEASURES OF EFFECTIVENESS — Criteria by which the employee's performance is evaluated. These are the key measures upon which merit is assessed.

A NOTE ABOUT MEASURES OF EFFECTIVENESS

Since these are the yardsticks by which performance is measured, they must be specific! A measure such as "maintain good quality" is too general. A specific measure of quality should be expressed. In writing measures of effectiveness, the supervisor should ask: When this responsibility of the individual is performed properly, what will take place?

A primary responsibility of each supervisor is the preparation **and revision** of position descriptions for the jobs of each subordinate. **It is extremely important that these descriptions be current, reflecting present expectations. They should be routinely reviewed and revised as job changes occur**. Prior to each performance review, supervisors should examine position descriptions to determine if the measures of effectiveness are still relevant and then choose those measures appropriate for inclusion on the performance assessment form. The annual performance review should also produce position descriptions that apply to the forthcoming review period.

Position descriptions should not be written by supervisors alone. Input from the Division office and the subordinate should always be sought. All parties should agree on the measures of effectiveness written on the position description. Position description revisions should be coordinated with the Compensation section of Personnel.

---

* From: Argonne National Laboratory (undated), "Three Steps to an Effective Performance Review: An Instructional Guide for Supervisors at the Time of The Annual Performance Assessment," author, Argonne, Illinois. Reprinted by Permission of Argonne National Laboratory.

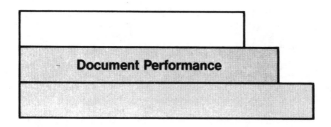

FILLING OUT A PERFORMANCE ASSESSMENT FORM can be a formidable task. However, this task can be made much simpler if the supervisor has done his or her homework by establishing and maintaining personal contacts with the employee and by evaluating the employee's performance throughout the review period. A requisite, therefore, is the noting, preferably in writing, of critical incidents in the subordinate's performance during the review period, including positive or negative comments expressed by others. This provides a resource for the documentation of performance required on the assessment form.

Using information gathered throughout the period reduces the possibility of violating a cardinal principle: **BE OBJECTIVE!** Nothing can undermine a supervisor/subordinate relationship faster than a performance review based on sheer opinion regarding the employee's traits or personality. Of importance is what the individual has accomplished in the past year.

THE PERFORMANCE ASSESSMENT FORM (AS SHOWN BELOW) REQUIRES THAT THE DEGREE TO WHICH EACH MEASURE OF EFFECTIVENESS HAS BEEN ACHIEVED BE RATED, FOLLOWED BY STATEMENTS WHICH SUBSTANTIATE AND DOCUMENT THE REASONS BEHIND THAT RATING.

MEASURE:

WEIGHT ☐   RATING: Low └─────────┴─────────┴─────────┴─────────┴─────────┘ High

PERFORMANCE DOCUMENTATION TO SUPPORT RATING:

There are spaces provided on the form for listing up to six measures of effectiveness. These should be taken directly from the position description. Attaching a weight to each measure is optional. Required is a rating of performance regarding that measure along a scale from "Low" to "High." In the section "Performance Documentation to Support Rating," the supervisor is required to document specific instances occurring since the last Performance Assessment that will substantiate the rating given. **A RATING WITHOUT DOCUMENTATION IS INCOMPLETE AND DOES NOT THOROUGHLY COMMUNICATE THE REASONS BEHIND THE ASSESSMENT.** This is particularly important in cases where documentation is necessary to substantiate future management actions.

The "Overall Relative Assessment of Performance," at the end of the form, should summarize the ratings for each measure of effectiveness and should correlate with the merit increase received by the employee.

EMPLOYEE ACCOMPLISHMENT STATEMENTS

Each employee should prepare a statement of accomplishments during the review period. This action is a vital link in the communications necessary for effective performance reviews. Though not specifically required by the Argonne performance assessment procedure, accomplishment statements give supervisors a summary of achievements during the review period as the subordinate sees them.

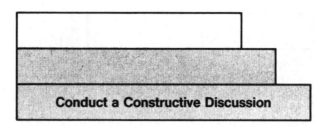

Conduct a Constructive Discussion

THE PERFORMANCE REVIEW DISCUSSION. This discussion should be built upon a foundation of free-flowing, timely communications during the review period. If it goes well, it can honestly summarize the employee's contribution, substantiate a merit increase or lack thereof, and provide the basis for improvements in performance. If done poorly, it can undermine relationships, discourage both supervisor and subordinate, and diminish the credibility of documentation of personnel actions.

The following checklist for the performance review discussion should be referenced before each talk takes place.

PREPARE — Good discussions don't just happen, they are planned! Inform the employee in advance. Review background material. Again review the position description and the completed assessment form. Set objectives for the discussion. Think it out. Jot down key questions and topics.

PICK A GOOD TIME AND PLACE — Hold the discussion where it will not be interrupted, where physical facilities and time do not present limitations.

FACILITATE SUPPORTIVE COMMUNICATIONS — Open the discussion by explaining the purpose of the talk, putting the employee at ease, and describing the review process, timing, and format. Stress again the importance of position descriptions and measures of effectiveness.

The goal is to keep defensiveness to a minimum. **Defensive** behavior occurs when an individual perceives or anticipates threat. People who become defensive, devote an appreciable portion of energy to defending their capabilities rather than listening to the supervisor. Communications are **supportive** when both parties engage in a mutually beneficial discussion of the work performed, the ratings, and the documentation of measures of effectiveness.

ENCOURAGE DISCUSSION — Ask open questions that stimulate response. Above all, **listen** and don't respond until you understand what the other person has said.

REVIEW THE PERFORMANCE ASSESSMENT FORM — Go over it together in detail. Allow the employee to insert legitimate additions or corrections. Have the employee sign the form, indicating that he or she has read it, not necessarily that he or she agrees with its contents. Allow the employee to make a copy if desired.

EMPLOYEE REBUTTALS

The employee who strongly disagrees with the performance assessment should be allowed, and encouraged, to write a rebuttal. This should be submitted within a week of the performance review discussion, should be attached to the performance assessment form, and should be made a permanent part of the performance assessment record.

ARGONNE NATIONAL LABORATORY
9700 South Cass Avenue
Argonne, Illinois 60439

	EES 0515
	JOB CODE

POSITION DESCRIPTION

	COST CODE

TITLE:	DATE:
Oceanographer/Physical (Descriptive)	01/22/85

BASIC PURPOSE:

To support energy resources and technology development by describing, quantifying, and evaluating physical oceanographic (and other geophysical) processes, including functioning as a project leader when so designated.

TYPICAL ACTIVITIES:

This position will gather and analyze data regarding the physical oceanographic and/or geophysical aspects of resource and technology development projects. Such data may come from existing sources; but in some cases, the position requires the oversight of and participation in the acquisition of physical data on transport and mixing in water. Interaction with others in the Geophysics and Engineering Section (both modelers and data acquisition personnel) is required. This position may require interaction with those involved with environmental assessment or compliance activities. Interfaces with sponsors and/or investigators from other agencies may be necessary in field activities. Preparation of reports on data acquisition and analyses is a function for this position.

WORK ENVIRONMENT:

Typical office setting. Field work and extended hours often required. Occasional travel for program reviews and technical conferences. As a project team member reports to project leader and as a project leader reports to the Section Leader for Geophysics and Engineering.

KNOWLEDGE, SKILLS AND EXPERIENCE:

This position requires:

1. Considerable knowledge of oceanographic problems in coastal waters;
2. Considerable knowledge of physical hydrologic processes;
3. Considerable knowledge of measurement techniques for tracers in water;
4. Good knowledge of measurement and analysis of data pertaining to geophysical, particularly hydrologic, processes;
5. Good knowledge of oceanographic/hydrologic equipment and devices;
6. Good knowledge of environmental concerns posed by energy resource and technology development;
7. Considerable skill in oral and written communication;
8. Considerable skill in establishing and maintaining effective interpersonal relationships;
9. Considerable skill in performing qualitative and quantitative data analysis;
10. Considerable skill in conducting physical measurements;
11. Working skill in using oceanographic/hydrologic measuring devices
12. Working skill in interpreting oceanographic data.

This level of knowledge and skill is usually attained through advanced formal education in oceanography (masters level) and several years of experience in physical oceanography/liminology/hydrology, including work with tracers.

Oceanographer/Physical (Descriptive) (Cont'd)

MEASURES OF EFFECTIVENESS:

1. Quality, quantity, and originality of publications with consideration given to the magnitude and complexity of the work, and emphasis on refereed publications in books, journals, and formal Argonne reports.

2.a. For research activities: quality and quantity of work, including: approaches taken, techniques applied or developed (including patents), and interpretation of results in general technical and project-specific terms.

2.b. For review activities: quality and quantity of work, including: thoroughness in dealing with relevant literature, and clarity and tactfulness of critiques.

2.c. For assessment activities: quality and quantity of work, including: relevance of approaches adopted, validity and utility of analytical techniques used, and degree to which assessments are accepted by professional community.

*3. Completion of project tasks within allotted time and budget to meet project goals and to provide sponsor satisfaction.

4. Initiative and resourcefulness in creating new or improved approaches to ongoing work, to provide better ways to pursue existing work or expand sponsor support.

5. Effective interaction with project and section members to accomplish project goals and enhance group research capabilities.

6. Communication of research, review, or assessment activities and results, in oral and written form, to other project personnel, the sponsor, and relevant professional community; organization of technical sessions and related outside professional activities, where applicable.

7. When designated a project leader, quality of leadership in planning project goals and implementing plans within project resources, and success in developing new or expanded sponsor support.

---

*Not used if number 7 chosen.

ARGONNE NATIONAL LABORATORY
MERIT REVIEW PERFORMANCE ASSESSMENT
STAFF AND SALARY EMPLOYEES

Employee's Name	Payroll No.	Job Classification

Division/Department	Evaluator	Review Period

1. MEASURES OF EFFECTIVENESS (from current position description)

A. MEASURE:

WEIGHT ☐ RATING: Low |_____|_____|_____|_____|_____| High

PERFORMANCE DOCUMENTATION TO SUPPORT RATING:

List Ways Employee Can Strengthen Performance in This Area:

B. MEASURE:

WEIGHT ☐ RATING: Low |_____|_____|_____|_____|_____| High

PERFORMANCE DOCUMENTATION TO SUPPORT RATING:

List Ways Employee Can Strengthen Performance in This Area:

C. MEASURE:

WEIGHT ☐ RATING: Low |_____|_____|_____|_____|_____| High

PERFORMANCE DOCUMENTATION TO SUPPORT RATING:

List Ways Employee Can Strengthen Performance in This Area:

D. MEASURE:

WEIGHT ☐ RATING: Low |_____|_____|_____|_____|_____| High

PERFORMANCE DOCUMENTATION TO SUPPORT RATING:

List Ways Employee Can Strengthen Performance in This Area:

E. MEASURE:

WEIGHT ☐ RATING: Low |_____|_____|_____|_____|_____| High

PERFORMANCE DOCUMENTATION TO SUPPORT RATING:

List Ways Employee Can Strengthen Performance in This Area:

F. MEASURE:

WEIGHT ☐ RATING: Low |_____|_____|_____|_____|_____| High

PERFORMANCE DOCUMENTATION TO SUPPORT RATING:

List Ways Employee Can Strengthen Performance in This Area:

2. SAFETY PERFORMANCE (Training of subordinates, corrective actions, use of personal protective equipment, etc.) Comment on how safety principles were applied in work area:

3. AFFIRMATIVE ACTION (for supervisory positions) Comment on how supervisor supported Argonne's Affirmative Action Program:

4. DEVELOPMENT PLANS: To assist employee in strengthening performance or to prepare for promotion:

5. OVERALL RELATIVE ASSESSMENT OF PERFORMANCE:

Low |_____|___|___|___|___|___|___|___|___|___|___| High

ADDITIONAL COMMENTS AND REACTIONS:

_____   _____   _____
Evaluator's Signature   Date   Employee's Signature
                                                       (indicating only having seen completed form)

____10
TECHNOLOGY TRANSFER

This chapter focuses on technology transfer for a mission-oriented research organization. A mission-oriented research organization has its objectives defined in specific organizational goals rather than in technical terms and is vertically integrated. In other words, these organizations span activities covering basic research, applied research, development, and even technical support of operational activities. Non-mission-oriented research organizations have their objectives defined primarily in scientific terms, for example, the study of high-energy physics, nuclear energy, toxic substances, atmospheric physics, and bioacoustics. Academic research is generally non-mission-oriented and is usually small-scale research carried out in academic departments of universities. Much of the technology transfer from non-mission-oriented research organizations to application in real-life situations is likely to occur via a buffer organization similar to a mission-oriented R&D organization, and hence the focus on such organizations.

For R&D organizations, technology transfer, or tech transfer, may be defined as the process by which science and technology are transferred from one individual or group to another that incorporates this new knowledge into its way of doing things.

10.1 TECHNOLOGY TRANSFER HYPOTHESES

The following general hypotheses are related to technology transfer:

- Technology transfer of research results is essential if a mission-oriented research organization is to be effective in fulfilling its task.

- The effectiveness of technology transfer provides the essential measure of productivity of a mission-oriented R&D organization.
- Effective technology transfer increases user involvement in the innovation process which, in turn, positively affects R&D productivity and has long-term benefits in terms of funding support from the sponsor groups.
- Institutional and organizational constraints, as well as improper planning for technology transfer, impede the process.
- Technology transfer techniques and approaches can be developed to facilitate the process.

10.2 STAGES OF TECHNOLOGY TRANSFER

Transferring technology from an R&D lab to manufacturing, marketing, and the ultimate user is an important function. Different organizational elements can play useful roles in successfully reaching this goal. To see how different roles and functions can best be organized, it would help to examine the stages or steps of technology transfer.

Rogers [1983, p. 20], suggests five main steps leading to the adoption of technology:

- Knowledge
- Persuasion
- Decision
- Implementation
- Confirmation.

Knowledge occurs when a potential user learns about the new technology and gains some understanding of its capabilities and usefulness. At this stage the user wants to know what the innovation is, what its capabilities are, and how it works. *Persuasion* occurs when the user forms a favorable or an unfavorable attitude towards the innovation. Here the user is looking at comparative advantages and disadvantages of the innovation. *Decision* occurs when the user engages in activities that lead to adoption or rejection of the innovation. *Implementation* occurs when the user incorporates the innovation into the way of doing things. *Confirmation* occurs when the user seeks to confirm the implementation decision and continues to use the innovation. This step is not always well understood, which is why many innovations first implemented are later discontinued. Certain activities to reinforce user acceptance of the innovation need to continue after implementation.

Adoption of innovation involves considerable uncertainty and thus some risk. The consequences of adoption in terms of its benefits are not always clear. Operational problems can often occur during the implementation stage, thus increasing costs and reducing benefits. Some of this uncertainty can be reduced by demonstration projects and by implementing the innovation on a partial basis. Organizations that do not reward prudent risk taking are less likely to adopt innovations.

Innovation adoption typically follows an S-curve. Rogers [1983, p. 247] describes five categories of adopters. Early adopters are usually prudent risk-takers, better informed and educated, and act as opinion leaders for the organization. The role of early adopters is to decrease the uncertainty about an innovation by adopting it and by making needed adjustments to the innovation to fit organization needs. Early adopters then communicate this information to other potential users within the organization and to peers outside the organization.

Adoption of innovation would normally require resources (people, funds, and time), some training in using the innovation, and, at times, some changes in the way organizations operate. This involves commitment to and acceptance of the innovation at both the individual and organizational levels. Organizational structure and its routine functioning provide stability and continuity to an organization. The adoption of innovation may seem to threaten this stability and continuity and thus it is understandable that there often is some resistance to innovation.

Some innovations may require manufacturing before they can be utilized by the ultimate user. For example, if the innovation involves a longer lasting light bulb or a complex instrument to monitor toxic wastes, the devices must first be manufactured before the user can implement them. Some innovations, such as computer systems, improved analysis procedures, or improved design criteria can be transferred to the user without manufacturing or other major intermediate steps. In both cases, before the innovation is implemented, the manufacturing department or the user has to become aware of the innovation and be persuaded to go on to the next steps: decision and implementation.

During the early steps—knowledge and presentation—marketing people can play an important role. Marketing people may, for example, develop information brochures or demonstrations that capture the imagination of the users. These activities could be sufficiently exciting that the users become very interested in the innovation, learn about its capabilities, form favorable attidues toward it, and are persuaded to take the initative to seek further information. As users move to the decision stage and beyond, the R&D group and other individuals intimately familiar with the innovation need to play the pivotal role.

10.3   APPROACHES AND FACTORS AFFECTING TECHNOLOGY TRANSFER

Roberts and Frohman [1982, p. 36] describe three general approaches used by industrial research organizatons to facilitate research utilization: These are the personnel approach, the organizational link-pins approach, and the procedural approach.

The Personnel Approach. The personnel approach involves movement of people, joint teams, and intensive person-to-person contact between the generator and user of the research. Suppose an R&D group develops an intelligent stand-along air-pollution monitoring device that has a built-in microprocessor capable of real-time analysis. The innovation is complex, requiring some modifications or debugging during manufacturing. Some key members of the R&D group may be transferred to manufacturing to facilitate the process. The enthusiasm and keen insight of the R&D group can thus be transferred to manufacturing, increasing the probability of effective technology transfer.

The Organizational Link-Pins Approach. This encompasses specialized transfer groups that contain engineering, marketing, and financial skills, use of integrators who act as third pary transfer coordinators, and new venture groups.

Some organizations may find that movement of people creates other unacceptable personnel problems or is not economical. A special "technology transfer group" is formed to specialize in moving innovations from R&D to demonstration, manufacturing, and to the ultimate user. It is important to recognize that a technology transfer group cannot consist of just a sales or public affairs office (PAO). In one case we studied, the PAO was driving the train and results, predictably, were disappointing. After the initial knowledge and presentation stages, further activities quickly faded away. The PAO group did not have the technical understanding to successfully carry out other tech transfer activities. Even at the knowledge and persuasion stages, misleading and at times erroneous information was provided to the user groups. This further reduced the probability of success for the follow-on stages. For a technology-based innovation, it is essential that knowledgeable engineers and scientists play a leading role in the technology transfer group at all stages. As the technology moves to the decision stage and beyond, PAO group's role is minimal.

The Procedural Approach. This includes joint planning, joint funding, and joint appraisal of research projects using research and user groups from manufacturing and marketing.

This procedural approach, which involves joint planning and participation in the innovation process by the user community, can be utilized quite effectively. User groups that include personnel from manufacturing, marketing, field users, corporate funding sponsors, and the research community can be organized for major R&D products. It is important to note that participants in these user groups still continue their normal duties. Their participation in the user group is an added responsibility. Researchers often comment on how many new ideas are generated as a result of their interaction with this user group. Such approaches require considerable organizational support, but the effort is worth the cost. In many cases, movement of people or formation of specialized technology transfer groups is simply not feasible due to organizational or cost considerations. Procedural approaches such as formation of user groups can serve as a tool for effective technology transfer without requiring movement of people or extra resources for establishing technology transfer groups. Procedural approaches can also be used to complement the other two approaches.

Cetron [1973, p. 11] describes a number of factors affecting technology transfer:

- National policies, laws, and regulations (e.g., taxes and tax credits, tariffs, and health and safety regulations)
- Corporate policies
- Market demand
- Scientific base of the nation and industry
- Level of R&D effort
- Education level
- Availability of capital.

10.4 ROLE OF THE USER

Von Hippel [1978, p. 31] makes a strong case for the role the user plays in the innovation process and in technology transfer:

We have found that 60 to 80% of the products sampled in those industries [manufacturing process equipment or scientific instruments] were invented, prototyped, and utilized in the field by innovative users before they were offered commercially by equipment or instrument manufacturing firms.

In the case of scientific instruments, Von Hippel [1978, p. 12] states:

In 81% of all the innovation cases studied, we found that it was the user who perceived that an advance in instrumentation was required; invented the instrument; built a prototype; improved the prototype's value by applying it; and diffused detailed information on the value of the invention and how the prototype device might be replicated. Only when all these steps were completed did the manufacturer of the first commercially available instrument enter the innovation process. Typically, the manufacturer's contribution was to perform product engineering work which, while leaving the basic design and operating principles intact, improved reliability, convenience of operation, etc.; and then to manufacture, market, and sell the improved product.

The implications of these findings are significant for some industries. Management strategies should be set up to discover and utilize user-developed innovations. The manufacturer's contribution to product engineering and to setting up the necessary facilities to manufacture and market the product are also significant. Issues of innovation ownership in terms of patent rights or trademarks need to be investigated before committing resources for manufacturing and marketing.

10.5 CHARACTERISTICS OF INNOVATION

Rogers [1983, p. 238] describes five different characteristics of an innovation, as perceived by the potential adopter, that affect its rate of adoption:

Relative Advantage: The degree to which the innovation is superior to ideas it supersedes.

Compatibility: The degree to which the innovation is consistent with existing values, past experiences, and needs of the user.

Complexity: The degree to which the innovation is relatively difficult to understand and use.

Trialability: The degree to which an innovation may be tried on a limited basis (in other words, without committing to full-scale, total operational change).

Observability: The degree to which the results from the use of an innovation are visible and easily communicated to users and other decision-makers.

Clearly, characteristics of an innovation play an important role in technology transfer. For example, before the user adopts new technology, the user has to weigh the extra effort and investment in adopting new technology against the *relative advantages* presented by the new technology. Since existing technologies can be modified and they can "stretch" to be more efficient, the new technology has to represent considerable advantages over existing ones before the extra effort involved in adopting this new technology would be considered a worthwhile undertaking.

Relative advantages relate to such items as reduced cost, increased profitability, increased convenience, reduced time, enhanced capability, and associated social status. While cost factors may stay the same or even increase, some innovations could provide relative advantage by reducing the time required to accomplish a mission or by markedly increasing product performance. For example, for military hardware such capabilities could provide a strategic or a tactical advantage, and thus facilitate adoption.

An innovation that is *compatible* with existing values and past experiences of the user is more likely to be adopted. For example, if the user has had a positive experience with innovations from a particular research laboratory, user adoption in the future will naturally be higher. The felt needs of the user can also play an important role. Sometimes external forces can create this need. For instance, regulatory requirements could create a strong need for adoption of advanced waste water treatment technologies.

Some innovations are complex because their capabilities are difficult to understand and may require specialized training, equipment, and user capabilities. For such innovations, efforts need to be made to communicate capabilities simply and to provide the necessary training and equipment to increase the adoption rate.

Users are often willing to try new technology but are not willing to make full scale and total operational changes, for obvious reasons. The risks outweigh the benefit to be derived. Therefore, when technology can be tried on a limited basis and if the changes can be made incrementally (*trialability*), the probability of its acceptance increases. Many innovations in office automation have followed this pattern.

If the benefits from the adoption of an innovation can be readily seen and easily communicated to potential users (*observability*) the rate of adoption is naturally greater. Hardware items fall in this category. Benefits from the adoption of software items (procedures, methodologies, and computer systems), however, are not as observable and not as easily communicated to potential users and thus have relatively slower rates of adoption.

10.6　ROLE OF MARKET AND PEOPLE

According to Roberts and Frohman [1982, p. 38], several studies provide persuasive evidence that market needs, rather than technological opportunities, provide the main pull and motivation for research project output utilizations. He found that 75% of the innovations judged most important by the company originated in response to perceived needs in the marketplace rather than any technological opportunities. Market factors and user needs are therefore important considerations in facilitating technology transfer.

The role of people in technology transfer has been well recognized. The existence of a *technology gatekeeper*, a person who links the organization to the outside world of scientific and technical knowledge, has been documented by Allen [1977, p. 141]. Roberts and Frohman [1982, p. 27] describes two other gatekeepers—market gatekeeper and manufacturing gatekeeper—who have relevance to technology transfer.

The market gatekeeper is a communicator who understands what competitors are doing, what regulators might be up to, and what is happening with regard to the marketplace. This type of a gatekeeper brings vital information to the R&D organization and keeps the R&D research focus on target and toward the kinds of activities that are likely to be accepted and implemented successfully.

The manufacturing or operations gatekeeper understands enough of the practical and constrained environment of manufacturing and of the operations of the user community to keep the R&D personnel well informed of the manufacturing and operations requirements. This individual makes sure that the concepts developed by R&D can either be manufactured profitably or made a part of the operation procedures of the user community.

As discussed previously, a strong case has been made for the crucial role people play in technology transfer. Roberts and Frohman [1982, p. 37] have stated: "Nothing transfers enthusiasm so well as working with or watching a person who has faith, conviction, and excitement about an idea." At times, moving research project personnel so they work more closely with manufacturing and marketing can help overcome many unforeseen transfer difficulties. This point is made by many authors; but moving people presents several practical, financial, and organizational problems.

When moving personnel, it is essential to have an effective plan for replacing the research personnel with others who can continue needed research activities. Sufficient investment inherent in movement and replacement of people is required. The goals and objectives of the affected individuals need to be considered. The effects of movement on employee motivation and future job opportunities and promotion potential (within the organization and outside the organization) need to be analyzed. In summary, the strategy recommended would be to move some research project personnel selectively for a short period to act as catalysts and mitigate other concerns associated with moving people.

10.7 BOUNDARY SPANNING

One main and perhaps crucial ingredient in technology transfer is *boundary spanning*. This requires some elaboration.

Engineers should be able to communicate effectively with other engineers, economists with other economists, and so on. Furthermore, an engineer with a specialization in air pollution control presumably can communicate better with another engineer in air pollution control than with an engineer specializing in groundwater hydrology. One could continue this argument further. The point is that with the increase in the complexity of science and technology, specialization has become necessary, and this increased specialization can inhibit communication. As discussed previously, an increase in communication among scientists and engineers is essential for the innovation process. The added problem in tech transfer is that the communication network needs to go beyond the research community to include the user community, the marketing people, and the manufacturing groups. This would require boundary spanning—going beyond the immediate boundary of one's discipline.

To be sure, it is not enough to just increase communication beyond the immediate boundary or group of R&D personnel. For the communication to be effective, it must result in the understanding of "user needs" and creative collaboration among the various groups (researchers, marketing, manufacturing, and ultimate users) to facilitate significant tech transfer.

Sole responsibility for boundary spanning or gatekeeping cannot be formally assigned to an individual. In an R&D organization, this will have to be one of the responsibilities that R&D personnel undertake as an integral part of the innovation process, albeit, some will do it more effectively than others. When utilizing any of the approaches for technology transfer (e.g., personnel, organization link-pins, procedural) participation of personnel who are able to span the boundary is likely to produce the best results.

10.8 ORGANIZATIONAL ISSUES IN TECHNOLOGY TRANSFER

In an article titled "Implementing New Technology," Leonard-Barton and Kraus [1985, p. 102] identify a number of organizational issues that affect technology transfer. Some of these are discussed and summarized below.

The technology transfer manager (or implementer of new technology) has to integrate the perspectives and needs of both the R&D personnel and users. The focus in technology transfer needs to be on *marketing* the product rather than *selling* it, with user needs and preferences given proper consideration. Like many other authors, Leonard-Barton and Kraus have identified involvement of opinion leaders in the user organization as a critical element for technology transfer success.

They point out that for implementing new technology, enthusiasm alone is not enough. New technology implementation usually requires a supportive infrastructure and the allocation of scarce resources for its implementation. Implementation teams for this purpose should include [Leonard-Barton and Kraus, 1985, p. 107]:

- A sponsor (a high level person who can help provide adequate financial and manpower resources)
- A champion (salesperson, problem solver)
- An integrator (manages conflicting priorities)
- A project manager (oversees the administrative details).

In addition, they suggested that sufficient authority needs to be vested in one member of this team with enough power in the organization to mobilize the necessary resources (both in the R&D and user organizations) to make things happen.

There is a natural tendency on the part of humans to resist change. Leonard-Barton and Kraus [1985, p. 108] state that "tacit resistance does not disappear but ferments, grows into sabotage, or surfaces later when resources are depleted." At times, the reasons for resistance relate to real or perceived problems that the new technology may cause:

- Loss of jobs
- Loss of control
- Loss of autonomy or authority
- Many benefits to the organization, but not many to the individuals involved.

In addition to resisters, another group that can adversely affect technology transfer efforts is referred to as the "hedgers" [Leonard-Barton and Kraus, 1985, p. 109]. Hedgers refuse to take a stand against an innovation so that others can address their objections, but they can affect the future of a new technology when they are a key link in the implementation plan. To overcome this, top managers, presumably in the user organization, should take some kind of symbolic action (memo, speeches, etc.) providing full support to the technology transfer effort [Leonard-Barton and Kraus, 1985, p. 109].

One of the key factors affecting technology transfer is the perceived risk and uncertainty associated with new technology. Adopters have to weigh expected benefits or rewards if adoption is successful, against perceived risks if the adoption is unsuccessful. In organizations where initiative is not valued highly and failures are severely criticized, adoption of new technology is not likely to be pervasive.

In one organization an employee commented that the way to get ahead was "don't rock the boat, keep a low profile, and don't make any mistakes." Naturally, in such organizations there will be resistance to change and adoption of new technology is going to be less likely. On the other hand, in organizations where employees are eager to understand and learn about new technology, where management recognizes that mistakes are likely during any change,where personnel are rewarded for prudent risk-taking, adoption of new technology is likely to flourish.

10.9 THE AGRICULTURAL EXTENSION MODEL

The government agency that has been most successful in technology transfer of research results is the Agricultural Extension Service. The approach used by the Agricultural Extension Service is commonly called "The Agricultural Extension Model," which consists of three main components [Rogers, 1983, p. 159]:

1. *A research subsystem*, which conducts agricultural research. This is a cooperative effort of the U.S. Department of Agricultural and the 50 state agricultural experiment stations.

2. *State extension specialists* who are stationed in state agricultural universities. They link the research group to the county extension agents.
3. *County extension agents*, who work as change agents with farmers, and
   other rural people at the local level.

Once an agricultural innovation reaches an individual, via the county
extension agent, horizontal transfer of the innovation takes place through
the peer networks.

The Agricultural Extension Service was established in 1914 "To aid in
diffusing among the people of the United States useful and practical information on subjects relating to agriculture and home economics, and to
encourage the application of same." Thus, the Agricultural Extension Service has a long and successful history of technology transfer. Unique among
its characteristics is the fact the budget for the extension service comes from
federal, state, and county governments [Rogers, 1983, p. 160].

Because of concerns among federal agencies and industry regarding the
lack of adequate mechanisms for transferring technology from the R&D
groups to the users, it has been asserted that the successful agricultural
extension model be replicated. Not withstanding the success of the agricultural extension model, the application of this model for other purposes has
not been very successful.

What are the reasons for this? One has to look at the unique characteristics of agricultural research and this model. In this case, the farmer is an
identifiable and a unique target of research, sustained level of funding is
available from the federal, state, and county governments, and there
is over 70 years of history and experience in implementing this model.
Many of these characteristics are not present in other technology transfer
situations.

10.10 NASA TECHNOLOGY TRANSFER ACTIVITIES

The National Aeronautics and Space Administration (NASA) has established a network of industrial application centers at six universities that
provides technical assistance and literature retrieval. The network is perhaps
the largest information storehouse of technical information in the world
[Ruzic, 1978]. Another method of transferring technology is the NASA-
funded biomedical and technology applications teams. These teams try to
apply technology to problems encountered in medical facilites and public
sector agencies.

A study of factors affecting adoption of NASA developed technology
indicates that a number of technical and economic factors impact the rate of
technology adoption [Chakrabarti and Rubenstein, 1976]. This study indicates that top management support is of primary importance in the success
of innovation adoption, also, technical and economic variables, organiza-

tional climate and involvement of the innovator in implementation of the technology affect the rate of technology adoption.

10.11 IBM CASE STUDIES

Cohen et al. [1979, p. 11], focusing on the transfer of technology from research to a profitable commercial enterprise, describe a study of 18 IBM projects; some of them were successful, while others failed. They produced valuable guidelines for moving technology from research to product development. This study can form an archetype for the development of guidelines for technology transfer that are responsive to the unique requirements of a given organization.

As a result of this study, factors identified that affect technology transfer are discussed in the order of their relative importance:

Technical Understanding

- It is necessary that research personnel fully understand the main technology before passing it on. Though this may seem obvious, it is not always the case.
- It is necessary to evaluate the benefits of new technology in comparison to what is already available and to other competitive advancements.
- One must identify where it will fit in the product line and what requirements must be met to reach the fit.
- One possible means of manufacturing needs to be exhibited.

Feasibility

- Both the research and the receiver unit must reach an agreement on what constitutes feasibility and then what should be established.
- Some estimate of cost effectiveness should be made.
- In some cases, feasibility implies acceptability by the end user. This would recognize some kind of joint study with real users to establish feasibility.

Advanced Development Overlap

- For projects being transferred out, some overlap of research activities may be needed either to support development or to explore advanced or related technologies.
- For systems work (computer software), creation of special advanced development effort is often the answer to problems of scaling-up or to answer questions of economic feasibility.

Growth Potential

- When projects are narrowly focused on a specific need and do not have paths to technical growth and product applicability, technology transfer may suffer. This is because existing technologies "stretch" themselves and the limited advantage offered by the new technology may not be sufficient to warrant change.

Existence of an Advocate

- A strong proponent activity is needed to help overcome many hurdles during the technology transfer process.

Advanced Technology Activities in a Development Laboratory

- In moving technology from research to manufacturing, advanced technology programs in the development laboratories are often necessary. (For some research organizations, research and advanced development units may work in the same group.)

External Pressures

- In some cases, parallel activity by a competitor may help provide the push for technology transfer; in others, regulatory requirements may necessitate adoption of new technologies, for example, advanced waste treatment technologies.

Joint Programs

- It was concluded that joint programs with receiver groups are good to have, but they do not ensure success.

Other secondary factors affecting technology transfer relate to timeliness, internal users, government contracts, high level involvement, individual corporate responsibility, and proximity. There was an interesting comment about proximity. For the IBM projects studied, in no case was the proximity of a development laboratory to a research laboratory an important factor for technology transfer. Being close was convenient, and saved money, but no transfer failed because of distance [Cohen et al., 1979, p. 15].

In thinking about the transfer of technology we must be careful not to give sole weight to technical and rational criteria. The following true story makes the point. In India, an agricultural team convinced a farmer to use some new seeds. The results were dramatic. Production was 10 times as great. In evaluating the event, the farmer was asked for comments. To the amazement of the questioner, he indicated he was not planning to use the seed again. "Why?" asked the city-raised Indian agricultural engineer. "Because I have no room to store that much extra production, my cows can't eat the plants that are left on the field after the crop is harvested and I have no way to get that much production to market." In other words, the engineer had used productivity as the *only* criterion, not taking into account social and collateral activities associated with the crop.

10.12 TECHNOLOGY TRANSFER STRATEGY

After reviewing all that has been written about the subject, one may feel a little overwhelmed by the many requirements necessary to transfer technology effectively. Trying to get several individuals to do some specific tasks for tech transfer, trying to get support from top management, trying to get the necessary financial resources, and then anticipating all the problems (for example, "hedgers", etc.) make tech transfer seem like a difficult, if not an impossible task. Because of the uncertainty associated with each step and because of the difficulties in finding the necessary people and resources on a timely basis, successful tech transfer may seem like an elusive dream. In practice, rarely does anyone have all the resources available for tech transfer except for those special projects that are necessary for the survival of the organization.

More often than not, technology moves from research and development to the user in small increments. The size of the transfer effort varies. For some large projects, resources required for effective tech transfer may indeed be extensive. For most projects, the tech transfer effort may have to be accomplished within existing resources, by fending off the skeptics who are opposed or simply reluctant to accept new technology and without all the support mechanisms at high levels of the organization.

No grand scheme or all encompassing formula for tech transfer is offered and none seems obvious. Based on the considerable practical experience of the authors in moving technology from a research organization to the user community, and after reviewing some of the insightful suggestions made by others, the following approach may allow one to develop a strategy in response to the unique requirements of the organization—its history, its culture, and its technology. A generalized tech transfer strategy development plan is depicted in Figure 10.1 and a description of major activities of this plan follows. To understand this approach clearly and to operationalize the concept, real research project execution and actual organizational experiences are needed. Hypothetical examples cannot easily convey the organizational and individual behavior contexts that effect tech transfer. Where possible some examples are presented, albeit these examples may not be applicable to all cases.

1 Tech Transfer Activities and Documents

Based upon the knowledge of the R&D staff and the user community, prepare a preliminary list of tech transfer activities and documents that

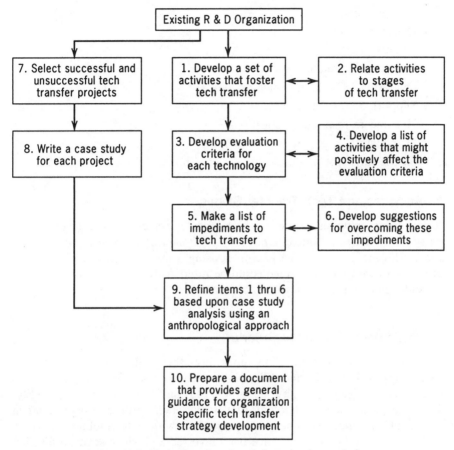

Figure 10.1. Technology transfer strategy development plan.

foster or enhance technology transfer. For larger and more complex projects, this list preparation may require extensive interviews; for smaller projects telephonic information from selected participants would be sufficient. The general approach of allocating resources based on the size and complexity of the project and, indeed, based on the availability of resources is the prudent course of action. (Discussion material presented earlier in this chapter could be used as a guide for this and other activities that follow.)

Some examples of tech transfer activities and documents are:

- User involvement in research project identification
- User involvement in research program execution
- Sponsor at high levels
- Effective information brochures, audiovisuals, etc.

- User manual
- Design criteria
- Patents
- Licensing for manufacture
- Operation and maintenance document
- Support center for training, etc.
- Hot line to respond to questions
- Demonstration projects
- Successful implementation for selected users

2 Activities and Tech Transfer Stages

Relate these activities to the five tech transfer stages or steps (knowledge, persuasion, decision, implementation, confimation) discussed earlier. Use some relevance scale. As an example, using a matrix, activities having the most relevance to a given stage could be rated A, those with least relevance C, and others without relevance left blank.

3 Technology Evaluation Criteria

It must be recognized that fundamentally, the ability to transfer a new technology is limited by its utility. Utility encompasses such items as relative advantage, marketability, economic feasibility, and user acceptability. Trying to push a new technology that is marginally utilitarian will result in failure in the end. At times one must deal with a technology in which considerable R&D resources have been invested and which seems utilitarian to the R&D community, but which the user community judges to be of marginal utility. It is a poor strategy for the R&D community and its top management to zealously push marginally useful technology without making a genuine effort to understand and to overcome the user community's objections. Not only is the effort likely to fail, but it could adversely affect future worthwhile efforts. In such situations, it would be prudent to recall that the focus of tech transfer is supposed to be on marketing the product rather than selling it. Thus, user needs and preferences should be given proper consideration. Emphasis then should be on activities (discussed earlier) that enhance user acceptance, though this is not always an easy course of action.

A list of evaluation criteria should be developed. Based on the discussion of characteristics of innovation and key issues in technology transfer, a suggested list follows:

Relative Advantage. To what degree is the innovation more advantageous to existing technologies? Does it save cost, time, or improve quality.

Compatibility. To what degree is the innovation compatible with existing values, experiences, capabilities, felt needs, and organizational and cultural settings?

Complexity. To what degree is the innovation complex and difficult to adopt by the users? What degree of specialized training is required before the innovation can be adopted? What specialized equipment is needed?

Trialability. To what degree can the innovation be tried on a limited basis?

Observability. To what degree can the advantages of the innovation be easily communicated to decision-makers and users?

Technical Understanding. To what degree does the research personnel fully understand the main technology?

Resource Requirement. What level of resources is required to implement the new technology? Is this resource requirement compatible with previous user experiences? Is the capital needed for the new technology available?

Advanced Development Concepts. Are the research activities going to continue to debug problems and further supplement the technology?

Growth Potential. Does the technology have a potential for growth and product applicability? Will the new technology overcome "stretching" of existing technology capabilities?

Advocate. Are there advocates at higher levels and at user level?

Market Pull. To what degree is there a market pull?

External Pressures. To what degree are there external pressures (such as regulations, competitor development, etc.)?

A numerical or relative importance scale rating scheme can be developed to evaluate a new technology vis-à-vis such criteria.

4 Activities to Enhance Evaluation Criteria

The purpose of the evaluation criteria is not necessarily to determine whether the project should be tech transferred or not, but rather to see how the viability of the tech transfer can be improved. It would seem that if the evaluation criteria are used to make a "go or no-go" decision, there may be a natural, though unfortunate, tendency on the part of the researchers to be less objective about the criteria. In actual practice this is a crucial point and needs to be emphasized. If, for example, the evaluation criteria show that the product (a new concept, process, system, or design) is not compatible with existing and past experiences, then the emphasis should be on how the innovation can be improved so that it becomes compatible.

5   Impediments to Tech Transfer

Make a list of impediments to tech transfer. This list should include organizational, resource requirements, and general behavioral-related items. In the earlier part of this chapter, much information is provided on this topic and can be used to generate a list that can be supplemented, depending on organization experience and project characteristics.

6   Suggestions to Overcome Tech Transfer Impediments

For every impediment to tech transfer, it would be useful initially to develop suggestions for overcoming the impediment. As an example, if at the higher management level there is a tepid response concerning the immediate benefits from the new technology, showing evidence of tangible, intangible, and unexpected benefits should help. Some examples of such benefits that might accrue from tech transfer include:

- Improved quality of the product.
- Increased market share due to improved quality.
- Flexibility to use the new technology for purposes other than those intended at this time.
- Strategic advantage over competitors if the new technology can provide the flexibility for necessary product lines.
- Reduced time required to do the job; even though savings in time have already been used as a savings in cost, reduced time can often provide a crucial advantage (for instance, in a military tactical situation).

7   Selection of Successful and Unsuccessful Projects

Based on the past experience of the R&D organization, select a number of projects in which tech transfer was or was not successful. The number of projects selected would depend on the total domain, diversity, and resource availability of the study. A minimum of three of each type of project is recommended, with a higher number of successful ones when more than three projects are selected.

8   Case History

Prepare a case history for each project. The examples provided in the referenced IBM projects [Cohen et al., 1979] should prove useful.

9   Refine Items 1 through 6

After analyzing the cases, items 1 through 6 should be modified. Considerable effort would be involved in executing this activity. Input from R&D

and user community personnel is needed. Emphasis here should be on doing qualitative, anthropological analysis. Quantitative analysis should be avoided unless sufficient quantifiable data are available.

10 Guidance Document for Tech Transfer

A guidance document should be prepared based on analysis performed to provide information for R&D performers. The focus of the document should be on flexible general guidance. Rigid, mandatory requirements will only be counterproductive. The document can provide a framework that allows R&D managers to develop policy, and implement strategies that foster technology transfer. The format of the document and level of detail will depend on the nature of technology, characteristics of the R&D organization, and the user community among other things.

It needs to be recognized that not all research outputs can or should be pushed to tech transfer. This is because need and technology may change during the R&D process, and R&D may not to able to produce what was thought possible during the planning stages. This type of uncertainty in R&D results should be accepted if an organization is ever going to undertake challenging R&D projects. Not being able to transfer technology successfully should not be viewed as a loss or necessarily a poor investment in the unsuccessful R&D project. Projects with unsuccessful tech transfer records can be useful as building blocks for future related research activities. There could be other unintended benefits to ongoing research efforts, though the links may seem less obvious at the time.

10.13 SUMMARY

In developing an effective management strategy for technology transfer, it is important to understand stages of technology transfer and fundamental issues and factors affecting adoption or rejection of new technologies. All these issues and factors that relate to the innovation itself, the adopter, and the organization are discussed in this chapter.

This chapter briefly describes tech transfer activities of the Agricultural Extension Service and NASA. The Agricultural Extension Service has been most successful in technology transfer of agricultural research to the farmer. Its work started in 1914. Recently, NASA has undertaken many activities in order to facilitate adoption of space technology for industrial and biomedical applications.

In the high tech area, effective and timely technology transfer from research to manufacturing is essential to maintain a competitive position in this industry. Eighteen IBM projects were studied by Cohen et al. [1979]: some were successful projects and others were not. Factors that affected technology transfer are discussed in detail.

Finally, this chapter presents an approach that should allow one to develop an effective strategy to meet the unique requirement of a given R&D organization.

Technology transfer is an issue on which many R&D managers and others involved in research have some interesting, useful, and insightful comments. Some of these comments follow:

"People by nature are conservative. therefore, reluctance to adoption of new technology is understandable."

"Because of some uncertainties involved in adopting new things, people are just not going to easily accept innovation."

"Changes and innovation are going to put some people to trouble so there will be resistance."

"Tech transfer becomes a question of personalities. Some people resist innovation and change so you really need a champion at a high enough level to push new technologies through."

"Organizations profess that they encourage adoption of new technologies but in practice initiative and risk-taking is not valued much or rewarded; mistakes are penalized quickly, promotions are given to managers who are caretakers and take little or no initiative or risk." "Some of the new technologies sound and look good, but when implemented, benefits end up being marginal and costs higher than expected. There just are too many uncertainties and hidden costs."

"Nothing encourages adoption of innovation more than external pressure from a competitor. If you don't change you may not survive."

"Time is a premium commodity, so new technology has to be convenient to adopt and benefits have to be transparent to the user."

10.14 QUESTIONS FOR CLASS DISCUSSION

1 From your experience as a consumer or a user of new technology, what kinds of factors persuaded you to adopt new technology? What factors worked against adopting new technology?

2 Now that you know about problems and issues related to technology transfer, take an R&D organization and develop a guidance document for facilitating technology transfer.

10.15 FURTHER READINGS

Chakrabarti, A. K. and A. H. Rubenstein. (1976). *Interorganizational Transfer of Technology—A Study of Adoption of NASA Innovations*. IEEE Transactions on Engineering Management V23N1, Feb. 1976.

Dorf, R. C. and K. K. F. Worthington. (1987). *Study of Technology Transfer Arrangements for Natural Laboratories*. Lawrence Livermore National Laboratory, Report No. UCRL-15967. NTIS 64-88-ISS24.

Interagency Study of Federal Laboratory Technology Transfer Organization and Operation. (1985). Federal Laboratory Consortium and Industry Working Group. Department of Energy Report No. DOE/METC-85/6019.

Rogers, E. M. (1983) *Diffusion of Innovations*, 3rd ed. New York: Free Press.

____11
ORGANIZATIONAL CHANGE IN R&D SETTINGS

This chapter is for those who are thinking of introducing change in their organization and is designed to give the manager a general, overall idea of what goes on in organizational change and how to evaluate it. When the change is substantial, the manager should get help from consultants either inside or outside the organization.

Organization change can focus on individuals, dyads (e.g., supervisor–subordinate); teams; or the whole organization. One can focus on cognitive skills (e.g., how to analyze a problem); affective changes (e.g., how to feel about one's competitors); or behaviors (e.g., how to behave correctly in particular situations). Thus, potentially, there are $4 \times 3 = 12$ kinds of organizational changes. However, to simplify this chapter we will discuss only some of these: changing individuals (cognitive, affective, behavioral), teams, or the whole organization.

Before deciding what aspect of the organization to improve it is important to analyze the strengths and weaknesses of the organization. A needs assessment is highly desirable. This can be done by interviewing at all levels of the organization, focusing on what is done well and what is done badly and needs improvement in the views of the participants.

In fact, such needs assessment should be done routinely every few years, because few R&D organizations are doing today what they did 5 years ago. Research projects, technology, and customer needs keep changing. To be responsive to such changes the organization needs to change.

The first step is to determine specifically what needs to change. Some behaviors can be changed directly; in some cases attitudes and values linked to many behaviors need to change. The strategic planning of the organization must be coordinated with the activities of each part of the organization. Then a needs assessment and a plan for change can be developed that can indicate whether people, teams, or the organization needs to change, and whether the change is mostly cognitive, affective, or behavioral. Standard operating procedures may need to be developed that will respond to the changed environment of the laboratory.

11.1 WHY ORGANIZATIONAL CHANGE

It is sometimes necessary to change the organization. The need for this change may be due to the following:

Change in the Stage of the Development of the Organization. The organization may have matured, may have become too large, or too static. Such changes may require new teams, work groups, different perspectives, or new managerial structures.

Program Fluctuation. In a dynamic R&D organization, it is not uncommon for the program to change. Considerable increase or decrease in a program may necessitate major change.

New Program Emphasis. Again, no research organization working on different programs at present can anticipate all new program emphases. As in any dynamic organization, the management must respond to changing needs. As the program emphasis changes, it becomes necessary to change the structure of the organization in response. In addition, structural changes and movement of people in the organization may be needed in order to provide visibility to new programs and a focal point for emerging requirements.

Customer Interface. When problems and issues with the sponsor interface exist, it is not uncommon for an R&D organization to restructure the organization to eliminate these problems.

Personnel Changes. Even if the total program and the focus of the research organization remain the same, some personnel changes (for example, loss of key personnel) could necessitate restructuring the organization.

Performance Problems. If some individuals or units are not performing well, some structural changes in the organization may be needed.

The Relationship of a Work Group to the Organization. If an R&D group within a research laboratory needs to relate differently to the main organization, major changes within the research group may be needed.

11.2 STEPS IN ORGANIZATIONAL CHANGE

Organizational change may involve implementation and understanding of the following steps:

Diagnosis. What is the problem? Can it be solved?

Resistance. Who has a vested interest in the status quo? If we change things, what are we going to change, and who will object?

Transfer. Introducing training, attitude change, or other new procedures.

Evaluation. Empirical determination of whether the change has been successful.

Institutionalizing. Establishing new norms and procedures, restructuring work, changing schedules to fit the new norms.

Diffusion. Telling others that the change was successful. Developing opinion leaders to increase the use of the successful methods.

11.3 PROBLEMS AND ACTION STEPS

There are a number of problems associated with implementing major organizational changes. Managers who are not sensitive to these problems and attempt to implement organizational changes in an autocratic manner will find themselves imposing an enormous cost on the organization, as well as to the individuals involved, and, indeed, to the very objectives that they had hoped to accomplish.

Management should provide an analysis indicating the need for organizational change and articulating the objectives and goals that need to be achieved as a result of this organizational change. Implementation of major changes in an organization can present significant problems and must be dealt with in such a way as to minimize their adverse impact on organization effectiveness.

Nadler [1982, p. 449] identified three major problems that occur when implementing major organizational changes:

Resistance to Change. Since change represents some uncertainty, it has an impact on the stability and security of the individuals affected. For the individual, this could mean finding new ways of coping with new situations and new environments.

Organizational Control. Organizational change may alter the existing system of management control and may change some of the existing power distribution. Organizational change may also make it difficult to monitor performance and make corrections during the transitions.

Power. Since an organization is in a way a political system consisting of different individuals, groups, and coalitions holding and competing for power, an organizational change that alters the power distribution is likely to cause some political activity.

Implications and specific action steps to overcome the problems are identified in Table 11.1. Each situation is different and each organization is unique with regard to its history, individuals involved, and specific problems being addressed by the organizational change. Consequently, the general action steps suggested can serve only as a guide for developing an organizational change plan and strategy.

11.4 INDIVIDUAL CHANGE

Discussed under individual change are cognitive, affective, and behavioral changes. Some R&D organization-related examples are also provided for these types of changes.

Cognitive Change

Individuals often need new ways of thinking, or new cognitive skills—for example, how to analyze particular technical problems. In research settings this is particularly common, since new techniques in laboratory work, or new developments in mathematics, or the scientist's discipline may require learning. Seminars, courses, and workshops are often used for such training. The lecture is one of the main methods of delivering cognitive information, but guided reading, working with a model that can demonstrate the new skills, discussions, doing problems, or presenting seminar papers are also quite effective. One must consider carefully the best mix of such activites, for the particular need.

In this age of computers, a particularly useful way is to present information in a programmed learning format. For example, a problem situation may be presented, and five possible courses of action may be suggested. The trainee must select one of these courses. After the course is selected the trainee receives feedback, indicating the strengths and weaknesses of the choice. If the most optimal choice was not selected, the trainee is asked to try another of the suggested options, and again receives feedback, until the optimal option has been selected, and then the most extensive feedback is offered. This approach can be made to look like a game. For example, if the trainee has selected a bad course of action, the feedback can be provided in an interesting and challenging manner without discouraging the trainee.

A computer does not have to be used. The same programmed learning format can be presented in a book. Even learning how to lead has been put in this format, in the so-called Leader–Match Leadership Training Program [Fiedler, Chemers, et al., 1977]. The program teaches managers how to analyze their leadership style and how to change the work environment to match their style. It has been evaluated and found to be useful (improved mine safety and productivity; see Fiedler et al., 1984). This technique was also used to teach managers going abroad to work in other cultures, and to

TABLE 11.1   Organizational Change Management and Action Steps[a]

Problem: Resistance.   Implication: Need to motivate change

ACTION STEPS

- Identify problems and issues that necessitate the need for change. Individuals affected need to be jolted out of the present complacency and stability.
- Affirmatively seek participation of the affected staff in the change. Focus on building ownership of the change among the participants so that they would be genuinely motivated to not only accept the change but make it work smoothly and effectively.
- Build in rewards for the behavior that is needed during the transition stage and after implementation. Restructure awards (e.g., pay, promotion, monetary rewards, job assignments, other recognitions) to support the direction of the transition.
- Allow time for dealing with the feeling of loss caused by the change. Show understanding and provide necessary information to help overcome the problems it might create.

Problem: Control.   Implication: Need to manage the transition

ACTION STEPS

- A critical step is to develop and communicate a clear image of the future. Recognizing that the transition and the implemented states are still dynamic systems, written information, which explains the reasons for the change, what the new organization would be like, how the transition will occur, and how individuals will be affected, should be provided.
- Include all changes needed to accommodate the new organization. This may include structural change, task change, change in the social environment, etc.
- Organizational management for the transition needs to include items such as a transition plan, a transition manager, and resources for the transition. At times, other transition management structures such as task forces or experimental units may be needed during the transition period.

Problem: Power.   Implication: Need to shape the political dynamics of change

ACTION STEPS

- Develop multiple and effective mechanisms (e.g., surveys, sensing groups, consultant interviews, formal reports on key milestones, informal channels) for generating feedback about the transition to management.
- Assemble and mobilize the key power groups in support of the change. Work with individuals adversely affected and develop ways to investigate any adverse effects caused by the change.
- Use leader behavior to generate enthusiasm and energy in support of change.
- Use positive symbols and language to generate support and enthusiasm for change.
- To build in some stability and minimize anxiety, provide some sources of stability (e.g., physical location, people, some programs, etc.) that stay unchanged. These should be identified and communicated to the organization members.

---

[a] Adapted from Nadler, [1982, p. 446].

learn something about the local customs and behaviors so as to improve their performance abroad [Triandis, 1977].

The in-basket technique is also useful in cognitive training. A manager is given a case and a series of communications, for example: a letter from a research program sponsor complaining about responsiveness, a request for information regarding an ongoing project, procurement documents, programming documents, information about upcoming meetings and visitors requiring immediate action, personnel documents, and telephone messages. The manager must decide which of the documents must be handled first, and how to deal expeditiously with them. This requires analysis of each item, decisions to delegate some items and the development of procedures for effective follow-through on all items.

Much of the written communication sent to a manager or principal investigator usually is deposited in the in-basket. Managers who do not respond effectively to this information cause inefficiencies and delays. Organizations also require effective information dissemination, which may require the manager to make phone calls, or write letters, Such actions can constitute correct responses to the in-basket training. It is particularly useful to teach managers which of the in-basket items must be handled immediately, which require more information, which can be delegated, and which require setting up follow-through procedures to be checked in the future. A common problem in organizations is that no effective follow-through mechanism exists and some items, while being acted on at different levels of an organization, are simply forgotten (i.e., fall in the cracks). This often causes a burden on the organization and dissatisfaction with the manager's performance. Failure to follow-through and respond to action items often increases the manager's own workload. New managers may not realize this, and thus the in-basket is an opportunity to teach them about the importance of follow-through.

The in-basket method has the advantage that it is very similar to the actual work of the manager. So, the training has validity and can be accepted easily by the manager. Experienced managers, who are known for the excellence of their management methods, may be used as instructors.

Affective Change

Changing the way people feel about particular activities, co-workers, or projects involves attitude change. Chapter 5 presented much information about this subject. One procedure that can be used to change emotions, not discussed so far, is sensitivity training. Sensitivity groups encourage people to provide candid assessments of the way they perceive others. They usually meet for 2 or 3 days, or a weekend, and provide an intensive experience. They are popular among those who wish to escape from loneliness, wish to receive warmth and support from others, and are supposed to teach people to tolerate anxiety, understand themselves better, change interpersonal behavior, and resolve conflict. Evaluations of these groups have generally not supported the expectation that people will change for the better. One of the problems is that institutions have well-established norms, and people have strong habits. Spending a weekend on this kind of training will not overcome habits that were developed over a long time. To change the norms one needs to work on groups or even departments rather than individuals and to provide training for everyone. Also, the consultants who do lead these workshops are not always well trained. When clients break down in the course of discovering something unpleasant about themselves workshop leaders are often unable to help them. Thus the casualty rate can be high and the objective benefits are often questionable.

Behavioral Change

Clinicians have developed very effective procedures for changing clients. However, these changes require quite a lot of one-on-one work, and are quite expensive for organizations. For example, Kanfer [1988] has developed a "self-regulation" approach that begins with the clinician working on the client's motivation to want to change. Next, the client is helped to see that certain settings, stimuli, and people are the causes of the undesirable behaviors. The client has to learn to avoid such situations, and thus master a particular technology that keeps the undesirable behaviors to a low probability.

Clients take responsibility for arranging contingencies, that is, placing themselves in situations where the undesirable cues are not present, so the behavior that needs to be suppressed is less likely to occur, and placing themselves in situations that contain the desirable cues, so that desirable behavior increases in probability. Once the desirable behavior takes place the clients learn to reward themselves. The clinician helps the client to set goals and to define the desired responses and the specific rewards to be administered after each goal has been reached. Thus clients learn to monitor their own performance, and to compare it to established criteria, as well as to self-administer rewards. Also, the client has to learn to resist temptation, that is, to avoid behaviors that are immediately enjoyable but detrimental in the long run. This requires learning to recall the distant undesirable effect at the moment a behavior is chosen. The amount of time required for an important change using this kind of approach is approximately 40 hours of clinician time. Thus, the cost is in the thousands of dollars. However, if the effectiveness of an important manager is reduced by the undesirable behavior, the organization may well be able to justify such expense.

11.5 GROUP CHANGE: TEAM BUILDING

One of the reforms frequently used in organizations is called team building. The team definition is simply "a group of people who must relate to each other in order to accomplish some task." Team building is the process of encouraging effective working relationships among members of the team and, also, reducing the barriers that may exist in effective cooperation of members of the team. There is no doubt that many teams do not work very well. Some people are not well integrated and team members do not plan together. They do not use their resources to achieve needed communication. Communication is often poor and people misunderstand or do not trust each other. A team facilitator can help members talk to one another so they can discover how much they have in common. For example, superordinate goals (goals desired by both teams that neither team can reach without the help of the other) might become salient, and members of the organization may realize that some of the mutual distrust they feel is not justified.

Since a lot of team building involves interactions with colleagues it is a very sensitive matter. It is true that if the reform does not work out as planned, the relationship may become worse than before.

In order for team building to be effective it is essential that the total culture of the organization support it. In fact, the emphasis on team building used today contrasts with the emphasis on sensitivity groups that was more prevalent about 20 years ago. This is a result of the realization that one has to work with the whole organization, rather than with just a few groups, if one is to be effective in changing the organization.

One of the problems management faces when it attempts changes is that the change may affect only isolated individuals. In the past, individuals from different parts of the organization were selected by management and sent for training. When these trainees were returned to the organization they found that the organization did not respond to the change that they had experienced. As a result, they went back to their old habits and the effect of the training was wiped out. In contrast to training specific individuals, team building involves training everybody who is part of the team; it also ensures that other groups, particularly other teams that are a part of the organization, receive the training.

An effective approach is to allow members of the team to talk to one another or send messages to each other concerning behaviors that they find desirable, objectionable, or neutral. One such technique is called "From Me to You." Each team member writes a message on a sheet of paper aimed at another team member. The message specifies behaviors that should be kept up ("keep doing that"), stopped ("stop doing that"), or started ("it would be nice if you did that"). Some of these behaviors can be job specific. Other behaviors might be social. For example, a subordinate may ask a boss for more frequent comment on the boss's perception of the subordinate's work performance or for an invitation to the boss's house once a year. These messages may be sent anonymously, or not, depending on the extent the team members are ready for the exchange of intimacies. A contract might be negotiated as a result of such exchanges. For example, "if you do more of this, I will do more of that" could be part of the agreement.

A related technique is role clarification. The trainer asks each member to identify the four or five people the member interacts with most frequently when on the job. The member then "visits" each of them and asks them to describe how they perceive the member's job. "What do you think I am supposed to do? With what frequency? When, where, how?" Such information defines the "emitted job role" as perceived by that person. By going on to all the relevant others (superiors, subordinates, and peers), the person can identify varieties of the "emitted role." Quite frequently there will be a discovery that the various important others define his/her role differently. Then it is possible to discuss the discrepancies with them as a group. The role can then be clarified.

Such role clarification can be very helpful in improving job relationships. The team member can negotiate a different role and align the subjective role with the emitted role. As a result, the enacted role can become a much closer version of the subjective role since the subjective role becomes more salient and clearer to everyone.

A usual approach to team building is to begin with a diagnostic phase, in which team members answer a questionnaire that indicates team problems and difficulties. Usually about 10 questions are asked about each of the following areas [Francis and Young, 1979]:

1. *Effective Leadership* e.g., "Team members are uncertain about their individual roles in relation to the team."
2. *Suitable Team Membership* e.g., "We need an input of new knowledge and skills to make the team complete."
3. *Team Commitment* e.g., "No one is trying hard to make this a winning team."
4. *Team Climate* e.g., "There is much stress placed on conformity."
5. *Team Achievement* e.g., "In practice the team rarely achieves its objectives."
6. *Relevant Corporate Role* e.g., "We do not work within clear strategic guidelines."
7. *Effective Work Methods* e.g., "Team members rarely plan or prepare for meetings."
8. *Team Organization* e.g., "We do not examine how the team spends its time and energy."
9. *Critiquing* e.g., "The team is not good at learning from its mistakes."
10. *Individual Development* e.g., "The team does not take steps to develop its members."
11. *Creative Capacity* e.g., "Good ideas seem to get lost."
12. *Intergroup Relationships* e.g., "Conflicts between our team and other groups are quite common."

If a team agrees with many negative statements in a particular area it indicates that some team building work is needed. Special exercises are available corresponding to each of these 12 areas. For example, the "From Me to You" exercise described above can be used to improve team climate.

Team building also involves communication exercises, reviewing the progress that is made in each of the areas that has been targeted for change, and, finally, taking a second measure with the questionnaire mentioned above. The second time, if the team checks fewer negative items that correspond to the 12 dimensions of team building, one can assume that some positive change has occurred. However, a multimethod approach to team change evaluation is recommended and should include a wide range of measurements.

The different phases of team building can include cognitive, affective, and behavioral changes. Specifically, after the administration of an instrument, such as the one previously described, there is bound to be some cognitive change, for example, "our team has a problem learning from its mistakes." The various team-building exercises change both affect (how people feel about themselves and their team colleagues) and behavior (how people respond to each other). Decisions by the team to institute new standard operating procedures result in behavior change. Of course, some behaviors are easier to change than others. If the behaviors are automatic, and determined by habits, there needs to be a substantial interference with the cue-behavior sequence to modify the behavior. Other behaviors are easy to change. For example, discovering that a task one finds unpleasant to do is undesirable from a wide variety of perspectives can easily lead to change.

11.6 ORGANIZATIONAL CHANGE

Two techniques: survey feedback and grid organizational development can, at times, be useful in understanding organizational problems and ways to overcome them. These techniques require administering a questionnaire and working with different levels of management. This means an experienced consultant would be needed to help implement these techniques.

Survey Feedback

In this case a consultant distributes a questionnaire throughout the organization, the data collected are aggregated in a variety of ways and fed back to the organization, which discusses them in several sessions. Much of the discussion turns out to be technical: it criticizes specific questions and indicates how they can be interpreted in different ways. The organization can obtain some benefit from this exercise, particularly when top management realizes that certain departments do have low morale, that communication upward is poor, that supervisors are really unaware of problems faced by subordinates, and that researcher ideas are not sought for organizational goal setting. Management can use survey results to focus on the problem and to introduce change using techniques such as team building.

Grid Organizational Development

This approach starts with top management and works through to the bottom of the managerial structure in an attempt to sensitize managers to the importance of the human factor and healthy relationships. Generally, managers are task oriented (otherwise they would not have gotten there), so the emphasis on human relationships sensitizes them to a dimension that they tend to underuse. The approach also provides training in conflict management, and is an opportunity to review policies, objectives, make plans, and evaluate changes that have already been made. In the hands of a good consultant this approach is quite helpful.

11.7   EVALUATING ORGANIZATIONAL CHANGE

The several kinds of changes outlined above need to be evaluated. The organization needs to know whether the costs of particular changes can be justified. It needs to assess what techniques of change work and what techniques are ineffective. Since each organization is to some extent unique, with its own culture, the fact that one technique worked in another organization does not mean that it will be effective in your own.

The most important attitude that managers need to develop about organizational change is that every change is an experiment. When we do an experiment we modify some independent variables and measure some dependent variables. Similarly when we undertake an organizational change (our independent variable) we must measure its effects on the organization (our dependent variable). The reason we do experiments is because we want to unlock the secrets of nature. Organizations are also part of nature. In fact, they are a very complex part of nature. Designing changes for organizations that will improve them is much more difficult than doing a chemistry experiment. So, we must be modest in our expectations, and not anticipate miracles. But with systematic change, and careful measurement, we should be able to sort the changes that are effective from the changes that are ineffective or hurt the organization.

Unfortunately, administrators often have the wrong attitudes about organizational change. Since they are the ones who approved the change they feel ego-involved. Since they want the change to succeed, they are unable to take an objective, open, experimental approach. Yet, that is exactly the approach that is needed. It is important that managers train themselves to see organizational change supportively, but also critically. If it fails, try again. In other words, the correct attitude is to view change as an experiment, which may or may not work. If all our experiments came out the way we expected, there would be no point in doing them! It is exactly because we get unanticipated results that we keep experimenting. Similarly, we should not assume that every innovation will benefit the organization, and we should not put down our peers or subordinates who fail to introduce successful innovations. In fact, if one never fails this may be a sign of too low a level of risk. The bold innovator has more failures than successes, but the few successes often change the world.

In sum, we must not expect that our first idea about organizational change is going to work. Try, and try again. Keep measuring what happens and you will gradually find out what works.

When doing evaluation research following organizational change, we need to use many methods and a variety of very different methods. For example, one may wish to measure job satisfaction, turnover rates, productivity rates, quality of publications, and many other dependent variables before deciding that a particular reform has or has not been successful.

In evaluating reforms one must also consider that any particular reform continues over time, and thus cannot always be evaluated at only one point. In fact, people who are specialists in evaluation research have distinguished between *formative* and *summative* evaluation. Formative evaluation examines the effects of the change as it happens. Thus one modifies the organizational change to take into account the results of the evaluation. In the case of summative evaluation, on the other hand, one waits until the change has occurred, and has been in place for some time, before making the evaluation.

Specialists in evaluation have used a variety of ways to make their evaluations. For example, some people advocate self–study as a means of getting the group affected by the change to assess how the particular reform has worked for them. Another approach consists of forming a blue-ribbon committee, usually consisting of people outside of the administrative unit in which the change has occurred, who come in, ask a lot of questions, and make a judgment as to whether the particular reform has been effective. Still another method is to look at particular data sets as criteria for an effective reform. These data sets may include the dollar amounts of grants and contracts obtained to support the research, the number of publications, judgments about the quality of the publications, the extent to which the persons or groups who were part of the changes are being quoted, or the reputation of the group. Still other possibilities include bringing in a specialist with an adversarial view, whose role is to discover that the reform is ineffective. This specialist is usually a critic of the reform, and may often uncover problems that the participants may not see. Still another approach is goal-free evaluation, in which the evaluator simply tries to find out what "really" is happening or has happened. The idea in this case is that the evaluator is an unbiased spectator who can evaluate the change most appropriately. There are also classical evaluation specialists, who utilize "experimental" and "control" groups or look at the results of change over time. They use the particular group's performance prior to the introduction of a reform as a control for the evaluation of the change that has occurred since the reform was introduced. Still another approach is the one used by anthropologists who look at what is happening, and describe it as well as they can from the perspective of the "natives" (the members of the organization). This is done without any idea about the antecedents or the correlates of the observations they make.

It is often the case that a combination of these approaches may be optimal in order to gain a really good understanding of the effects of the reform.

Another issue in evaluation research is the question of whose perspective to take more seriously. For example, in a department in a particular organization, the members of the department may represent one perspective, top management may represent a different perspective, the supervisor of the department may have a third perspective, and the peers in other departments may have a fourth perspective. Who is to say whose perspective should be taken more seriously? Should one weigh the various perspectives to get a single index that reflects the particular reform?

11.8 SUMMARY

Organizations often need to be changed. One needs to understand problems associated with organizational change and the action steps that might help overcome these problems. Some individual changes can be accomplished through training, whereas others require extensive one-on-one clinical work. Some group change can be accomplished by team building techniques; other techniques for organizational change involve survey feedback and grid organizational development. These aspects of individual and organizational change are discussed in this chapter. Evaluation of the change is necessary to ascertain that desired objectives are reached. Different procedures for evaluating change are outlined in the chapter. A combination of these approaches needs to be used to cover many perspectives and to reduce bias.

11.9 QUESTIONS FOR CLASS DISCUSSION

1 Suppose you were going to do some "team building" in your R&D lab. What would be the steps?

2 What would be some considerations that may militate against team building?

3 What criteria for effective team building would you use?

4 Review the methods of evaluation of an organizational change. Which method should be used for which condition?

11.10 FURTHER READING

Francis, D. and D. Young (1979). *Improving Work Groups*. San Diego, CA: University Associates.

Nystrom, P. C. and W. H. Starbuck (1981). Remodelling organizations and their environments. *Handbook of Organizational Design*, Vol. 2. Oxford University Press.

APPENDIX: RESEARCH, DEVELOPMENT, AND SCIENCE POLICY

We have added this appendix because we felt that researchers need to see how their activities relate to social goals, and must be able to understand trends that shape science policy. Since they do have some choices of how they will spend their time, they must be able to influence funding for their research. Science policy should not be shaped only in the nation's capital. Unfortunately, one of the major problems in the United States has been insufficient participation by scientists in the formulation of this policy. In discussing research goals with colleagues, supervisors, subordinates, and science policy formulators, researchers need to know something about the formulation of science policy. In a democracy, if government alone is left to decide such matters, it will result in second-rate policy. Participation by scientists is necessary for the sound development of such policy. To do this effectively, scientists need to understand:

- Relationships between science and technology
- Need for investment in basic research
- R&D expenditures and economic development
- R&D expenditures internationally and nationally.

Some of the information in this appendix provides a global view of international and national investment in research. While this may seem to be of little utility to a principal investigator or a research manager, there is no question that the information included here provides a broad understanding of the research enterprise and its implication for science policy and has a number of possible uses at certain times or at some levels. Some suggestions on how a principal investigator or a research manager can use this information follow.

A persuasive case has been made that investment in R&D plays a crucial role in the economic well-being of a nation, the profitability of a business enterprise, and the effectiveness of a technology-based governmental agency. There is evidence that the return on R&D investment in industry is higher than investment in other activities [Nadiri, 1980]. R&D managers can use this information to develop a strategy for making a case for their own program.

Using national information as a model, the R&D manager of a research group or a laboratory may want to conduct a study to check the effectiveness of its research activities. For example, return on investment (ROI) of selected completed research projects can be analyzed. To minimize biases, some research organizations have a third party conduct such ROI studies. In conducting such a study, tangible benefits accrued from the utilization of the research output are documented and analyzed through direct discussions with the users and costs are determined through discussions with the research group. In one case, such an activity demonstrated that the return on investment from completed research projects was, on the average, 30 to 1. As a note of caution, since only completed research projects can be analyzed and since there is a natural bias built into selecting more successful projects than others, the overall return on investment may be somewhat lower than such a study has shown. In any case, such information can provide a powerful argument for convincing research sponsors to provide the necessary resources.

Research requires considerable resources; it is indeed an expensive activity. The data we present here may be used to support the need for realistic budgets that may seem inflated to those who are unfamiliar with R&D. For research excellence, it is necessary to attract talented scientists and have well-equipped laboratories. None of this is possible without sufficient funding. Seeking funds for research is also an excellent way to test the market and user response to previous research outputs. Making a successful case for research funding and convincing sponsors and customers of the considerable benefits that R&D output provides is, in the final analysis, an effective feedback mechanism that is healthy for all concerned.

Discussion of university–industry linkage should be of interest to principal investigators and research managers. Organizations interested in university linkages should find many useful ideas for leveraging R&D investment by working cooperatively with the university community.

A.1 RELATIONSHIP BETWEEN SCIENCE AND TECHNOLOGY

There is consensus in the literature and among knowledgeable scientists that technology stimulates science. As Bondi [1967] put it: "It is certainly a matter of experience that every time our experimental technique has taken a leap forward, we have found things totally unexpected and wholly unimaginable before. I see no reason whatever to expect that future improvements in experimental techniques will not have the same effect." This comment reminds us of the advances in astronomy after the development of the telescope, in bacteriology after the invention of the microscope, and so on. Innumerable other examples are possible.

On the other hand, in the opinion of some it is not so clear that science stimulates technology. Price [1965] examined citation patterns in both scientific and technological journals and did not find a link; Langrish [1971] argued that the role of universities in industrial innovation is limited. While university research can be justified on other grounds, such as the training of students [Allen, 1977], it is not possible to justify it as a stimulant to innovation alone. On the other hand, Gibbons and Johnston [1974] found that one-sixth of the information needed to solve technological problems came from scientific journals.

The best conclusion, it seems, is to think of the scientific and technological systems as mutually supportive and interacting mechanisms. Science, technology, and the market are interrelated [Freeman, 1982] and in developing science policy we ought to consider support for both science and technology. Achieving a balance in support for both requires additional considerations.

A.2 BASIC RESEARCH—WHO NEEDS IT?

The conduct of basic research that does not have immediate commercial benefit raises questions such as "Who needs it?" and "Why do it?"

In the public sector, as in the industrial sector, decision-makers are often concerned with current problems and issues. Since basic research involves discovering fundamental mechanisms rather than achieving practical applications, and there is considerable uncertainty and risk, it is not difficult to understand why support for basic research is not always as strong as one might expect.

Personnel involved in basic research need the resources to undertake such activities. In addition, scientists want freedom to investigate the topics they deem worthwhile. Basic research requires a great deal of time, but decision-markers tend to be impatient. Also, decision-makers faced with distributing scarce resources among competing requirements may find it difficult to support basic research. This problem needs to be understood and further analyzed.

One could argue that if resources are not invested in basic research, the foundation necessary for technological innovation (infrastructure for training scientists and engineers, trained personnel, and new inventions) would be missing. On the other hand, without technological innovation and investment in technology, the increase in productivity and the general economic well-being of society would be missing. After all, commercialization of technology is the engine that produces resources for use in basic research and for investment in the future. While the scientific community may want the decision-makers to understand the importance of basic research for the long-term viability of an industrialized society, it is equally important that scientists understand the importance of the innovation process, which turns outputs from research and development into useful commercial products so that the extra resources needed for basic research can become available.

Basic research focuses on the development of new knowledge, much of which is embodied in scientific information that cannot be made into a marketable private property. As Merton [1973, p. 273] has suggested, the findings of science are a product of collaboration within the scientific community. Discoveries are the property of the commons, and the rights to these properties are assigned to the wider scientific community. This implies that in most cases the output from basic research is not marketable. This raises questions such as:

- Who should fund basic research?
- How should the resources devoted to basic research be determined?
- How should efficiency in the use of these resources be achieved?

Funds for Basic Research

There seem to be three major possible funding sources: private enterprise through the free market economy, governmental agencies, and nonprofit foundations. It is useful to examine which sources are most likely to fund activities that will improve society.

Arrow [1974, pp. 144–163], discussing the allocation of resources for invention, has treated this subject very elegantly and thoroughly. He suggests that the possible failure of perfect competition to achieve optimal resource allocation through the free market system is related to several factors. His discussion is too technical for review here, but the conclusion is clear: the free market system is not going to be able to allocate the necessary resources to basic research activities. In addition, no matter what the demand for the output of basic research might be, it would be less than optimal in a free market system, for two reasons: "(1) since the price is positive and not at its optimal value of zero, the demand is bound to be below the optimal; (2)...at any given price, the very nature of information will lead to a lower demand than would be optimal" [Arrow, 1974, p. 154]. What this means is that even if the free market system could provide the necessary basic research funds, this would not be in the best interest of society since the basic research output would be utilized at a level that is less than optimal for society. As discussed later in this appendix, noncommercial sources have historically been the major funding sources of basic research. And this not only makes sense, but is desirable from a societal viewpoint.

It is important to note that sometimes the output from basic research is needed to conduct applied research and that science (the output from basic research) and technology interact with the market or human needs to foster the innovation process. Logically, the only basic research supported by industry then would be in areas where investment in basic research is essential to complete product developments that have present or potential commercial benefits.

In discussing this issue of basic research, Professor Andrew Schofield of Cambridge University pointed out that in pursuing new knowledge, in addition to the wages paid to a researcher and the capital invested in laboratory facilities, there is the fundamental issue of the individual scientist's motivation and drive to discover. Many scientists invest considerable personal time, effort, and emotional energy in pursuing new knowledge regardless of its marketability or immediate utility. This investment by the individual scientist may be far more important than the institutional investment in basic research. Management practices that recognize this and foster an innovative environment—via job design, organization development, and reward system—may result in increased effectiveness of institutional investment in basic research.

Level of Resource Allocation

Because of the reasons cited above, private enterprise is not able to allocate the necessary resources for basic research using the efficient competitive market processes, except where basic research is needed for commercial product development. Any time government or other nonprofit organizations find themselves engaging in such activities, the level of resource allocation becomes a problem. Other surrogate measures and social needs have to be used, recognizing that the level of resource allocation in such cases cannot be as efficient or as self-correcting as the market mechanism. Discussion of some of these measures and needs follows:

Economic Considerations. Presumably, resources should be allocated so that the expected marginal social benefit exceeds or equals the marginal social benefit of competing usages. Because of considerable uncertainty and other complexities, these computations may simply be based on a preference index, which might itself be determined by the expected economic benefits.

Its Contribution to Social Welfare. As Freeman [1982, p. 201] has stated, "The advance of science and technology must find its support and its justification, not merely in the expectation of competitive advantage, whether national or private, military or civil, but far more in its contribution to social welfare, conceived in a wider sense." One of the colleagues at

Cambridge University stated that basic research should be looked at as "an important cultural activity. If one is looking for direct returns, one is not likely to see a penny back." Therefore, decisions on allocating resources for basic research have to consider its enormous social welfare benefits.

Based on Comparative Needs. One could look at the historical record or compare percentage of gross national product devoted to basic research by other nations, and the impact of varying percentages of investment in basic research on economic productivity and the social welfare of society.

Other Considerations. In discussing this with some eminent R&D managers (identified in the Preface), a number of other practical considerations emerged, as reflected in the following comments:

> Basic research investment runs 10–15% of total R&D and depends on:
>
> "Do we have the people who are interested?"
> "Do we have the people who have the time?"
> "Do we have the people who are able to conduct basic research?"
>
> This really determines the level of basic research funding in most cases.

As discussed in Chapter 1, a scientist who engages in a mix of basic and applied research is likely to be more productive than one who does not. Therefore, even for a profit-oriented industrial organization, allowing the scientist to undertake some basic research, regardless of its profitability or immediate utility, is best for all concerned. This will keep the scientist at the cutting edge of the discipline, provide a higher level of motivation, and, inevitably, result in greater productivity in the applied aspects of the research as well.

Efficient Usage of Basic Research Investment

At the macro level, efficient usage is partially achieved by establishing an appropriate science policy. For basic research, by and large, payment is independent of the results achieved. So, the traditional market mechanism is irrelevant. There are, however, other mechanisms that ensure efficiency at the macro and micro levels:

- The peer review process to determine the merits of proposed basic research projects.
- Awarding research contracts to those who have previously performed research successfully.
- The ethos of the scientific community (universalism, communalism, disinterestedness, and organized skepticism) that provides a vigorous review and analysis mechanism contributes to efficiency.

- Suggestions presented in this book, for creating a productive and efficient R&D organization, might be helpful.

Peer review and other processes mentioned here have historically worked well, but they tend to be a bit conservative and they lack flexibility. Major breakthroughs are unlikely to be anticipated by a committee. In an R&D organization a portion of total R&D funding can be provided to managers at different levels as discretionary funds to be used for high risk research projects. Our experience indicates that this approach has proved very fruit-ful. It reduces the lead time required for the normal funding cycle for a project and provides the flexibility so necessary to undertaking high-risk, exploratory research requiring relatively low investment.

A.3   UNIVERSITY–INDUSTRY LINKAGE

As participants in a Technological Innovation Symposium savored the food and drink in the Fellows' Dining Room at Churchill College (Cambridge University), Maurice Goldsmith [1970, p. xiii] stated that "it was easier to accept why the 'educational purists' of the past, in such a cloistered, culti-vated atmosphere, had been able to contribute to Britain's slow decline in industrial efficiency by insisting on the separation between the university, technology, and industry."

If a university can contribute to the decline of a major world industrial power like Great Britain, presumably the same university has the potential to contribute to the rise of a nation to a world industrial power. This would further point to the importance of the university community contribution to innovation and industrialization. Cambridge University provides an example of university–industry cooperation that is worth noting.

The Cambridge Phenomenon

Notwithstanding Goldsmith's comments, the fact is that few universities, if any, have contributed so much to Britain's industrial efficiency, economic well-being, and technological leadership as has Cambridge University. Dur-ing World War II, Cambridge scientists helped develop technologies such as the radar, telecommunication, and nuclear physics that helped provide the allies with a winning edge! At present, the well-known "Cambridge phe-nomenon," which has helped foster development of many science parks around Cambridge, has resulted from the collaboration between the Cam-bridge University community and industry. Capital investment for the in-frastructure (land, buildings, and laboratory facilities) for one of the largest science parks around Cambridge was provided by one of the colleges of Cambridge University [Wicksteed, 1985].

In fostering university–industry links, Cambridge University consciously avoided a structured and detailed policy governing these ties. On the issues of intellectual property rights, risk and liability, and industrial liaison, the university position evolved as follows.

Cambridge believes that the ownership of intellectual properties rests with the individual University member, unless the contract governing the work in which the know-how is acquired specifies otherwise. The University does not exercise any control over or have a financial interest in the exploitation of an academic's know-how, unless the academic asks the University to play such a role. It is felt that successful exploitation must ultimately depend on the motivation and skill of the academic.

Cambridge University has consistently taken a relaxed and liberal attitude toward the time spent by faculty on outside work. It is presumed that outside activities will be beneficial to teaching and research activities.

The University does not accept any legal liability for work done by faculty members for outside organizations. Naturally, if the rewards accrue to the academics, the latter must accept the risks too and make their own arrangements for professional liability, and so on.

The Cambridge experience shows that a relaxed attitude and the simplicity of this industrial liaison arrangement have helped nurture a culture that encourages and is supportive of university links with industry [Wicksteed, 1985, p. 77]. As exemplified by the Cambridge phenomenon the university–industry link positively affects the institution's responsibilities for teaching, research, and public service. In addition to direct economic benefits to the nation, this link enhances the faculty's intellectual and technical capabilities.

Science Parks

In the United States, high technology enclaves include "Silicon Valley" in California, Route 128 in Boston, the Research Triangle Park in North Carolina, and others. In 1940 Santa Clara County, where Silicon Valley is located, was a peaceful agricultural region with a population of only 175,000. It is now one of the densest concentrations of high technology enterprises in the world and has reached a population of over 1 million. A recent estimate puts the number of high technology firms in Silicon Valley at a little over 1200, employing around 190,000 persons [*Washington Post*, December 3, 1984]. This development has been fostered by the presence of major universities such as Stanford and the University of California, Berkeley. Similarly, the Route 128 phenomenon has been helped by the proximity of MIT and other universities in the Boston area. The size and scope of spin-off industries in both Silicon Valley and Route 128 are far more extensive than the industrial parks around Cambridge. In the United States there are other university locations as well where there is a concentration of high technology industry, though none on the scale of Silicon Valley or Route 128.

University–Industry–Government Interaction

As discussed in *Science Indicators* [1985, p. 108], the American system of university–industry research connections is without parallel in the world. The system is complex, involving individual, institutional, and corporate responses to many needs and opportunities. This interaction may consist of general research support to universities in the form of monetary gifts, equipment donations, endowment funds, construction of research facilities, or exchange of personnel. It may also take the form of cooperative research support through research consortia, cooperative research centers, and university-based institutes serving industrial needs.

The American university and government relationship is unique. As discussed by Donald Kennedy [1985, p. 480], the President of Standford University, the federal government could have established a set of quasi-independent laboratories in cooperation with the industrial sector, like the Max Planck Institutes in Germany, or it could have established large government laboratories. Instead, for publicly supported fundamental research, the government has historically relied on the university community. This approach guaranteed that new discoveries in science and the training of such scientists could take place at the same locations—the great American universities.

President Derek Bok [1982, p. 153], of Harvard University, has suggested several mechanisms for improving university–industry linkages. Some examples are industrial scientists teaching as adjunct professors and thereby contributing to the academic program of the department while providing a channel of communication between the university and an industrial laboratory; arranging postdoctoral programs for industrial scientists at universities; university scientists working as consultants to industry, thus bringing recent developments and critical judgments from the university to industry, or performing contract research for industry; combined university–industry–government research programs; or the establishment of high technology research enterprises by faculty members themselves as exemplified by the Cambridge phenomenon discussed earlier.

Science and technology, as we have seen, contribute to national economic efficiency and productivity. The expediency and efficiency with which we are able to translate scientific knowledge into innovation—commercially useful products and processes—forms the mechanism for this increase in national productivity and economic well-being. The universities employ outstanding scientists and engineers who perform the research that forms a basis for the innovation process. An industry or a government research laboratory that fosters interaction between its scientists and the university community is bound to improve its research productivity and quality. In addition, unique laboratory research facilities at the universities, and the personnel needed to operate such facilities, would be quite expensive if not impossible to duplicate at most commercial or governmental laboratories. In many cases, therefore, especially for basic and related applied research projects, sponsors can leverage their investment by providing research grants to a university.

There are many other ways commercial or governmental research laboratories can leverage their investment in research:

- Providing seed money to a university researcher to explore an area of interest to an industrial consortium. If research results are promising, other agencies such as the National Science Foundation (NSF) may provide funding to continue the effort.
- By providing support to carry out, beyond the basic research stage, research activities originally funded by NSF or other noncommercial organizations.
- By providing graduate student support for research projects. This engages not only the student but a significant effort of faculty in a research area at a very nominal cost. Experience shows this has other benefits as well, such as the availability of trained scientists in areas of interest to the sponsor.
- By jointly building and operating some aspects of a research facility and thus sharing equipment, personnel, and costs. There are numerous successful examples of such endeavors. These activities are easier to manage if the governmental research facility is co-located with the university.
- By exchange of research personnel.

A.4 Technical Innovation and Economic Development

Labor, capital investment, availability of natural resources and raw material, technical innovation, and management skills all contribute to high productivity and economic development in a nation. Here the discussion will focus on the role R&D plays in technological innovation and economic development.

The discussion on the output of science and technology pointed out that R&D productivity to some degree can be measured by output in terms of scientific literature, patents, and the gross domestic product of each employed person. A general relationship or correlation between investment in R&D and these three items seems to exist. This general correlation can never be precise because factors other than R&D (such as capital, quality of the labor force, social, economic, and political factors, among other variables) also play a major role. There is also the phenomenon of economic cycles. Studies conducted by the Systems Dynamic Group at MIT suggest that economies move through long waves of approximately 50 years duration. In the early part of the cycle productivity per person increases. This upswing is due to an increase in capital investment per person, but after the accumulation of the physical facilities and the capital investment, adding more capital does not necessarily add to productivity [Rothwell and Zegwell, 1982, p. 39].

Technological innovation as discussed previously combines understanding and invention in the form of socially useful and affordable products and processes. To produce this basic understanding and invention, investment in basic research is required. One could argue that the investment in one country could be in basic research, but that the benefits might accrue to another country that combines the results of basic research to produce useful and commercially profitable products and processes. In any case, looking at the world as a complete system, investment in R&D is necessary for innovation.

In examining the role of technology in enhancing productivity for the private, nonagricultural sector of the U.S. economy, we see that from 1909 to 1949 the cumulative percentage change in output per work-hour amounted to 80.9% [Rothwell and Zegwell, 1982, p. 24]. Of this, 87.5% of the total increase in output per work-hour was due to technical change; the rest was due to increased capital per work-hour. Another study conducted by Denison and reported by Rothwell and Zegwell [1982, p. 25] indicates that between 1929 and 1957 the contribution of technology to total growth was about 20%.

Commenting on the role of technological innovation in economic development, Charpie [1970, p. 3] states that in industrialized economies, all of the studies show that 30–50% of long-term economic growth stems from innovation that either improves productivity or leads to new products, processes, or completely new industries. It is further suggested [Charpie, 1970, p. 51] that technology affects international trade in several ways. International payments for technology such as patent royalties, payments for technical know-how, and so on flow predominantly to the nations that invest heavily in research and development, that is, the innovative nations. According to OECD figures, for example, the United States receives 10 times as much in technological payments from abroad as it makes in such payments to other nations [Charpie, 1970, p. 5].

Possession of high technology capacity has worked to the advantage of innovative industrialized nations in many other ways. When low-technology natural products are produced in low labor-cost countries, industrialized countries can overcome the labor cost disadvantage by producing high technology products for export, thus more than replacing the import balance. An example is the export of synthetic fiber from the United States to countries where low technology, labor-intensive cotton and wool were produced for export to the United States [Charpie, 1970, p. 5]. Nations that have demonstrated the highest innovative performance and investment and that have the necessary infrastructure for R&D are most likely to come on new opportunities that further improve their technological position in the world [Charpie, 1970, p. 5].

While in the short run economic progress may be made by applying the existing scientific knowledge base, in the long run, this simply is not possible. Freeman states [1982, p. 5]:

> It is only to assert the fundamental point that for any given technique of production, transport or distribution, there are long-run limitations on the growth of productivity, which are technologically determined. No amount of improvement in education and quality of labor force, no greater efforts by the mass media, no economies of scale or structural changes, no improvements in management or in governmental administration could in themselves ultimately transcend the technical limitations of candlepower as a means of illumination, of wind as a source of energy, or iron as an engineering material, or of horses as a means of transport. Without technological innovation, economic progress would cease in the long run and in this sense we are justified in regarding it as primary.

It is important to note that factors such as the education and training of the labor force, an efficient industrial infrastructure (such as transportation and communication networks), capital investment, and management skills all contribute to economic productivity. But without new inventions, and the scientific base to produce them, economic growth and productivity simply will not continue to increase.

In summary, while investment in R&D is correlated with improved economic performance, the broad trends outlined here suggest that the United States is losing ground in relation to other industrial countries.

A.5 Analysis of Investment in Basic Research

Reviewing the basic research investment in the United States, we find that in 1960, 9% of total U.S. R&D support was applied for this purpose. From 1976 on it has been approximately 12% of the total U.S. R&D effort [*Science Indicators*, 1985, p. 37]. This indicates a significant increase in support of basic research.

In the United States, the federal government continues to be the primary source of basic research support, providing two-thirds of the total funding [*Science Indicators*, 1985, p. 37]. This is quite understandable. Results of basic research are a property of the commons and these results are shared widely and without regard to commercialization. Since no property rights can normally be attached to the basic research output, significant investment by industry in basic research is unlikely. What investment industry does make in basic research serves the special needs of some high technology companies. The reasons for such investment may relate to (1) industry recognition of the link between science and technology and, in turn, the link between basic research and innovation; (2) the need to have a diverse portfolio of activities to increase research productivity; (3) industry recognition that providing opportunities for conducting basic research is essential to keeping high calibre scientists; and (4) attempts to reduce the time between basic research output and innovation by funding its own, rather focused, basic research to achieve a competitive advantage.

Federal government and industry investment in basic research is necessary to:

- Support the science and engineering (S/E) education process and to train the needed S/E manpower;
- Provide a vigorous link between invention and innovation;
- Maintain international competitiveness for industry;
- Provide technologies for critical national needs such as public health and national defense.

National investment in basic research, thus, benefits industry and the public and, therefore, is an important element of national science policy.

A.6   R&D EXPENDITURE

Investment in R&D in the United States and other countries has increased in recent years. Figure A.1 shows the total R&D expenditure in the United States and in four other major industrialized countries. The expenditures as shown in Figure A.1 have been converted into constant 1982 U.S. dollars, taking into account inflation and differences in the power of the national currencies of the countries involved.

Studies show that firms receive a rate of return of 30% for the typical R&D project, while the rate of return to society is even higher [Nadiri, 1980]. Of course, if more firms engaged in R&D and at a higher level, it is very likely that the rate of return would become lower. However, the fact that return on investment is now high suggests that we have not yet reached optimal levels of R&D activities. This does not imply that consulting engineering and professional firms, or small industries could always profitably engage in internally funded basic or applied research. The size of the firm, technology of the enterprise, availability of resources for investment in research, the competitive market situation, the need for R&D activity, and an effective R&D organization within the firm should be evaluated before undertaking an investment in R&D.

Perhaps one of the best measures of R&D activity in a country is the number of scientists and engineers (S/E) employed in conducting R&D. Figure A.2 shows the relative R&D efforts of six countries as indicated by the proportion of the labor force employed as scientists and engineers in R&D. Figure A.3 shows national expenditures for performance of R&D as a percentage of GNP for selected countries. Figures A.2 and A.3 show that

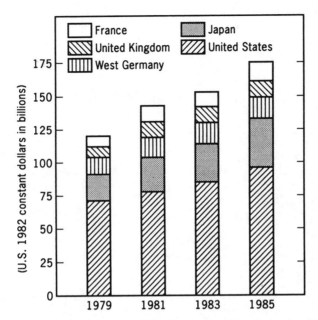

Figure A.1. Expenditures on research and development in selected countries. Foreign currency data are converted into U.S. dollars using current purchasing power parities. The data are then converted to 1982 dollars using the U.S. GNP deflator. *Science and Engineering Indicators*, 1987, p. 3.)

the Soviet Union appears to maintain a relatively large R&D effort in science and technology.

In the United States, R&D investment reached a level of about 132 billion dollars in 1988. Information regarding trends in R&D investment in current and constant 1982 dollars is shown in Figure A.4. The relative distribution of R&D expenditures in 1985 by source, performer, and type of R&D is shown in Figure A.5. That year half of the R&D activities in the United States were supported by industry. As one would expect, industry-supported R&D focused on developing commercial products for marketing in the United States and overseas, whereas federally supported R&D focused on areas such as defense, health, space, energy, agriculture, and other noncommercial but nationally important areas.

The U.S. Office of Management and Budget (OMB) divides the federal budget into functional categories that reflect areas of U.S. federal government responsibility. Of the 16 major categories that contain R&D programs, national defense receives the largest share of U.S. federal investment in R&D, and health accounts for the next largest. Relative distribution in 1986 of U.S. federal funds for R&D by selected budget function is shown in Figure A.6. U.S. government budget authority for national defense and nondefense purposes over the years in constant 1972 dollars is shown in

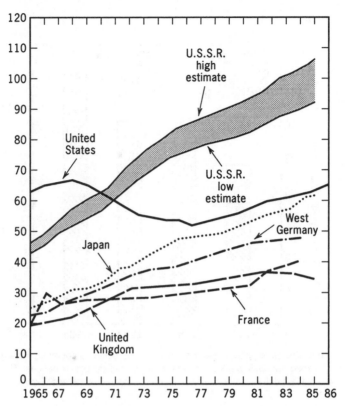

Figure A.2. Scientists and engineers engaged in R&D per 10,000 labor force population. (Source: *Science and Engineering Indicators*, 1987, p. 5.)

Figure A.7. U.S. federal government support for nondefense R&D declined in constant dollar terms at an average annual rate of 1.8% between 1976 and 1986. A comparison showing the federal obligations for research and development in constant 1972 dollars for 1980 and 1986 for selected major federal agencies is shown in Figure A.8.

U.S. government policy has sought to increase funding for basic research within all federal agencies and especially for research at academic institutions. In addition, the industrial sector is expected to expand its support for basic research at universities in an effort to further strengthen the science and technology base so necessary for sustained industrial development. Figure A.9 shows national expenditures for academic R&D by source in current and constant 1972 dollars.

Since defense-related R&D is not primarily oriented toward a nation's trade competitiveness, its public health, or other nondefense objectives, a comparison of nondefense R&D expenditures to GNP may be of interest. Figure A.10 provides this information. It is interesting to note that the ranking of countries based on the proportion of GNP devoted to nondefense R&D expenditure is similar to their ranking by the percentage of national

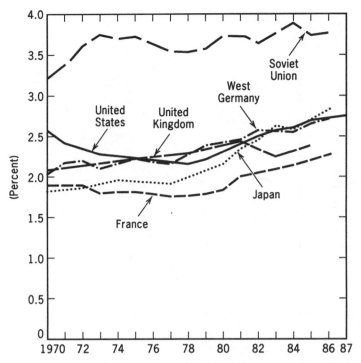

Figure A.3. R&D expenditures as a percentage of GNP, by country. (Source: *Science and Engineering Indicators*, 1987, p. 3.)

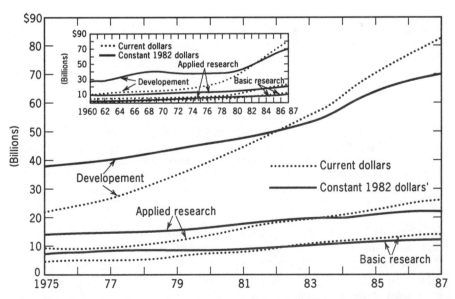

Figure A.4. National R&D expenditures by character of work. GNP implicit price deflators are used to convert current dollars to constant 1982 dollars. Estimates are shown for 1985, 1986, and 1987. (Source: *Science and Engineering Indicators*, 1987, p. 4.)

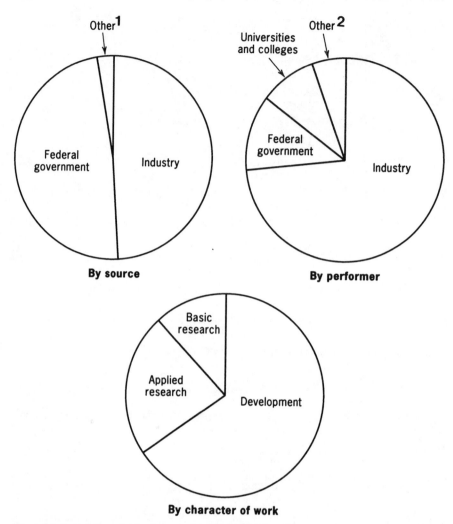

Figure A.5. Relative distribution of national R&D expenditures by source, performer, and character of R&D: 1985. [1]Includes universities and colleges and other nonprofit institutions. [2]Includes federally funded research and development centers administered by universities and other nonprofit institutions. Based on estimates for 1985. (Source: *Science Indicators*, 1985, p. 33.)

R&D expenditure financed by industry. For instance, in 1981, between 41 and 49.5% of the national R&D effort was financed by private industry in the United States, the United Kingdom, and France, while in West Germany and Japan, private industry investments were 57 and 62%, respectively [*Science Indicators*, 1985, p. 6].

All of the major market economies spend about the same proportion of their GNP (2.4–2.7%) on all research and development (see Figure A.3).

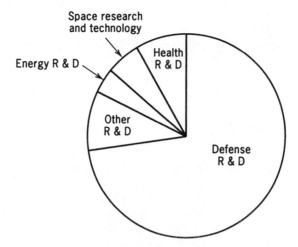

Figure A.6. Relative distribution of federal funds for research and development by budget functions: 1986. (Source: *Science Indicators*, 1985, p. 38.)

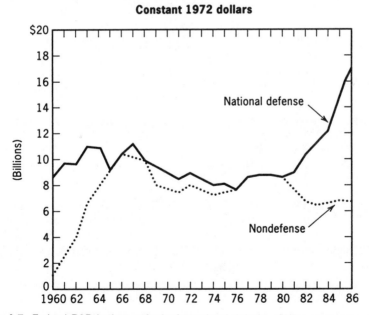

Figure A.7. Federal R&D budget authority for national defense. GNP implicit price deflators are used to convert current dollars to constant 1972 dollars. (Source: *Science Indicators*, 1985, p. 39.)

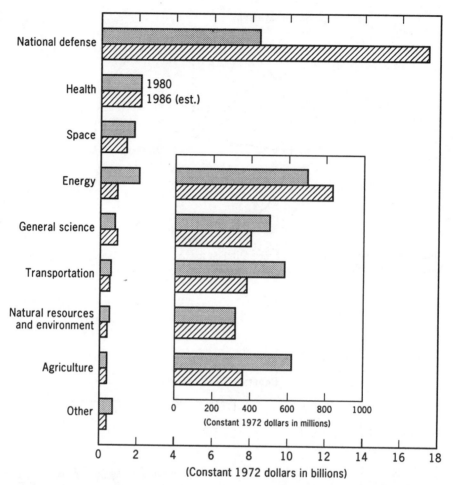

Figure A.8. Federal obligations for research and development in constant 1972 dollars. GNP implicit price deflators are used to convert current dollars to constant 1972 dollars. (Source: *Science Indicators*, 1985, p. 40.)

Because of the great differences between the Soviet system and the market economies, direct comparisons of R&D expenditures are not possible [*Science and Engineering Indicators*, 1987, p. 3]. It is significant to note, however, that funding of defense-related R&D for 1986 represented between 49 and 55% of total government R&D funding in the United States, the United Kingdom, and France. At the same time, this expenditure was only 9% in West Germany and an even smaller 2% in Japan. This trend has essentially continued in the 1980s. Clearly, as the share of national R&D effort devoted by a country to defense-related activities increases, resources available to business-related research activities decrease. Historically, the

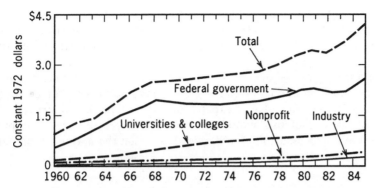

Figure A.9. National expenditures for academic R&D by source. GNP implicit price deflators are used to convert current dollars to constant 1972 dollars. (Source: *Science Indicators*, 1985, p. 108.)

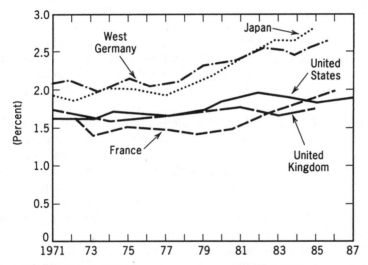

Figure A.10. Nondefense R&D expenditures as a percentage of GNP, by country. (Source: *Science and Engineering Indicators*, 1987, p. 3.)

reasons that West Germany and Japan spend less on defense-related R&D are the legal and constitutional constraints placed on these countries by the Allies at the end of World War II [*Science Indicators*, 1985, p. 6].

Data show that countries that spend proportionally less of their national R&D resources on defense enjoy the greatest GNP and productivity growth rate [Rothwell and Zegwell, 1982, p. 26]. Clearly, there are many technical spinoffs from defense-related R&D. This, however, is not an efficient way to develop new technology, and the *opportunity cost* to economic growth of defense-related R&D is clearly high [Rothwell and Zegwell, 1982, p. 26].

In developing national science policy, it is important to understand the critical need for R&D investment in defense-related activities. National policies in the United States and other industrialized countries with similar international responsibilities (e.g., United Kingdom and France) favor such expenditures. This is one area where the federal government, and not industry, must assume its proper responsibility and provide for an adequate national defense. Since R&D expenditures can increase productivity, R&D expenditures on defense-related activities can therefore reduce the proportion of GNP allocated to defense, and thus lessen the nation's total defense burden.

A.7   R&D PRODUCTIVITY

In this section, the emphasis is on R&D productivity at the national level. R&D productivity at the organizational level is discussed in Chapter 3. R&D organization productivity is defined as an *organization effectiveness vector* that includes quantifiable and nonquantifiable organization outputs, and this vector reflects the quality, and the relationship of outputs to organizational goals and objectives. Individual researcher productivity follows the general pattern of organization effectiveness vector and is discussed in Chapter 9.

Figures A.1 through A.4 provide information about the magnitude of selected countries' R&D investments. In addition to the monetary investment, in the long run, the ability of a nation to conduct research in science and technology is constrained by the ability of the nation's education system to produce the necessary science- and engineering-trained manpower.

It is difficult to compare the training of engineers and scientists from one country to the other, as the curricula are different and the quality of training and resulting degrees conferred convey different meanings. Consequently, a high number of engineers and scientists trained by a country may not predict the strength of the country in science and technology. This, however, is an indication of disciplinary emphasis by the country and, over time, this is bound to affect the ability of the country to conduct research in science and technology. Therefore, it is important to note that, as compared to the United States, the Soviet Union confers over twice as many first degrees every year in the S/E (science and engineering) disciplines (Figure A.11). In addition, Soviet education is concentrated heavily in engineering. For instance, 39% of all baccalaureate degrees awarded in the Soviet Union in 1982 were in engineering, as compared to only 7% in the United States. Japanese higher education also seems to concentrate on training in the engineering disciplines. In 1982, with only half the population of the United States, Japan awarded approximately 74,000 engineering degrees compared to only a total of 64,000 in the United States. Figure A.11 provides information regarding first degrees conferred by higher education institutions in natural

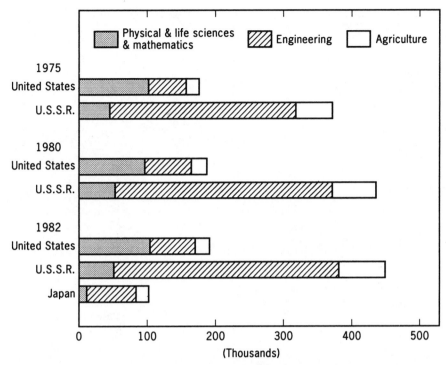

Figure A.11. First degrees conferred by higher education institutions in natural sciences and engineering for selected countries. (Source: *Science Indicators*, 1985, p. 7.)

sciences and engineering for selected countries. This trend continues in the 1980s.

In addition to the number of engineers and scientists produced by a nation, R&D productivity is also a function of the quality of the training, effectiveness of R&D management, availability of modern research equipment, and computer technology. Some surrogates of R&D productivity could be [*Science Indicators*, 1985, p. 8] scientific literature, the number of patents, and the overall economic activity represented by the gross domestic product (GDP).

Scientific Literature

The relative strength of a country's R&D activities can be measured, to some degree, by its share of publications in the world's leading scientific journals. The United States share of world scientific and technical articles for selected fields for the years 1973, 1981, and 1984 is shown in Table A.1. Further, the contribution to science represented in an article may be indicated by the number of times it is cited in subsequent publications (Table

TABLE A-1   U.S. Share of World Scientific and Technical Articles[a] by field

Field[b]	1973 (%)	1981[b] (%)	1984[b] (%)
All fields	38	35	35
Clinical medicine	43	40	41
Biomedicine	39	39	39
Biology	46	38	37
Chemistry	23	20	21
Physics	33	28	27
Earth and space sciences	47	42	41
Engineering and technology	42	41	40
Mathematics	48	38	37

[a] Based on the articles, notes, and reviews in over 2100 of the influentual journals carried on the *Science Citation Index* Corporate Tapes of the Institute for Scientific Information. From (*Science and Engineering Indicators* [1987, p. 12].
[b] Uses over 3500 of the influential journals carried on the 1981 *Science Citation Index* Corporate Tapes of the Institute for Scientific Information.

A.2). The data presented in these two tables would indicate that the U.S. research endeavor has a major impact on science and also on subsequent science. The U.S. share of citations in each field is between 18 and 80% higher than the U.S. share of publications.

Patents

Data on patent activity permit some overall comparisons of the output of inventors in different countries. Significant inventions are patented in the host country and in other countries as well. Thus, the number of external patent applications is weighted in favor of commercially or technically significant inventions. Figure A.12 shows the trend for external patent applications for residents of selected countries. This figure shows that Japanese inventive activity continues to increase as compared to the performance of the United States and other selected countries. The data are even more dramatic if we take patent applications per capita. The United States used to have 67 applications per 100,000 of population in the late 1960s and it is now down to 31 per 100,000; Japan used to have 28 per 100,000 in the late 1960s and it is now up to 35 per 100,000. These changes may be due to the rapid changes in technology that do not make it worthwhile to apply for patents. Perhaps, many people exploit their inventions without patents since the delay in obtaining one can substantially reduce the commercial value of the idea. Nevertheless, this change must affect the Japanese inventors just as much as it does American ones. The fact that the Japanese rate is now higher than the American per capita rate should be a matter of concern to American science policymakers.

TABLE A-2 Relative Citation Ratios[a] **for U.S. Articles**[b] **by Field: 1973 and 1980**

Field[3]	1973	1980
World citations to U.S.		
All fields	1.40	1.40
Clinical medicine	1.36	1.35
Biomedicine	1.42	1.40
Biology	1.08	1.15
Chemistry	1.66	1.75
Physics	1.53	1.54
Earth and space sciences	1.38	1.44
Engineering and technology	1.28	1.24
Mathematics	1.24	1.22
Non-U.S. citations to U.S.		
All fields	1.03	0.85
Clinical medicine	1.02	0.82
Biomedicine	1.09	0.92
Biology	0.69	0.55
Chemistry	1.20	1.01
Physics	1.18	0.99
Earth and space sciences	1.06	0.96
Engineering and technology	0.90	0.61
Mathematics	0.89	0.64

[a] A citation ratio of 1.00 reflects no over- or underciting of the U.S. scientific and technical literature, whereas a higher ratio indicates a greater influence, impact, or utility than would have been expected from the number of U.S. articles for that year. For example, the U.S. chemistry literature for 1973 received 66% more citations from the world's chemistry articles published in 1973. From (*Science Indicators* [1985, p. 8]).
[b] Based on the articles, notes and reviews in over 2100 of the influential journals carried on the 1973 *Science Citation Index* Corporate Tapes of the Institute for Scientific information.

Economic Activity

In a real sense, successful inventive and innovative activity over time should result in increases in an economy's ability to produce goods and services at low cost. Increasing productivity and the resulting improvements in the standard of living for the nation's citizens are clearly the important benefits of an R&D activity. Consequently, one measure of the impact of science and technology on society is the value of the production accounted for by each employed person. Gross Domestic Product (GDP) measures the value added by industry and individuals in each country. In addition to the input provided by science and technology, *GDP per employed person* reflects factors such as availability of natural resources, expertise of the work force,

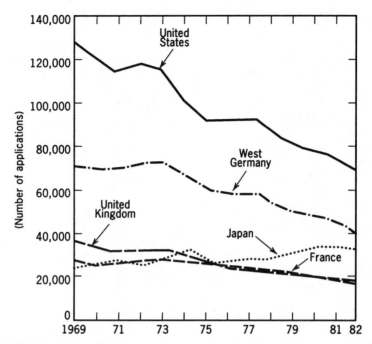

Figure A.12. External patent applications by residents of selected countries. (Source: *Science Indicators*, 1985, p. 9.)

investment in industry, and many other social and economic factors. Among the many sources of productivity growth, science and technology have been identified as major causal factors. GDP, therefore, to some extent represents the strengths of science and technology of a nation. Real GDP per employed person in selected countries is shown in Figure A.13. These GDP figures are based on currency exchange rates in effect in 1985. With a major adjustment in West German and Japanese currency exchange rates and due to the continued growth of their economies, West German and Japanese GDP per employed person is expected to equal or surpass the United States in the early 1990s.

A.8   SOME EUROPEAN PERSPECTIVES ON INNOVATION

Many Europeans feel that Americans are better than they are at adapting and exploiting technology and that there is a good working relationship between the university community and industry in the United States. Goldsmith [1970, p. xvi] stated that American skills lie in adapting and exploiting rather than in creating. To support this statement, he gave a number of examples of recent European developments that have had a major impact

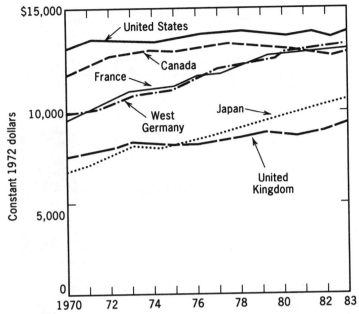

Figure A.13. Real gross domestic product per employed person in selected countries. GNP implicit price deflators are used to convert current dollars to constant 1972 dollars. (Source: *Science Indicators*, 1985, p. 9.)

on American engineering techniques: the triple-deck railway wagon for transporting automobiles (German), the horizontal climbing crane (French), the flotation process for plate glass (British), the basic oxygen furnace (Austrian), the Hovercraft (British patent), an the fundamental digital computer (British).

Notwithstanding American ability to adapt and exploit technology developed elsewhere, let us examine American ability to create and invent. American share of world scientific and technical articles (Table A.1), relative citation ratio for U.S. articles (Table A.2), external patent applications (Figure A.12), and the number of prestigious awards (see Figure A.14 for Nobel Prizes for Scientific Discoveries) earned by American scientists would indicate that American scientists are indeed leaders in inventing and creating new knowledge. Perhaps many scientists and engineers in America feel, and rightfully so, that the emphasis on American investment in R&D needs to be strengthened further so as to sustain and enhance this leadership position. To the extent that this is not happening, many may feel that the United States is falling behind. Some examples cited are the relatively small number of engineers trained in the United States (as compared to Japan and the Soviet Union), outdated laboratory facilities at universities, and little or no increase in the number of U.S. citizens who are full-time S/E graduate

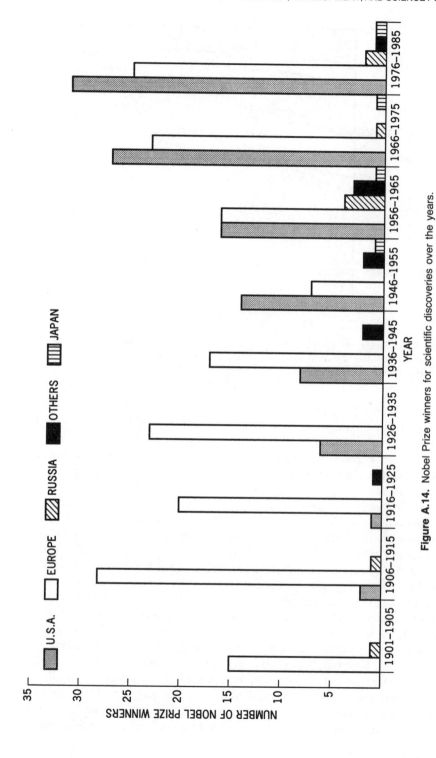

Figure A.14. Nobel Prize winners for scientific discoveries over the years.

students in doctorate-granting institutions [*Science Indicators*, 1985, p. 102]. One factor in the recent decline of American innovation may be the improvement in the conditions of scientific work in other countries, which has reduced the "brain drain" to the United States.

Nevertheless, some Europeans feel that the climate for research, development, and innovation is more favorable in the United States than in most European countries. The following are some examples [Charpie, 1970, p. 9]:

- The U.S. tax code provides an assured flow of high-risk investment capital to those would-be innovators who are able to establish contact with adequate venture capital sources. The capital gains provisions of the U.S. tax law provides an incentive for taxpayers in high income brackets to assume substantial investment risks in anticipation of sharply reduced tax rates on high profits. With the 1987 tax reforms, this, of course, has changed.

- America has a tradition of publicly appreciating and recognizing the success of antiestablishment people. In addition, the mobile, less-structured American society is technologically sophisticated and is receptive to new ideas and inventions. American society is conditioned to give praise and prestige according to accomplishments and it does not ignore a person of humble beginnings who chooses to fight the system and thus achieves success.

- One of the most important factors is that in America a would-be entrepreneur is surrounded by an environment that provides much evidence of successful entrepreneurship.

A.9 R&D EXPENDITURE AND SCIENCE POLICY

The information and analyses presented here should provide an overview of the considerable investment industrialized nations are making in R&D. The importance of this investment in both basic and applied research cannot be overstated. Discussions related to the importance of basic research and the impact of technical innovation on economic development may provide some information useful for developing a national science policy.

R&D Expenditures and Society

An analysis of R&D investment by the major industrialized countries gives an indication of the emphasis each nation places on its needs and the priorities each nation has established among competing social needs. Since investment in R&D affects the innovation process and thus the goods and services available to consumers, *the nature of R&D investment may to a large degree determine the real choices available to society*. Consequently, R&D

investment at the national level cannot be viewed primarily in terms of profitability.

Freeman [1982, p. 201] argued that:

> The advance of science and technology must find its support and its justification, not merely in the expectation of competitive advantage, whether national or private, military or civil, but far more in its contribution to social welfare, conceived in a wider sense. The funding of R&D is extremely important for these basic goals.

Because of the problems of the commons and other associated issues, there is a tendency for R&D investments in industry and in government to focus primarily on short-term projects and not on problems of the environment, resource conservation, and the like. As Freeman [1982, p. 402] has stated:

> Present R&D project selection techniques are biased overwhelmingly towards technical and short-term competitive economic criteria. This is true of both capitalist and socialist economies. An extremely important problem for research and social implementation is the evolution of quite new techniques of selection and assessment which could be applied both in the private and public sectors. These should take into account aesthetic criteria, work satisfaction criteria, environmental criteria and other social costs and benefits which today are almost excluded from consideration.

Only when a national science policy explicitly recognizes that market rate of return cannot properly account for the investment needed either in basic research or applied research, can we begin to develop a broader and a more comprehensive approach to investment in research. This argument does not necessarily lead to more investment in research. Instead, it may lead to modifying some of our priorities and it may lead to analyzing both monetary and human capital investments in R&D explicitly.

R&D Expenditures on Space and Defense

Let us take the case of major research and development efforts that are undertaken to focus on national priorities such as space or defense. Without making any political judgments, although these can be important, it would be salutary to look at investments beyond the monetary aspects—the investment of scientific talent incurred for these activities. Commenting on the recent Strategic Defense Initiative, the Nobelist John Bardeen states that investment in this research program alone is larger than the entire amount spent by the government for all nonmilitary research, including the National Science Foundation and the National Institute of Health. Perhaps, he states, the country can afford this $30 billion investment in *monetary terms*, but not in the *diversion of the top talent* of scientific manpower to such activities [Bardeen, *Daily Illini*, April 21, 1986]. Further commenting on a similar experience in the early 1960s, Bardeen [*Daily Illini*, April 21, 1986] has stated that the Apollo Program in the early 1960s was a great technical success, but the real cost to the United States was far greater than the dollars spent might indicate.

It was during the 1960s that the aerospace industry expanded rapidly to meet military and space needs and drew the scarce top technical talents from civilian and other human needs. This, in turn, provided an opportunity to nations (such as Japan and Germany) to establish a lead in the civilian based industries and markets. Large undertakings such as the Apollo Program historically have caused perturbations in the supply and utilization of top technical talent, so that the aerospace or military industry grew faster than could be sustained in the long run. Within a decade of its expansion in the early 1970s, highly trained engineers, ill-suited for civilian needs, were being laid off by the aerospace industry.

No one questions the importance of national defense. Indeed, it is one of the most important priorities for a nation and especially so for a superpower like the United States. As a matter of national policy, however, it is important to consider not only the expenditures in major research programs of the magnitude of the space or Strategic Defense Initiative, but also the investment of top scientific talent in such activities. The perturbation their programs cause in the utilization of scientific talent is an important consideration. It would seem that a vigorous debate on these issues is essential so that various national priorities are appropriately balanced. Such a debate should bring into consideration a science policy that explicitly addresses the issue of top *talent diversion* to different national efforts in addition to the *monetary aspects*. Educational and training programs could then be geared to produce the necessary technical talent, perturbations could be minimized, and essential defense needs, along with other nonmilitary and human needs, could be effectively satisfied. This would produce a more sustainable defense policy, which would be less costly to the nation because engineers and scientists highly trained and experienced in addressing military needs will not be rendered useless when there are major funding shifts and because the resources and manpower normally wasted in startups and winddown activities for large project undertakings for space and defense will be eliminated or minimized.

Choices among Competing Priorities

As the cost of specific projects (e.g., the supercollider) increases some critics claim that "big science" threatens to eliminate "small science." Thus it seems that establishing science policy will eventually require making choices among competing national priorities. Is there a role for the science community for making these choices and formulating a national science agenda? In an address to the members of the National Academy of Science, Frank Press [1988] stated that "we must also be willing, for the first time, to propose priorities across scientific fields.... We can do so in a manner that is knowledgeable, responsible and useful. We should accept the challenge." If the science community does not get involved in proposing priorities and in formulating a national science agenda, others will set this agenda without critical analysis and proper knowledge. Such a national agenda is not likely to have the support of the science community, confidence of the public, or the long-term commitment of the nation for financial support.

In making choices among competing national needs and proposing priorities across the scientific fields a set of credible evaluation criteria is needed. The weight given to various elements of the criteria would naturally differ among scientists themselves and other decision-makers. It should, however, not be too difficult to reach an agreement on the major elements of such criteria.

Dutton and Crowe [1988] have proposed a set of evaluation criteria (see Table A.3) with a series of questions under each of the main elements. They propose that each major research program of national significance be evaluated using such criteria so that comparable judgments can be made across programs.

A.10 SUMMARY

In summary, science and technology are closely interrelated. Investment in R&D is essential for economic development and for sustaining economic growth. The level of support should be determined by the social benefits of competing usages of the funds. The few clues that we have at present suggest that in the United States the benefits from increased support of R&D will be greater than the benefits that society will derive from competing usages of the funds. Discussion of university–industry linkage and the Cambridge Phenomenon is included for those interested in these aspects. Suggestions for improving this linkage and the ways industry can leverage its investment in R&D by working cooperatively with the university community are also mentioned.

Views on R&D expenditure and science policy, the topic discussed at the end of this appendix, naturally vary. Public policy decisions related to science policy and research expenditure affect resources available for conducting research and the emphasis of such research. Consequently, participation of engineers and scientists in the policy-making stage, where trade offs between competing demands are considered, needs to be reemphasized and institutionalized.

R&D scientists and engineers constitute a substantial portion of the American electorate. Over 1.3 million people, in a country where half the population usually does not vote, can be a critical force in some elections. The data presented here suggest that the United States lead in science is slipping. Furthermore, too much is spent on research that has little potential

TABLE A-3   Evaluation Criteria for Research Programs of National Significance

Scientific Merit

1. SCIENTIFIC OBJECTIVES AND SIGNIFICANCE

   What are the key scientific issues addressed by the initiative?

   Why are these issues significant in the context of science?

   To what extent is the initiative expected to resolve them?

2. BREADTH OF INTEREST

   Why is the initiative important or critical to the discipline proposing it?

   What impact will the science involved have on other disciplines?

   Is there a potential for closing a major gap in knowledge either within a discipline or in areas separating disciplines?

3. POTENTIAL FOR NEW DISCOVERIES AND UNDERSTANDING

   Will the initiative provide powerful new techniques for probing nature? What advances beyond previous measurements can be expected with respect to accuracy, sensitivity, comprehensiveness, and spectral or dynamic range?

   Is there a potential for insight into previously unknown phenomena, processes, or interactions?

   Will the initiative answer fundamental questions or stimulate theoretical understanding of fundamental structures or processes related to the origins and evolution of the universe, the solar system, the planet Earth, or life on Earth?

   In what ways will the initiative advance the understanding of widely occurring natural processes and stimulate modeling and theoretical description of these processes?

   Is there a potential for discovering new laws of science, new interpretations of laws, or new theories concerning fundamental processes?

4. UNIQUENESS

   What are the special reasons for proposing this initiative ? Could the desired knowledge be obtained in other ways? Is a special time schedule necessary for performing the initiative?

Social Benefits

1. CONTRIBUTION TO SCIENTIFIC AWARENESS OR IMPROVEMENT OF THE HUMAN CONDITION

   Are the goals of the initiative related to broader public objectives such as human welfare, economic growth, or national security? Will the results assist us in planning for the future?

   What is the potential for stimulating technological developments that have application beyond this particular initiative?

   Will the initiative contribute to public understanding of the physical world and appreciation of the goals and accomplishments of science?

2. CONTRIBUTION TO INTERNATIONAL UNDERSTANDING

   Will the initiative contribute to international collaboration and understanding?

   Does the initiative have any aspects requiring special sensitivity to the concerns of other nations?

TABLE A-3 *(cont).*

3. CONTRIBUTION TO NATIONAL PRIDE AND PRESTIGE

How will the initiative contribute to national pride and to the image of the United States as a scientific and technological leader?

Will the initiative create public pride because of the magnitude of the challenge, the excitement of the endeavor, or the nature of the results?

Programmatic Concerns

1. FEASIBILITY AND READINESS

Is the initiative technologically feasible?

Are new technological developments required for the success of the initiative?

Are there adequate plans and facilities to receive, process, analyze, store, distribute, and use data at the expected rate of acquisition?

Is there an adequate administrative structure to develop and operate the initiative and to stimulate optimum use of the results?

2. SCIENTIFIC LOGISTICS AND INFRASTRUCTURE

What are the long-term requirements for special facilities or field operations?

What current and long-term infrastructure is required to support the initiative and the processing and analysis of data?

3. COMMUNITY COMMITMENT AND READINESS

Is there a community of outstanding scientists committed to the success of the initiative?

In what ways will the scientific community participate in the operation of the initiative and the analysis of the results?

4. INSTITUTIONAL IMPLICATIONS

In what ways will the initiative stimulate research and education?

What opportunities and challenges will the initiative present for universities, federal laboratories, and industrial contractors?

What will be the impact of the initiative on federally sponsored science? Will new components be required? Can some current activities be curtailed if the initiative is successful?

5. INTERNATIONAL INVOLVEMENT

Does the initiative provide attractive opportunities for involving leading scientists or scientific teams from other countries?

Are there commitments for programmatic support from other nations or international organizations?

6. COST OF THE PROPOSED INITIATIVE

What are the total direct costs, by year?

What are the total costs, by year, to the federal budget?

What portion of the total costs will be borne by other nations?

Reprinted by permission, *American Scientist*, journal of Sigma xi, "Setting Priorities Among Scientific Initiatives," by John A. Dutton and Lawson Crowe, 76:600–601 (1988).

for technological innovation spin-offs, while other countries, such as Japan, are graduating more engineers than the United States, produce more patents per capita, and do more research in areas that have such spin-offs. These trends must be reversed. In a democracy, such changes come from concerned segments of the electorate. It is you, the reader, and others like you, that can initiate the needed policy changes.

REFERENCES

Albert, R. (1983). The cultural sensitizer or culture assimilator. In D. Landis and R. Brislin (Eds.), *Handbook of Intercultural Training*, Vol. 2. New York: Pergamon.

Alderfer, G. P. (1972). *Existence, Relatedness and Growth*. New York: Free Press.

Allen, T. J. (1970). Communication networks in research and development laboratories. *R&D Management*, **1**, 14–21.

Allen, T. J. (1977). *Managing the Flow of Technology: Technology Transfer and the Dissemination of Technological Information Within The Research and Development Organization*. Cambridge, MA: MIT Press.

Allen, T. J., M. L. Tushman and D. M. S. Lee (1979). Technology transfer as a function of position in the spectrum from research through development to technical services. *Academy of Management Journal*, **22**(4), 694–708.

Allio, R. J. and D. Sheehan (1984). Allocating R&D resources effectively. *Research Management*, **27**(3), 14.

Andrews, F. M. (1979). Motivation, diversity and the performance of research units. In F. M. Andrews (Ed.), *Scientific Productivity*. Cambridge University Press.

Andrews, F. M. and G. F. Farris (1967). Supervisory practices and innovation in scientific terms. *Personnel Psychology*, **20**, 497–515.

Anthony, R. N. and R. E. Herzlinger (1975). *Management Control in Non-Profit Organizations*. Homewood, IL: Richard D. Irwin.

Arrow, K. J. (1974). *Essays in the Theory of Risk-Bearing*. Amsterdam: North Holland; New York: America Elsevier.

Atchison, T. and T. W. French, (1967). Pay systems for scientists and engineers. *Industrial Relations*, **7**, 44–56.

Bailyn, L. (1984). *Autonomy in the Industrial R&D Lab*. Unpublished paper, Sloan School of Management, Massachusetts Institute of Technology, TR-DNR-#30.

254

Bailyn, L. and J. T. Lynch (1983). Engineering its difficulties. *Journal of Occupational Behavior*, **7**, 263–283.

Balkin, D. B. and L. R. Gomez-Mejia (1984). Determinants of R&D compensation strategies in the high tech industry. *Personnel Psychology*, **32**, 635–650.

Barron, F. (1969). *Creative Person and Creative Process*. New York: Holt, Rinehart & Winston.

Bass, B. (1985). *Leadership and Performance Beyond Expectation*. New York: Macmillan.

Baumgartel, H. (1957). Leadership style as a variable in research administration. *Administrative Science Quarterly*, **2**, 344–360.

Becker, L. J. (1978). Joint effect of feedback and goal setting on performance: A field study of residential energy conservation. *Journal of Applied Psychology*, **63**, 428–433.

Bell, D. (1973). *The Coming of Post-Industrial Society—A Venture in Social Forecasting*. New York: Basic Books.

Bell, J., R. Herman and C. Sutton (1986). The acid test of innovation. *New Scientist*, **6**, March, 34.

Bennis, W. (1984). The four competencies of leadership. *Training and Development Journal*, August, 14–19.

Blake, R. R. and J. S. Mouton (1986). From Theory to Practice in Intergroup Problem Solving In S. Worchel and W. G. Austin (Eds.), *Psychology of Intergroup Relations*. Chicago: Nelson-Hall.

Blake, S. P. (1978). *Managing for Responsive Research and Development*. San Francisco: W. H. Freeman.

Bok, D. C. (1982). *Beyond the Ivory Tower*. Cambridge: Harvard University Press.

Bondi, H. (1967). *Assumption and Myth in Physical Theory*. Tarner Lectures. Cambridge University Press.

Boorstin, D. J. (1983). *The Discoverers*. New York: Random House.

Boring, E. G. (1950). *A History of Experimental Psychology*. New York: Appleton-Century-Crofts.

Brickman, P., J.A.M. Linsenmeier and A. G. Mc Carneins (1976). Performance enhancement by relevant success and irrelevant failure. *Journal of Personality and Social Psychology*, **33**, 149–160.

Brooks, H. (1968). *The Government of Science*. Cambridge, MA: The MIT Press.

Brooks, H. (1973). Knowledge and action: The dilemma of science policy in the '70s. *Proceedings of the American Academy of Arts and Scientists*, **102**(2), Spring 1973: The search for knowledge.

Brown, J. K. and L. W. Kay (1987). *Tough Challenges for R&D Management*. Ottawa, Ontario. The Conference Board of Canada.

Carson, J. W. and T. Rickards (1979). *Industrial New Product Development: A Manual for the 1980s*. New York: Gower Press.

Cetron, M. J. (1973). Technology transfer: Where we stand today. Joint Engineering Management Congress 21st, pp. 11–28.

Chakrabarti, A. K. (1974). The role of champion in product innovation. *California Management Review*, **XVII**(2).

Chakrabarti, A. K. and A. H. Rubenstein (1976). *Interorganizational Transfer of Technology—A Study of Adoption of NASA Innovations*. IEEE Transactions on Engineering Management V 23N1, Feb. 1976.

Chakrabarti, A. K. and R. D. O'Keefe (1977). A study of key communicators in research and development laboratories. *Group and Organizational Studies*. September.

Charpie, R. A. (1970). Technological innovation and the international economy. In M. Goldsmith (Ed.), *Technological Innovation and the Economy*. London: Wiley-Interscience.

Cheng, J. L. C. (1984). Paradigm development and communication in scientific settings: A contingency analysis. *Academy of Management Journal*, 27, 870–877.

Cialdini, R. B. (1985). *Influence*. Glenview, IL: Scott, Foresman.

Cohen, H., S. Keller and D. Streeter (1979). The transfer of technology from research to development. *Research Management*, 22(3), May, 11–17.

Cunningham, J. B. (1979). The management system: Its functions and processes. *Management Science*, 25(7), 657–670.

Dalton, G. W. (1971). Motivation and control in organizations. In G. W. Dalton and P. R. Lawrence (Eds.), *Motivation and Control in Organizations*. Dorsey Press. Homewood, Illinois

Davis, E. E. and H. C. Triandis (1971). An experimental study of black-white negotiations. *Journal of Applied Social Psychology*, 1, 240–262.

David, P. and M. Wilkof (1988). Scientific and technical information transfer for high technology: Keeping the figure in its ground. *R&D Management*. 18.1.

Dunnette, M., J. Campbell and K.T. Jaastad (1963) The effect of group participation on brainstorming effectiveness for two industrial samples. *Journal of Applied Psychology*, 47, 30–37.

Dutton, J. A. and L. Crowe (1988). Setting priorities among scientific initiatives. *American Scientists*, November–December, 76.

Ellis, L. W. (1984). Viewing R&D projects financially. *Research Management*, March–April, 27(2), p. 29.

Evan, W. M. (1965a). Superior-subordinate conflict in research organizations. *Administrative Science Quarterly*, 10, 51–64.

Evan, W. M. (1965b). Conflict and performance in R&D organization: Some preliminary findings. *Independent Management Review*, 7, 37–46.

Farris, G. F. (1982). The technical supervisor: Beyond the Peter Principle. In M. L. Tushman and W. L. Moore (Eds.), *Readings in The Management of Innovation*. Boston, MA: Pitman Publishing.

Fiedler, F. E. (1967). *A Theory of Leadership Effectiveness*. New York: McGraw-hill.

Fiedler, F. E. (1986a). The contributions of cognitive resources and leader behavior to organizational performance. *Journal of Applied Social Psyhology*, 16, 532–548.

Fiedler, F. E. (1986b). Lecture at American Academy of Management. Chicago, August.

Fiedler, F. E., M. Chemers and L. Mahar (1977). *Improving Leadership Effectiveness: The Leader–Match Concept*. New York: Wiley.

Fiedler, F. E., C. M. Bell, M. M. Chemers and D. Patrick (1984). Increasing mine productivity and safety through management training and organizational development: A comparative study. *Basic and Applied Social Psychology*, **5**, 1–18.

Fiedler, F. E., W. A. Wheeler, M. M. Chemers and D. Patrick (1987). Managing for mine safety. *Training and Development Journal*, September, 40–43.

Fineman, S. (1980). Stress among technical support staff in research and development. In C. L. Cooper and J. Marshall (Eds.), *White Collar and Professional Stress*. New York: Wiley.

Fisher, W. A. (1980). Scientific and technical information and the performance of R&D groups. In B. V. Dean and J. L. Goldhar (Eds.), *Management of Research and Innovation. Time Studies in the Management of Sciences*, Vol. 15, pp. 135–150. New York: North-Holland.

Foa, U. and E. Foa (1974). *Societal Structures of the Mind*. Springfield, IL: Thomas.

Francis, D. and D. Young (1979). *Improving Work Groups*. San Diego, CA: University Associates.

Freeman, C. (1982). *The Economics of Industrial Innovation*, 2nd ed. London: Franes Pinter.

French, J. R. P. and R. D. Caplan (1973). See T. Keenan [1980] for summary.

Fusfeld, A. R. (1981). Guidelines for project selection. MIT R&D 1981, Summer Session Notes.

Gibbons, M. and R. D. Johnston (1974). The roles of science in technological innovation. *Research Policy*, **3**, 220–242.

Gibson J. E. (1981). *Managing Research and Development*. New York: Wiley.

Goldsmith, M. (1970). Introduction. *Technological Innovation and the Economy*. London: Wiley-Interscience.

Gordon, W. J. (1961). *Synectics*. New York: Harper & Row.

Guetzkow, H. S. and P. Bowman (1946). *Men and Hunger: A Psychological Manual for Relief Workers*. Elgin, IL: Brethen.

Hackman, J. R. and G. Oldham (1980). *Work Redesign*. Reading, MA: Addison-Wesley.

Hall, D. T. and R. Mansfield (1975). Relationships of age and security with career variable of engineers and scientists. *Journal of Applied Psychology*, **60**, 201–210.

Herold, D. M. and C. K. Parsons (1985). Assessing the feedback environment in work organizations: Development of the job feedback survey. *Journal of Applied Psychology*, **70**, 290–305.

Hersey, P. and K. H. Blanchard (1982). *Management of Organizational Behavior* 4th ed. Englewood Cliffs, NJ: Prentice-Hall.

Holt, K., H. Geschka and G. Peterlongo (1984). *Needs Assessment*. New York: Wiley.

Ilgen, D. R., C. D. Fishber and M.S. Taylar (1979). Consequences of individual feedback behavior in organization. *Journal of Applied Psychology*, **64**, 349–371.

Isen, A. M., et al. (1985). The influence of positive effect on the unusualness of word associations. *Journal of Personality and Social Psychology*, **48**, 1413–1426.

Jackson, B. (1983). Decision methods for selecting a portfolio of R&D projects. *Research Management*, Sept–Oct, 21. Vol 26, No 5 pp. 21–26.

Jackson, S. E. and R. S. Schuler (1985). A meta-analysis and conceptual critique of research on role ambiguity and role conflict in work settings. *Organizational Behavior and Human Decision Processes*, **36**, 16–78.

Jain, R. K., L. V. Urban and G. S. Stacey (1980). *Environmental Impact Analysis— A New Dimension in Decision Making*. Van Nostrand Reinhold.

Janis, I. L. (1972). *Victims of Groupthink: A Psychological Study of Foreign-Policy Decisions and Fiascoes*. Boston: Houghton Mifflin.

Jaques, E. (1961). *Equitable Payment*. New York: Wiley.

Kanfer, F. H. (1988). Contributions of a self-regulation model to the conduct of therapy. Invited address to the Midwestern Psychological Association, April 28, in Chicago.

Katz, D. and R. Kahn (1980). *The Social Psychology of Organizations*. New York: Wiley.

Katz, R. and T. J. Allen (1982). Investigating the not invested here (NIH) syndrome: A look at the performance, tenure, and communication patterns of 50 R&D project groups. *R&D Management*, **12**(1), 7–19.

Katz, R. and T. J. Allen (1985). Project performance and the locus of influence in the R&D matrix. *Academy of Management Journal*, **28**, 67–87.

Katz, R. and M. Tushman (1981). An investigation into the managerial roles and career paths of gatekeepers and project supervisors in a major R&D facility. *R&D Management*, **11**(3), 103–110.

Keenan, T. (1980). Stress and the professional engineer. In D. C. Cooper and J. Marshall (Eds.), *White Collar and Professional Stress*. New York: Wiley, pp. 189–210.

Keeney, R. L., and H. Raiffa. (1976). *Decisions with Multiple Objectives: Preferences and Value Tradeoffs*. New York: Wiley, pp. 6, 68.

Keller, R. T. and W. E. Holland (1975). Boundary-spanning roles in a research and development organization: An empirical investigation. *Academy of Management Journal*. June, **18**(2).

Kennedy, D. (1985). Government policies and the cost of doing research. *Science*, **227**, 480–484, February.

Krawiec, F. (1984). Evaluating and selecting research projects by scoring. *Research Management*, March–April, **27**(2), 21.

Landis, D. and R. Brislin (1983). *Handbook of Intercultural Training*, 3 vols. New York: Pergamon.

Langer, E. J. (1983). *The Psychology of Control*. Beverly Hills, CA: Sage.

Langrish, J. (1971). Technology transfer: Some British data. *R&D Management*, **1**, 133–136.

LaPorte, T. R. (1967). Conditions of strain and accommodation in industrial research organizations. *Administrative Science Quarterly*, **12**, 21–38.

Lawler, E. E. (1973). *Motivation in Work Organizations*. Monterey, CA: Brooks/ Cole, p. 9.

Lawler, E. E. III (1986). *High Involvement Management*. San Francisco: Bass.

Lawrence, P. B. and W. J. Lorsch (1967). *Organization and Environment*. Boston: Harvard University Press.

Leonard-Barton, D. and W. A. Kraus (1985). Implementing new technology. *Harvard Business Review*, Nov–Dec, 102–110.

Likert, J. F. (1967). *The Human Organization*. New York: McGraw-Hill.

Lincoln, J.F. (1951). *Incentive Management*. Cleveland: Lincoln Electric Co.

Locke, E. A. (1968). Toward a theory of task motivation and incentives. *Organizational Behavior and Human Performance*, **3**, 157–189.

Locke, E. A., K. N. Shaw, L. M. Saari and G. P. Latham (1981). Goal setting and task performance: 1969–1980. *Psychological Bulletin*, **90**, 125–152.

Locke, E. A., E. Frederick, E. Buckner and P. Bobko (1984). Effect of previously assigned goals on self-set goals and performance. *Journal of Applied Psychology*, **69**, 694–699.

Loher, B. T., R. A. Noe, N. L. Moeller and M. P. Fitzgerald, (1985). A meta analysis of the relation of job characteristics to job satisfaction. *Journal of Applied Psychology*, **70**, 280–289.

MacKinnon, D. W. (1962). The nature and nurture of creative talent. *American Psychologist*, **17** 7.

Marcson, S. (1960). *The Scientist in American Industry*. Princeton, NJ: Princeton University Press, pp. 78–151.

Marquis, D. G. and D. L. Straight (1965). *Organizational Factors in Project Performance*. Cambridge, MA: MIT Working Paper No. 133–165.

Maslow, A. (1954). *Motivation and Personality*. New York: Harper (2nd ed., 1970).

McCain, G. (1969). *The Game of Science*. Belmont, CA: Wadsworth, p. 59.

McGregor, D. (1972). An uneasy look at performance appraisal. *Harvard Business Review*, Sept–Oct., 133–138.

Merten, U. and S. M. Ryu (1983). What does the R&D function actually accomplish. *Harvard Business Review*, July–Aug.

Merton, R. K. (1973). In N. W. Storer (Ed.), *The Sociology of Science: Theoretical and Empirical Investigations*. Chicago: The University of Chicago Press.

Mintzber, H. (1973). *The Nature of Managerial Work*. New York: Harper & Row, pp. 56–58.

Mintzberg, H. (1975). The manger's job: Folklore and fact. *Harvard Business Review*, July–Aug., No. 75409, 49–61.

Morton, J. A. (1971). *Organizing for Innovation*. New York: McGraw-Hill.

Mosbacher, C. G. (1988). R&D funding in U.S. will hit $132 billion in 1988. *Research and Development*. January.

Murphy, K. R., W. K. Balzer, M. C. Lockhart and E. J. Eisenman (1985). Effects of previous performance on evaluations of present performance. *Journal of Applied Psychology*, **70**, 72–84.

Nadiri, M. I. (1980). Contributions and Determinants of research and development expenditures in U.S. manufacturing industries. In G. M. von Furstenberg (ed.), *Capital Efficiency and Economic Growth*. Cambridge, MA: Bollinger.

Nadler, D. A. (1982). Concepts for the management of organizational change. In G. L. Lippitt (Ed.), *Implementing Organizational Change*. Jossey-Bass, San Francisco.

Naisbitt, J. (1982). *Megatrends*. New York: Warner Books.

Newton, T. J. and A. Keenan (1985). Coping with work related stress. *Human Relations*, **38**, 107–126.

Newton-Smith, W. H. (1981). *The Rationality of Science*. London: Routledge and Kegan.

Organization of Economic Cooperation and Development (OECD). (1970). *The Measurement of Scientific and Technical Activities*.

Osborn, A. F. (1957). *Applied Imagination*, rev ed. New York: Scribner.

Osborn, A. F. (1963). *Applied Imagination*. New York: Charles Scribner.

Pelz, D. C. (1956). Some social factors related to performance in a research organization. *Administrative Science Quarterly*, **1**, 310–325.

Pelz, D. C. and F. M. Andrews (1966a). Autonomy, coordination and stimulation in relation to scientific achievement. *Behavioral Science*, **2**, 89–97.

Performance Appraisal, Harvard Business Review (1972). Collection of Thirteen Papers, No. 12101.

Peters, T. J. and R. H. Waterman (1982). *In Search of Excellence—Lessons from America's Best Run Companies*. New York: Haper & Row.

Price, D. J. D. (1965). "Is technology independent of science?" *Technology and Culture*, 553–568.

Press, F. (1988). *The Dilemma of the Golden Age*. Address to the Members of the National Academy of Science, 26 April 1988.

Quinn, J. B. (1985). Managing innovation: Controlled chaos. *Harvard Business Review*, May–June, 73–84.

Rahim, A. (1983). A measure of styles of handling interpersonal conflict. *Academy of Management Journal*, **26**, 368–376.

Regis, E. (1987). *Who Got Einstein's Office*? New York: Addison-Wesley.

Ritti, R. (1982). "Work goals of scientists and engineers," in M. L. Tushman and W. L. Moore (Eds.), *Readings in the Management of Innovations*. Boston: Pitman.

Roberts, E. B. (1978). What do we really know about managing R&D? Interview with Michael Wolff. *Research Management*, **21** Nov, (6), 6–11.

Roberts, E. B. and A. L. Frohman (1982). Strategies for improving research utilization. *Innovation/Technology Review*. Page 3–9.

Roberts, E. B. and A. R. Fusfeld (1981). Staffing the innovative technology-based organization. *Sloan Management Review*, Spring, 19–34.

Rogers, E. M. (1983). *Diffusion of Innovations*, 3rd ed. New York: Free Press.

Rosenbaum, M. E., D. L. Moore, J. L. Cotton, M. S. Cook, R. A. Hieser, M. N. Shovar and M. J. Gray (1980). Group productivity and process: Pure and mixed reward structures and task interdependence. *Journal of Personality and Social Psychology*, **39**, 626–642.

Rosovsky, H. (1987). "Deaning." *Harvard Magazine*, Jan–Feb.

Rothwell, R. and W. Zegwell (1981). *Industrial Innovation and Public Policy*: *Preparing for the 1980 and 1990s*. Westport, CT: Greenwood.

Ruzic, N. (1978). *How to Top NASA Developed Technology*. Research Management, V 21N6, Nov. 1978.

Saari, L. M. and G. P. Latham (1982). Employee reactions to continuous and variable ratio reinforcement schedules involving a monetary incentive. *Journal of Applied Psychology*, *67*, 506–508.

Salter, M. S. (1971). Management appraisal and reward systems. *Journal of Business Policy*, **1**, (4), 41–51.

Schmitt, R.W. (1985). Successful corporate R&D. *Harvard Business Review*, May–June, p. 124.

Schriesheim, J., M. A. Von Glinow and S. Kerr (1977). Professionals in bureaucracies: A structural alternative. In P. C. Nystrom and W. H. Starbuck (Eds.), *Perspective Models of Organizations*. New York: North-Holland.

Science and Engineering Indicators (1987). (National Science Board). Washington, D.C.: U.S. Government Printing Office.

Science Indicators, The 1985 Report (1985). (National Science Board). Washington, D.C.: U.S. Government Printing Office.

Shanklin, W. L., & J. K. Ryans, Jr. (1984). Organizing for high-tech marketing. *Harvard Business Review*, Nov–Dec., p. 164.

Sloan School of Management (1979). *Massachusetts Institute of Technology (MIT) Class Notes*.

Smith, G. C. (1970). Consultation and decision processes in an R&D laboratory. *Administrative Science Quarterly*, **15**, 203–215.

Snyder, M. (1979). Self-monitoring processes. In L. Berkowitz (Ed.), *Advances in Experimental Social Psychology*, Vol 12. New York: Academic Press, pp. 86–131.

Souder, W. E. (1975). State dominant (S-D), process-dominant (P-D) and task-dominant (T-D) models of the new product development (NDD) process: Some straw-men models and their contingencies. *Technology Management Studies Group Paper*, November 1.

Souder, W. E. and A. K. Chakrabarti (1980). Managing the coordination of marketing and R&D in the innovation process. In B. V. Dean & J. L. Goldhar (Eds.), *Management of Research and Innovation. Times Studies in the Management Sciences*, Vol. 15, pp. 135–150. New York: North-Holland.

Spector, P. E. (1982). Behavior in organizations as a function of employee's locus of control. *Psychological Bulletin*, **91**, 482–497.

Sutton, C. (1986). Serendipity or sound science? *New Scientist*, **27**, Feb, 30.

Szilagyi, A. D. and W. E. Holland (1980). Changes in social density. Relationships with function interaction and perceptions of job characteristics, role stress and work satisfaction. *Journal of Applied Psychology*, **65**, 28–33.

Thompson, J. D. (1967). *Organizations in Action*. New York: McGraw-Hill.

Thompson, P. H. and G. W. Dalton (1976). Are R&D organizations obsolete? *Harvard Business Review*, **54**, Nov, Dec, 105–116.

Thomson, W. J. (1983). Effects of control on choice of reward and punishment. *Bulletin of Psychonomic Society*, **21**, 462–464.

Triandis, H. C. (1971). *Attitude and Attitude Change*. New York: Wiley.

Triandis, H. C. (1977). *Interpersonal Behavior*. Monterey, CA: Brooks/Cole.

Triandis, H. C. (1980). Values, attitudes and interpersonal behavior. *Nebraska Symposium on Motivation, 1979*. Lincoln, NE:University of Nebraska Press.

Triandis, H. C., R. Hall and R. B. Ewen (1965). Member heterogeneity and dyadic creativity. *Human Relations*, **18**, 35–55.

Tushman, M. L. (1982). Managing communication networks in R&D laboratories. In M. L. Tushman and W. L. Moore (Eds.), *Readings in the Management of Innovation*. Marshfield, MA: Pitman.

Twiss, B.C. (1986). *Managing Technological Innovation*, 3rd ed. London: Pitman.

Von Hippel, E.A. (1978). Users as innovators. *Technology Review*, Jan, 31–37.

Vroom, V. and P. W. Yetton (1973). *Leadership and Decision Making*. Pittsburgh: University of Pittsburgh Press.

Walters, J. E. (1965). *The Management of R&D*. Washington: Sparten Books, p. 77.

White, S. E., T. R. Mitchell and C. H. Bell, Jr. (1977). Goal setting, evaluation apprehension, and social cues as determinants of job performance and job satisfaction in a simulated organization. *Journal of Applied Psychology*, **62**, 665–673.

Whyte, W. F. (1948). *Human Relations in the Restaurant Industry*. New York: McGraw-Hill.

Wicksteed, S. Q. (1985). *The Cambridge Phenomenon*. London: Brand.

Winchell, A. E. (1984). Conceptual systems and Holland's theory of vocational choice. *Journal of Personality and Social Psychology*, **46**, 376–383.

Winkofsky, E. P., R. M. Mason and W. E. Souder (1980). R&D budgeting and project selection: A review of practices and models. *TIMS Studies in the Management Sciences*, **15**, 183–197.

Worchel, S. and W. G. Austin (1985). *Psychology of Intergroup Relations*. Chicago: Nelson-Hall.

AUTHOR INDEX

SUBJECT INDEX